DROITWICH SPA

THE POSTCARD COLLECTION

PAUL JONES LRPS

AMBERLEY

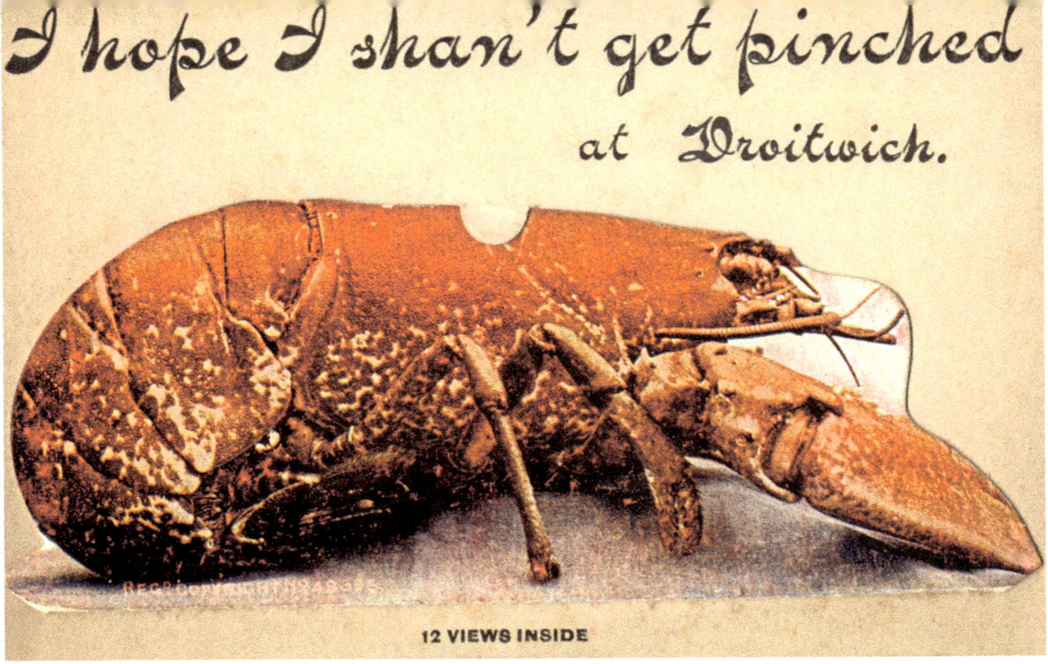

ACKNOWLEDGEMENTS

I am most grateful to Julia Skinner of the Francis Frith Collection for supplying the copyright criteria information for their collection. All Frith's images in this publication have been reproduced from originals that are over seventy years old, and are therefore out of copyright. Avoncroft Museum of Historic Buildings have also been most helpful by providing a photograph of the wooden crown from Ombersley, enabling it to be positively identified. I would also like to thank David Hawkes for the information relating to Gable House in St Peter's Walk, Michael Bowles for the Noake family information, and Barbara Middlemass for some of the Impney information.

First published 2017

Amberley Publishing
The Hill, Stroud, Gloucestershire, GL5 4EP
www.amberley-books.com

ISBN 978 1 4456 6414 9 (print)
ISBN 978 1 4456 6415 6 (ebook)

British Library Cataloguing in Publication Data.
A catalogue record for this book is available from the British Library.

Origination by Amberley Publishing.
Printed in Great Britain.

CONTENTS

	Introduction	4
CHAPTER 1	High Street and Friar Street	6
CHAPTER 2	The Vines, Dodderhill and the Salt Industry	18
CHAPTER 3	Queen Street, St George's Square and the Royal Brine Baths	26
CHAPTER 4	St Peter's and the Holloway	32
CHAPTER 5	Victoria Square and St Andrew's Brine Baths	38
CHAPTER 6	Ombersley Street and Ombersley Road	53
CHAPTER 7	Worcester Road, the Park and Witton	58
CHAPTER 8	Impney and Westwood	63
CHAPTER 9	Villages around Droitwich	69
CHAPTER 10	Mystery Images	94

INTRODUCTION

It was John Brettell who first brought old Droitwich images to a wider audience with his first book entitled *Droitwich in Old Photographs* in 1987, and he followed this just a few years later with *Around Droitwich* in 1989. Since then, several other books have followed, including *Droitwich a Pictorial History* by Lyn Blewitt and Bob Field in 1994, and Amberley's *Droitwich Through Time* in 2014.

In this volume I have included previously unpublished images, as well as a few favourites for their historical value, and though most are drawn from my postcard collection I have also included images from my collections of original prints, ephemera, and photographs.

Droitwich is, of course, most famously known for its brine, both as an industry and as a health resort. The Royal Brine Baths, previously known as the Saline Baths, was established in 1836 after Dr William Robeson Jaques successfully treated many patients during the cholera epidemic of 1832. Jaques's treatment, however, is not the beginning of the story – as is often assumed. On 30 May 1829 the *Worcester Herald* published the following article:

> We have heard that the project is entertained, in most respectable quarters, of forming, upon a liberal scale, hot and cold baths near Droitwich, to be supplied from the salt springs which rise in such a lavish abundance in that vicinity. Of the efficacy and great utility of salt-water bathing in many of the severer afflictions incident to humanity, we believe no doubt to be entertained, but such is the inland situation of this and adjacent counties, and such is their distance from the sea side, as to offer, in numerous cases, insuperable obstacles to the invalid's resorting thereto for the re-establishment of his health. It would afford us much satisfaction, therefore, to learn of the project alluded to being in a train for carrying into effect, looking upon it as one calculated to be of infinite public benefit and convenience, and which we think also could not fail of handsomely remunerating those who might embark therein.

In 1850, the following description of the salt trade was published in the local Post Office Directory:

> The brine, which contains one-fourth its weight of salt, rises spontaneously to the surface from springs about 110 feet below the surface: but steam pumps are used [*see* page 21], by which the brine is conveyed into a large pan, under which is a furnace, causing the water to evaporate; the salt particles being crystallised, remain at the bottom of the pan in thin crusts, somewhat like ice; they are then taken out with long ladles, placed in wooden boxes, and taken into the drying room (which is kept at a high temperature), and where they form those solid blocks which may be seen at every retailer's throughout the kingdom.

Droitwich, as both a resort and an industrial town, has inspired a number of writers in the past, including the now largely forgotten Eliza Margaret Jane Humphreys (née Gollan), who used the nom de plume of Rita. Rita was born at Gollanfield, Inverness, in 1850 and achieved writing success at the age of twenty-seven with her first novel in 1877. She was certainly a very famous and popular author during her lifetime, and it was in 1906 that Rita stayed at the Worcestershire Brine Baths Hotel in Droitwich (a visit that is listed in the *Droitwich Guardian's* Brine Baths Visitors' Record) in order to take the brine cure for her rheumatism.

The town and its surroundings soon began to evolve into the setting for her next novel, *A Man of No Importance* (first published in 1907), in which Droitwich is transformed by Rita into Salwych. Many familiar places within Droitwich and its environs are beautifully described by Rita in this novel, though most of the place names have been slightly altered.

During her 1906 visit to Droitwich, Rita received treatment for rheumatism at the Royal Brine Baths, and it was here that she met two employees of that establishment – my great-great-grandmother Eliza Skerrett and Eliza's brother-in-law Charles John Skerrett. At some point Rita decided to use them as models for characters in her new novel – forming them into Michael and Betty Chance. Charles and Eliza are illustrated on page 31 of this book, and Eliza and another brine baths employee, May Morton, can be seen on page 39 of *Droitwich Through Time* – standing next to the brine baths entrance.

The main characters of the book are Marah and Conall, and upon Conall's visit to the Royal Brine Baths, he is 'confronted by his friend of the lane [Betty Chance] and the previous night. In her clean print gown and neat apron and cap she looked just the sort of buxom comfortable person to cheer up an invalid, or wait on physical afflictions ... He was following her up one passage and down another. He saw a range of doors – some open and some closed'. At a later point in the story, Rita also refers to the twenty-minute sandglasses that were used to time treatment at the brine baths.

In this description of the Vines area from Rita's book, Dodderhill becomes Dodshill:

> They [Marah and Conall] paused a moment on the bridge spanning the dark sluggish waters of the canal. It was a weird and ugly spot. Even the sunshine seemed unable to lighten it or give a touch of cheerfulness to its aspect. To the left lay the miry banks by which the barges were moored. Ugly crooked houses shadowed the narrow lane ... The dark chimneys of the Salt Works, the heaps of refuse, the piles of unused brine, the melancholy waiting barges, the steam and smoke that shrouded it all as with the mantle of some brooding genie – all these were significant of the trade of the town, as well as of a certain monotony of dreary lives spent in that service, and rewarded with no greater benefit than the bare means of subsisting in its melancholy atmosphere.

It should be remembered that the brine industry was already in decline in Droitwich when Rita visited in 1906, and a number of the salt works lay derelict.

To conclude this introduction, I personally feel that the following description of the High Street by Rita beautifully sums up the character of the town:

> The old black and white houses leaned against each other as if seeking support ... The general aspect was that of a place recovering from a mild shock of earthquake which had shaken it gently, but not destructively, into an attitude of seeming helplessness. Everything inclined from strict canons of the perpendicular ... Roofs and chimneys were a variety of stunted or crooked shapes, and narrow lanes burrowed from right to left to where the sluggish canal waters on the one side, or the public park and avenues on the other, sounded their note of prosperity.

CHAPTER 1

HIGH STREET AND FRIAR STREET

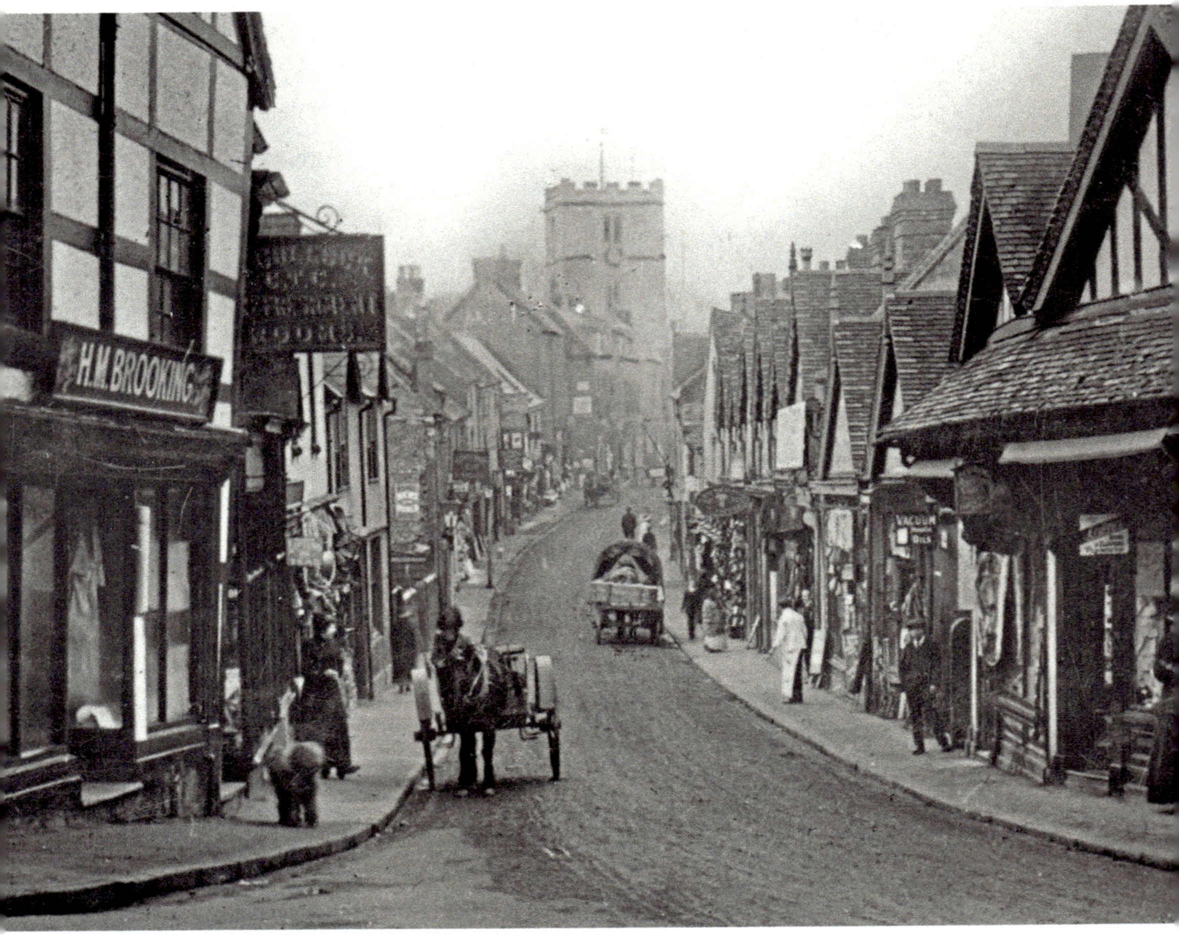

Droitwich High Street

In this charming scene of Droitwich High Street taken in the early 1900s, Bullock's refreshment rooms can be seen behind H. M. Brooking's business on the left. Bullock's Café and bakery expanded into Brooking's former premises in 1932, thus becoming an establishment known and loved by many. Note also that St Andrew's Church tower, which was lowered in 1926–27, is seen here at its full height.

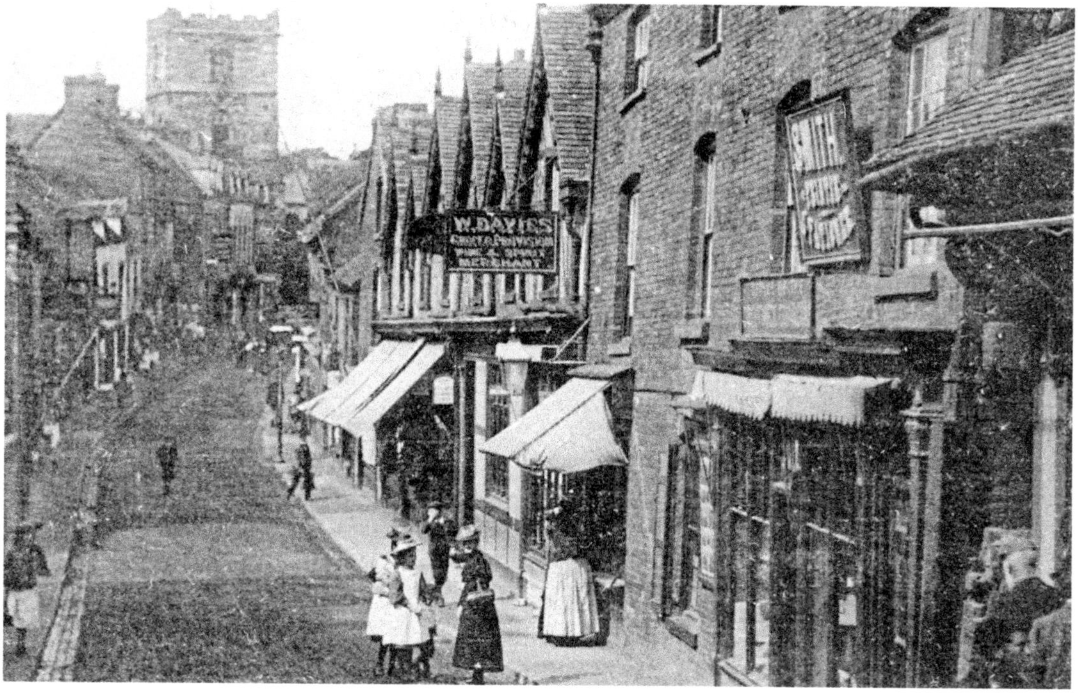

High Street

A much earlier view of Droitwich High Street is shown above, in which Smith's the printers can be seen on the right. Smith's were publishers of the *Droitwich Guardian* for many years, and moved into Queen Street after their High Street premises were demolished and replaced with two new units in 1904. By the time that the below image was taken, the two new units had been constructed, one of which became Machin's in 1906. George Wythes of the Hawthorns Worcester Road owned the grocer's business (right) which, after his early death in 1896, passed to his wife, who continued to trade with no change of name to the business.

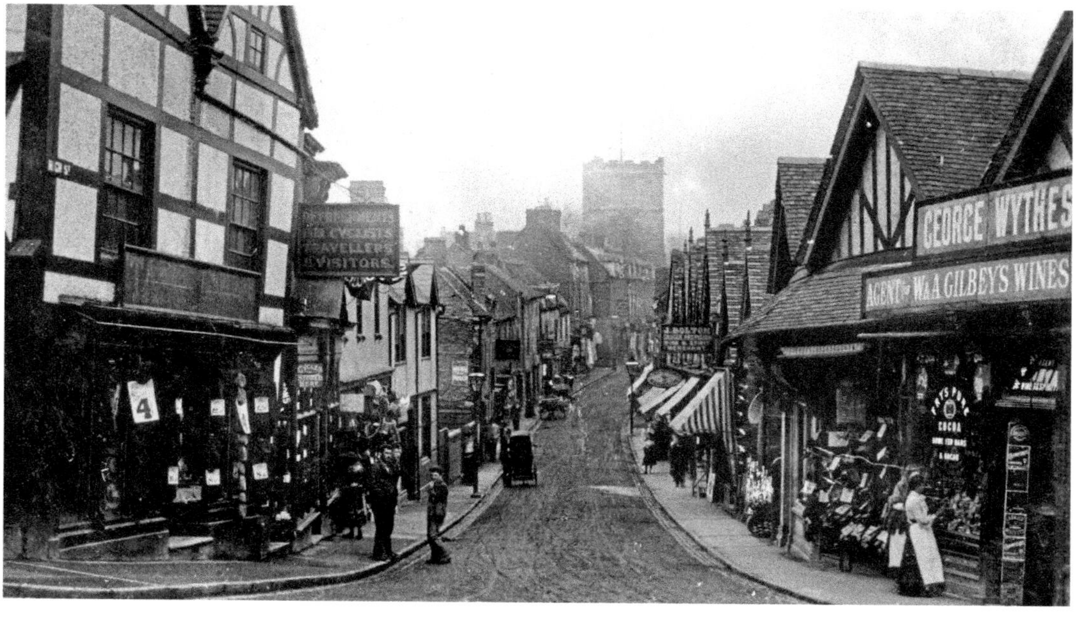

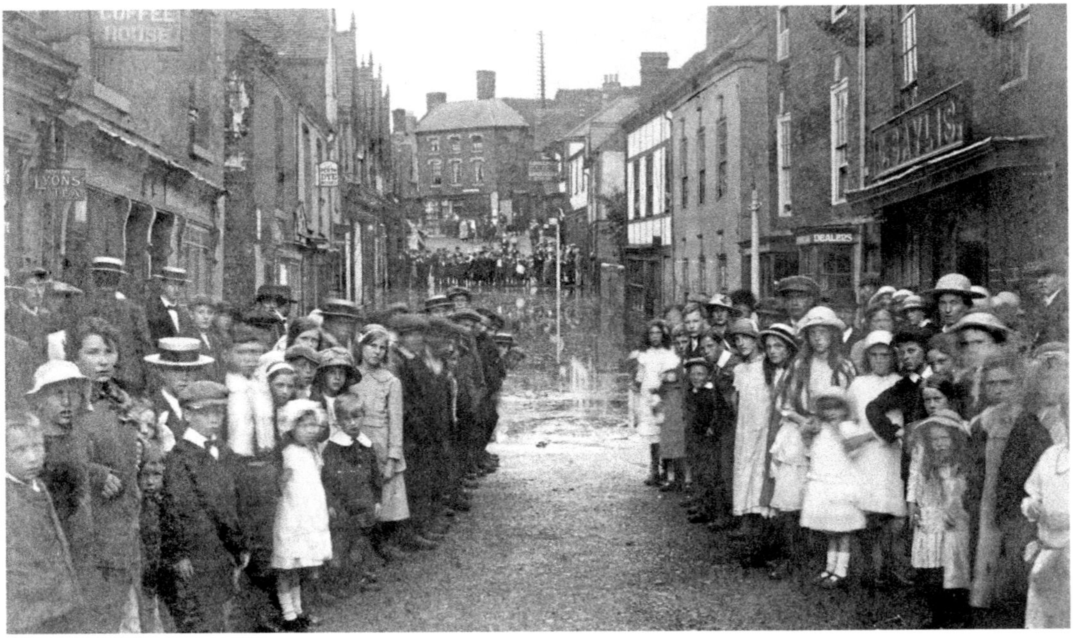

High Street Floods

Two shots of the High Street floods are shown here – above in 1916 and below in 1924. The above shot looks east towards buildings on Queen Street, which were cleared in a road-widening scheme in the 1930s. Further clearance was to take place in 1951. The image below looks west towards numerous flooded shops, including Machin's (right of centre). The High Street also flooded in 1904 and 1960 during the last century, and most recently in 2007. It was due to the flood of 2007 that the local historian Nelly Copson had to be rescued by firemen from her High Street home, and much of her archive was lost forever.

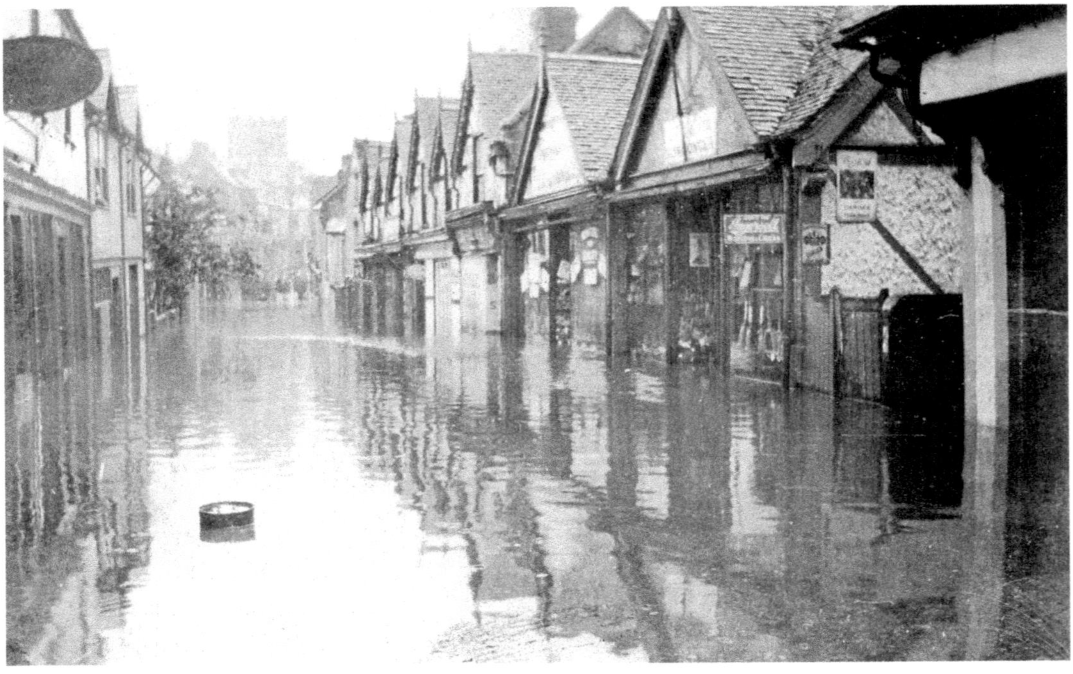

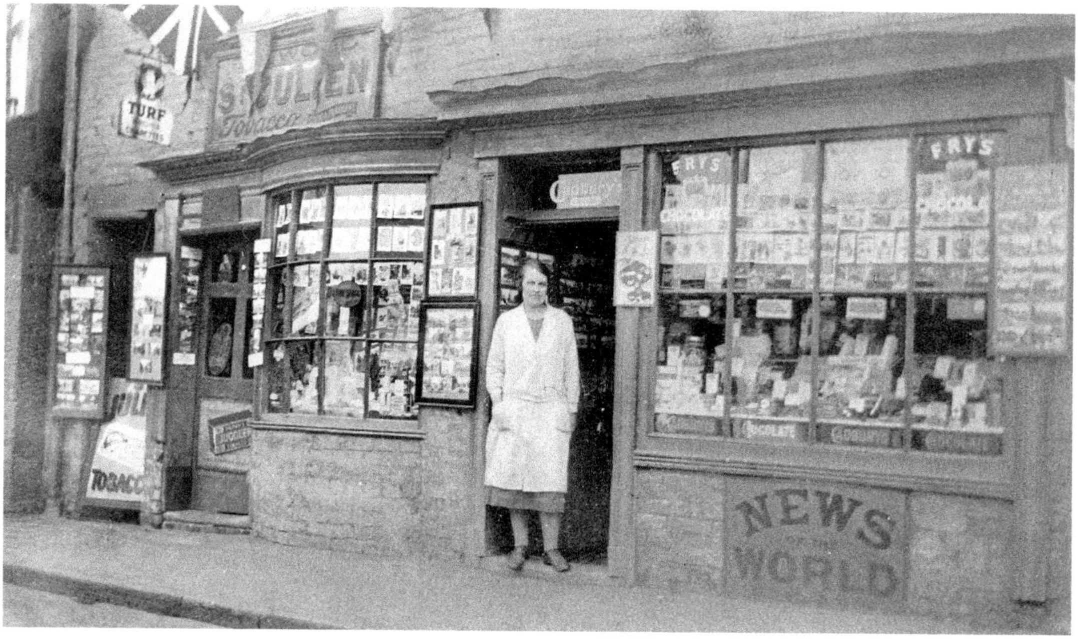

Elizabeth 'Lizzy' Wood

In the image above taken during the 1930s, Elizabeth 'Lizzy' Wood can be seen standing in the doorway of her sweetshop at No. 14 High Street. She also ran the tobacconist's shop next door at No. 16, and flitted from the counter of one shop to the other via a connecting doorway, while customers had to use the separate external doorways. In the below image taken from the doorway of Lizzy's shop during the same period, Osbourne's greengrocer and fruiterer can be seen (far left) on the corner of Gurney's Lane. The bunting was probably put up for the jubilee of 1935 or coronation of 1937.

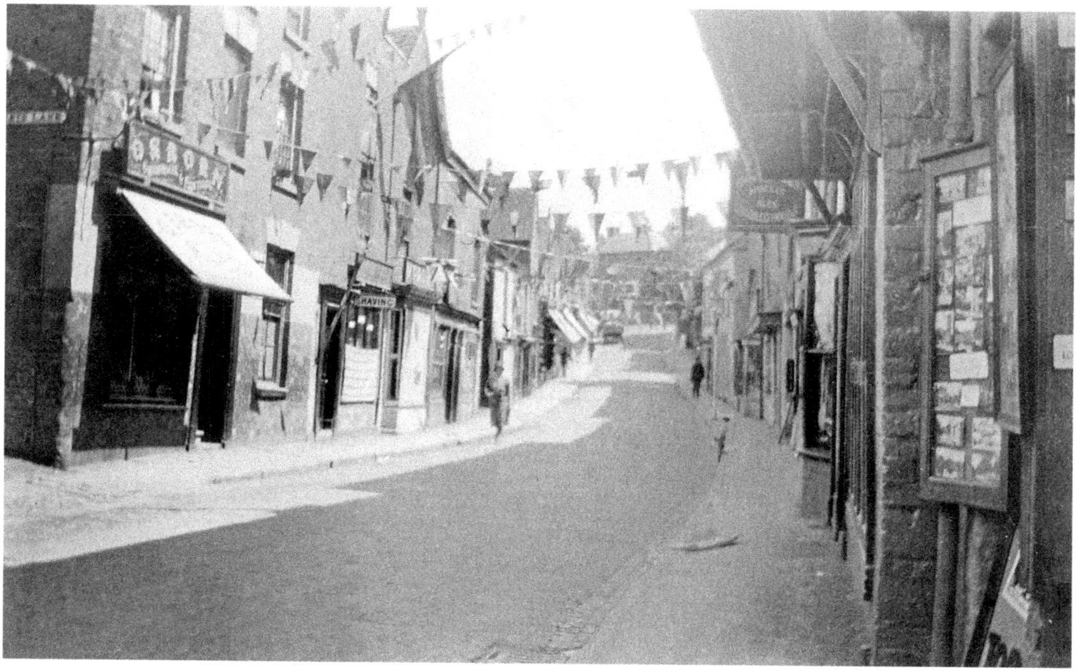

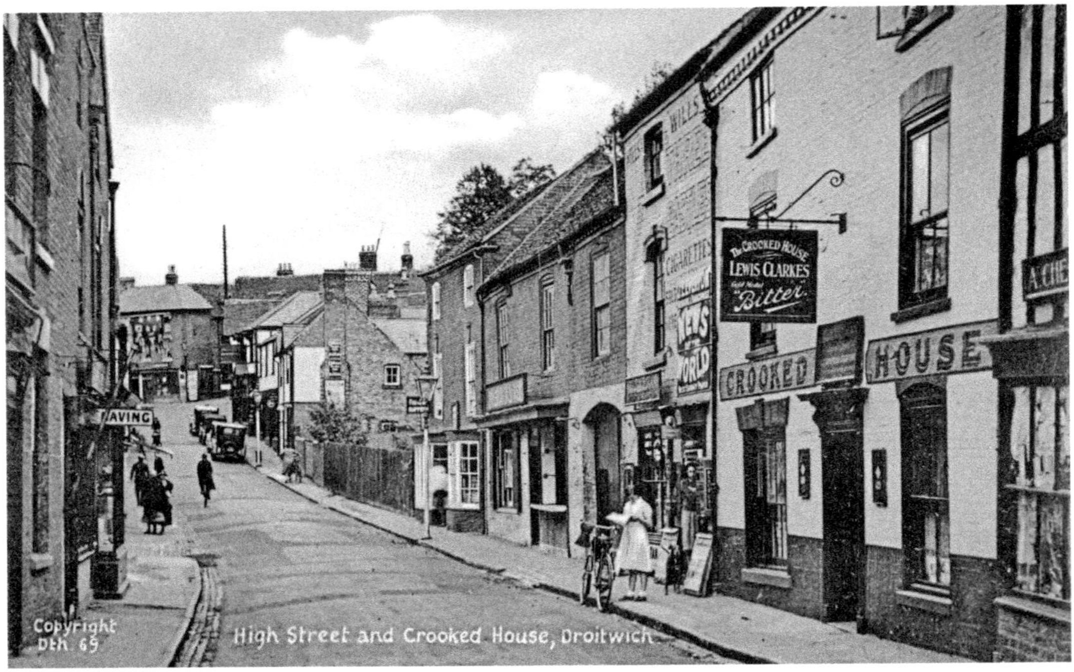

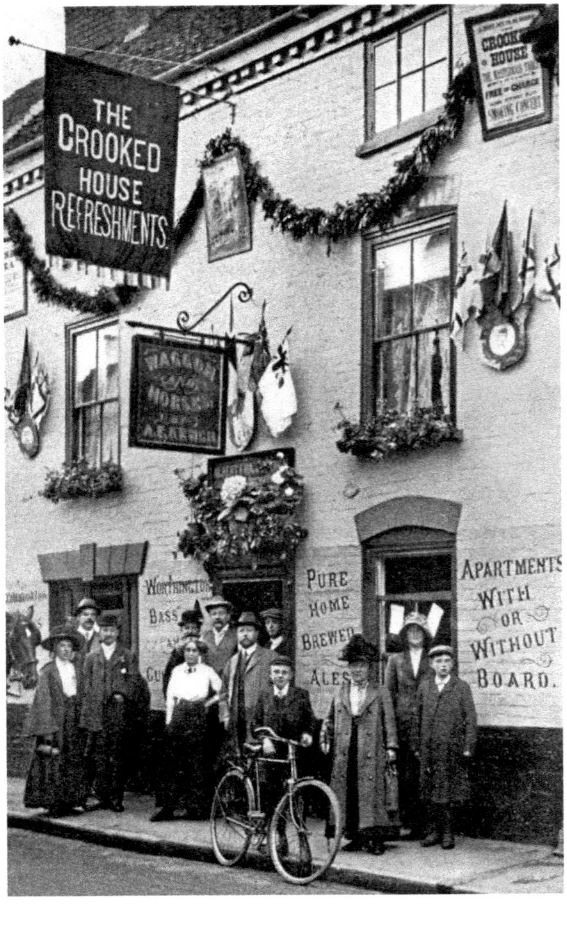

The Crooked House

In the above *c.* 1930 image of the High Street, the Wagon and Horses or 'Crooked House' can be seen on the right. During the 1970s and 1980s, the gap in the High Street (left of centre) was the site of the open market, and the buildings that now infill this gap are called Old Market Court. The second shot shows the Crooked House decorated for the local agricultural show, which was held from 4–6 June 1912. At this point in time Mr Kench was the proprietor, and it was he who saw many of the windows of the pub smashed during the Droitwich riot of 1910, which was caused by certain election issues.

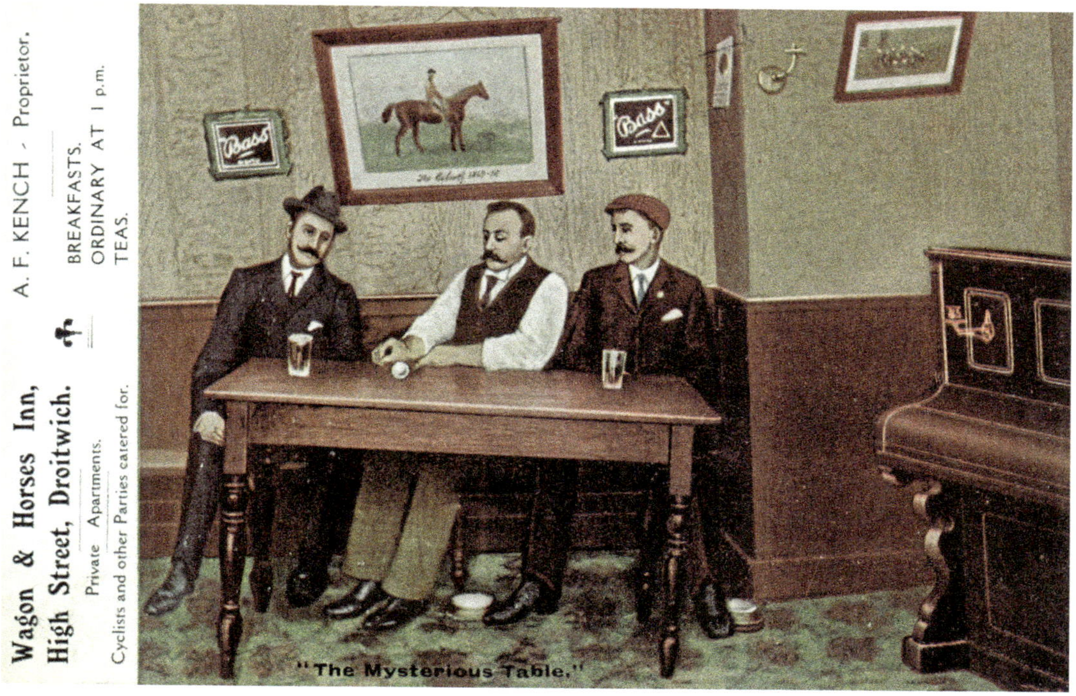

The Crooked House

The 'mysterious table' is shown above, on which a billiard ball seemed to roll uphill! This, of course, was an optical illusion caused by the crooked nature of the surroundings. Sadly, the pub closed in 1962, and the building is now known as Hereford House. The billiard ball is on permanent display in Droitwich Heritage Centre, and those wishing to see the illusion for themselves can see it at another Crooked House in Himley Staffordshire. The second image reproduced here shows one of the corridors of the Crooked House, and possibly Mr A. F. Kench himself, who became manager of the pub in 1891.

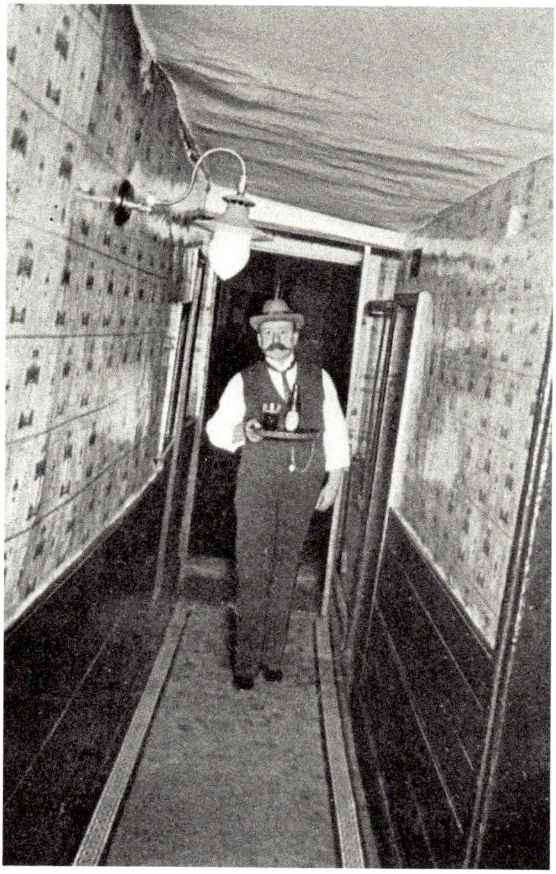

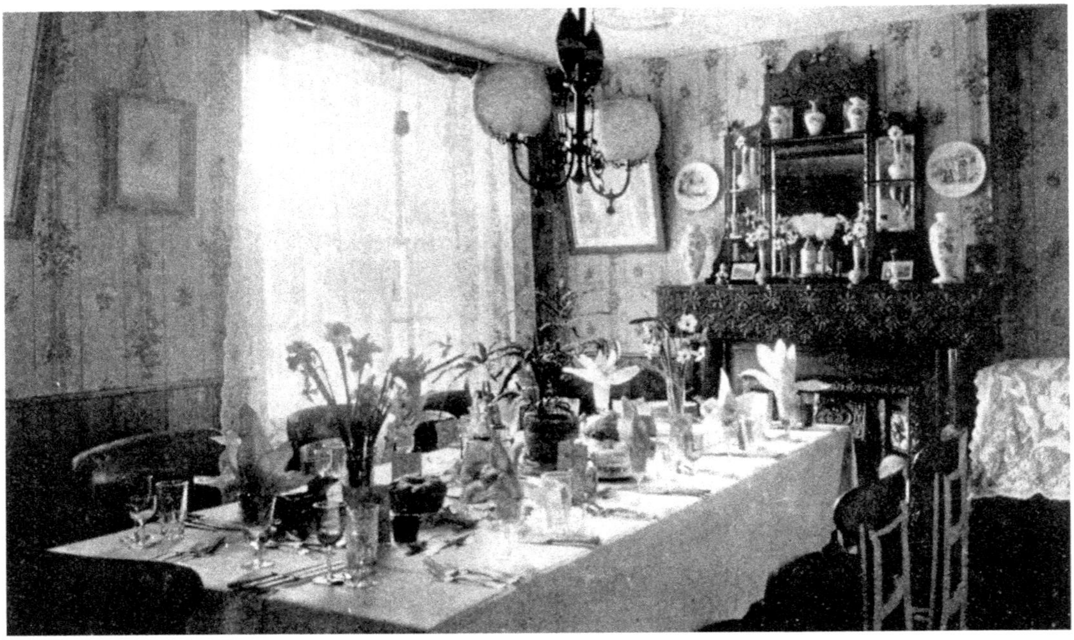

The Crooked House and St Andrew's Church

The dining room of the Crooked House is shown in the image above. This room is referred to in a booklet of the period as follows: 'It will be noticed that the unevenness of the floor necessitated removing the casters from the one side of the table.' The image below shows the gaslit interior of St Andrew's Church on the corner of the High Street and St Andrew's Street. The gas company in Friar Street Droitwich was established in 1836, and the centre of the town illuminated by gas in 1837. The Church's east window (centre) was replaced by the current First World War memorial window in 1928.

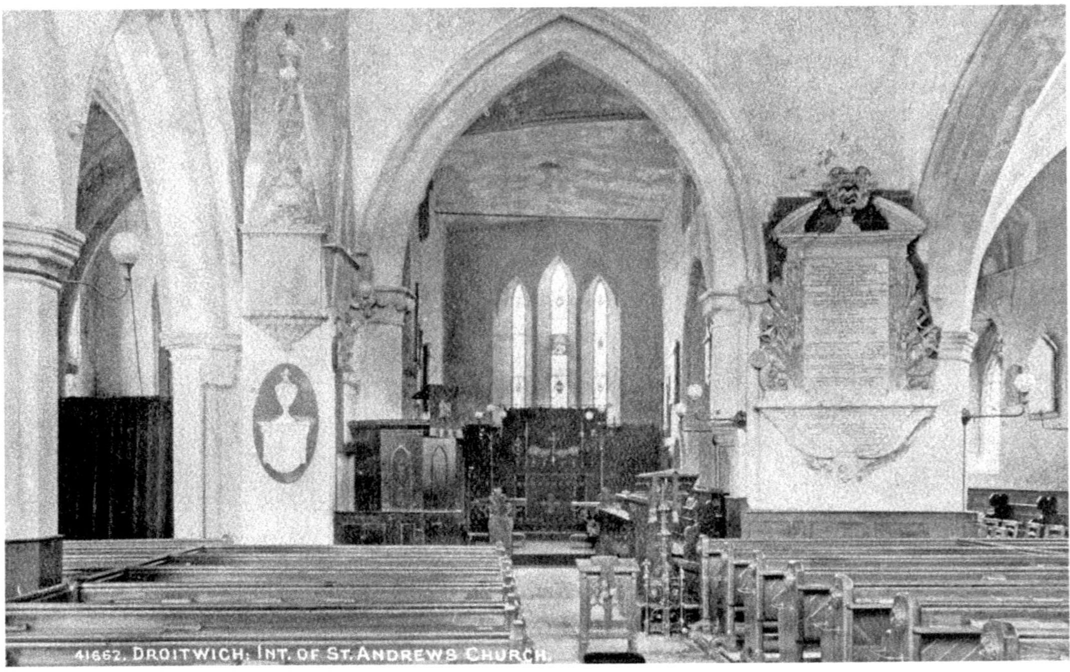

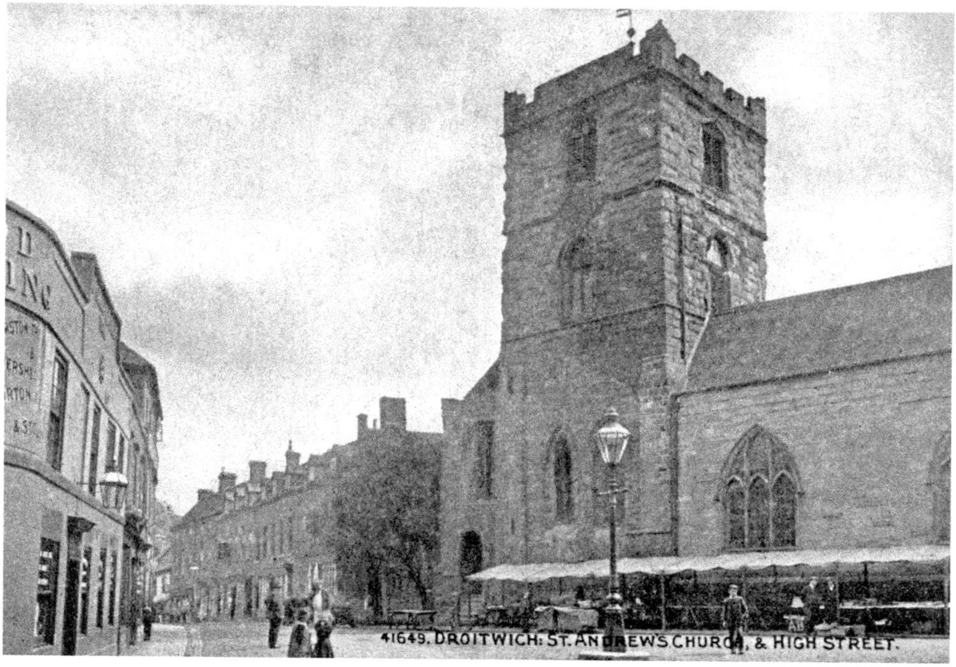

St Andrew's Church

Two exterior views of St Andrew's Church are reproduced here. The image above was taken in the early 1900s, and the old market that once clung to the church's north wall can be seen (right), as can the curved structure of the Star and Garter pub (left). In the image below, from around 1920, the Star and Garter can again be seen (left of centre) and the original wooden First World War memorial is also visible to the left of the church's doorway. This was replaced in the early 1950s by the current memorial in Victoria Square. The building to the far left was once the workshop of local cabinetmaker William Fowkes.

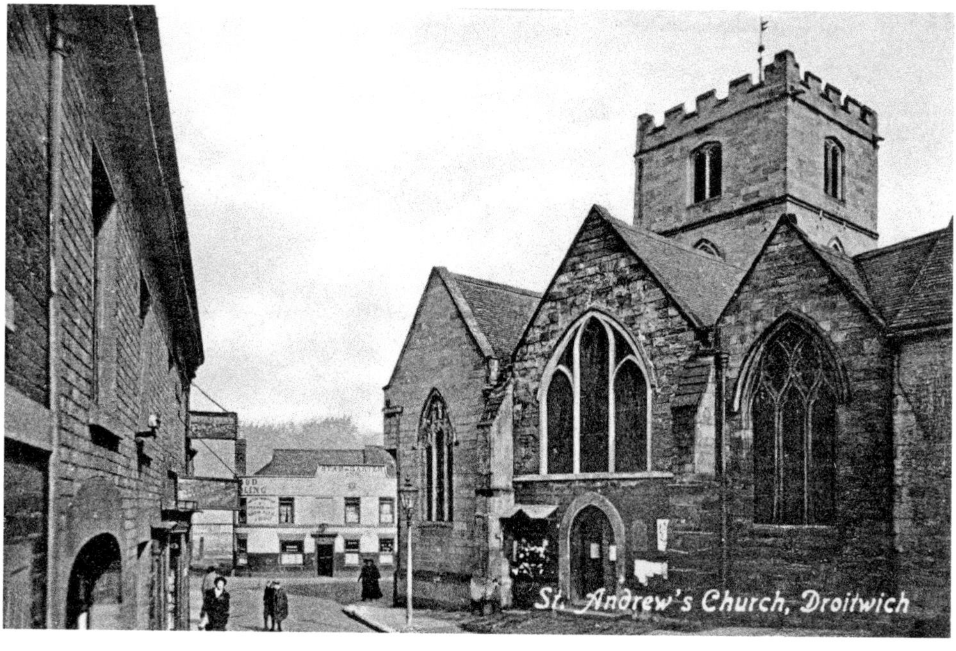

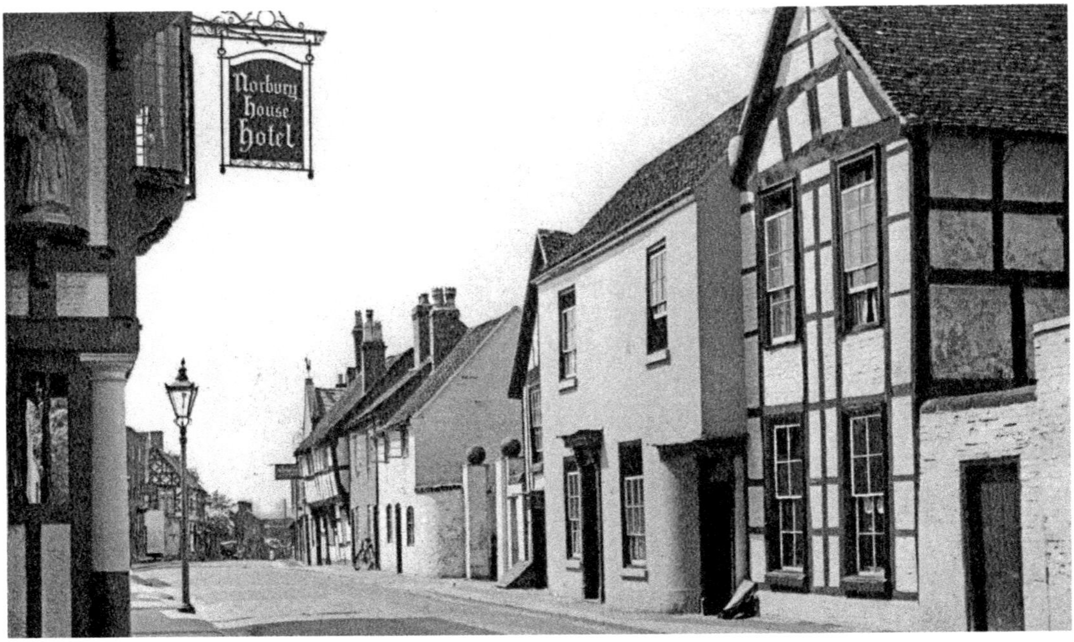

Friar Street

Chorley House can be seen on the right in the above view of Friar Street dating from the 1930s. This high-status timber-framed building was demolished in 1962 after efforts to save it failed. Priory House can be seen behind the lamp post, and the porch of the original Norbury House Hotel to the far left – though the porch itself was a later addition. The site of the original hotel building is now occupied by Priory Lane's junction with Friar Street, leaving only the hotel's luxury extension, which dates from the mid-1930s. Below is a charming sketch of the Norbury House Hotel's dining room.

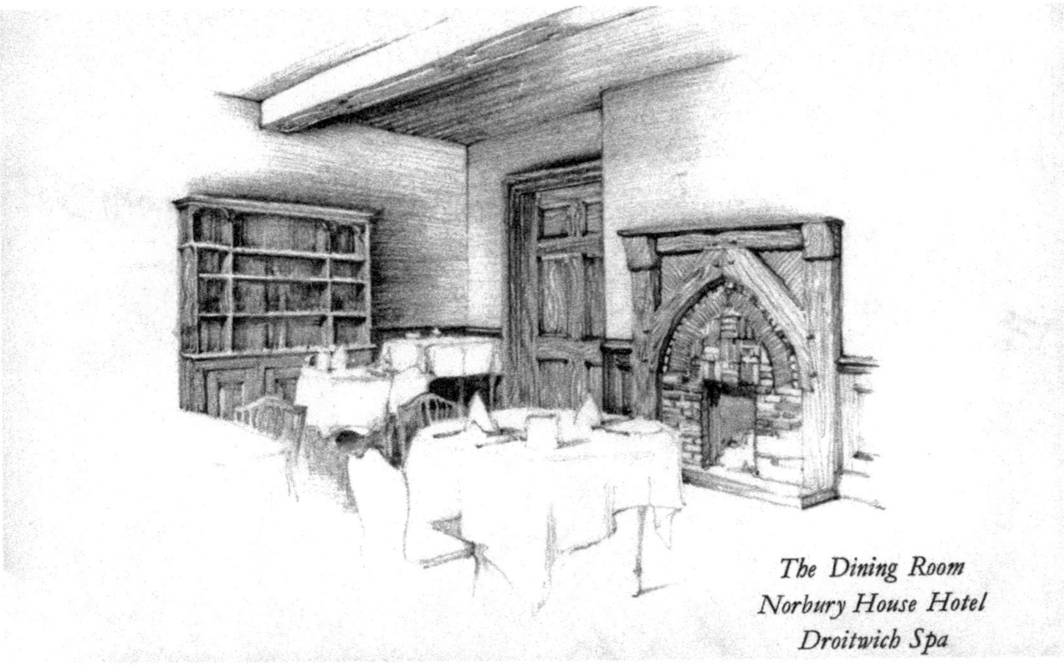

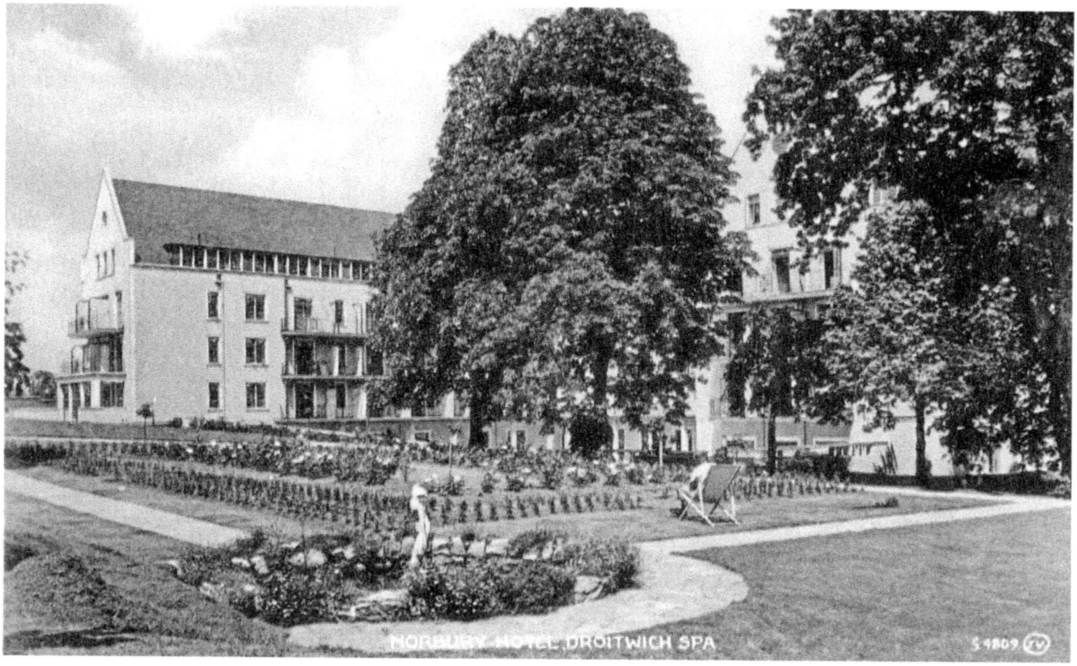

Norbury House Hotel

The two shots shown here of the luxury extension to the Norbury House Hotel were taken in around 1936. The walls were originally painted a light cream colour, but this has worn off over the years. The hotel's formal gardens in the foreground have been replaced by Priory Lane and the 1970s shopping precinct. This expanded hotel, on which many hopes were pinned, was very short-lived, as it was requisitioned during the Second World War, became council flats and offices in 1970, and is now an apartment block. The ever-popular Norbury Theatre has occupied part of the west wing since the early 1960s.

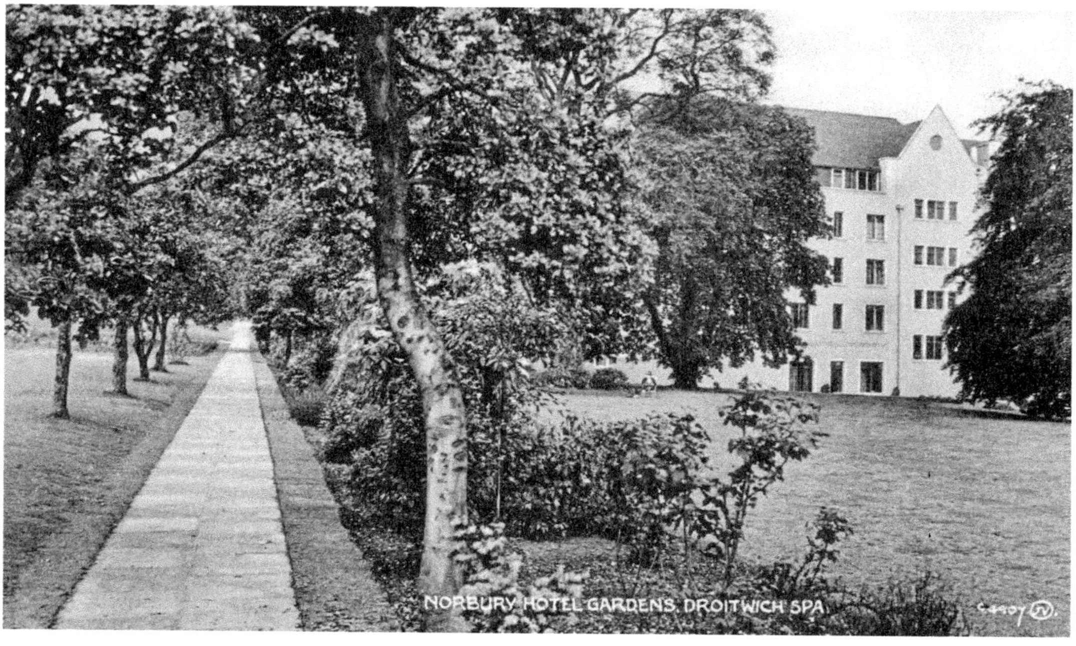

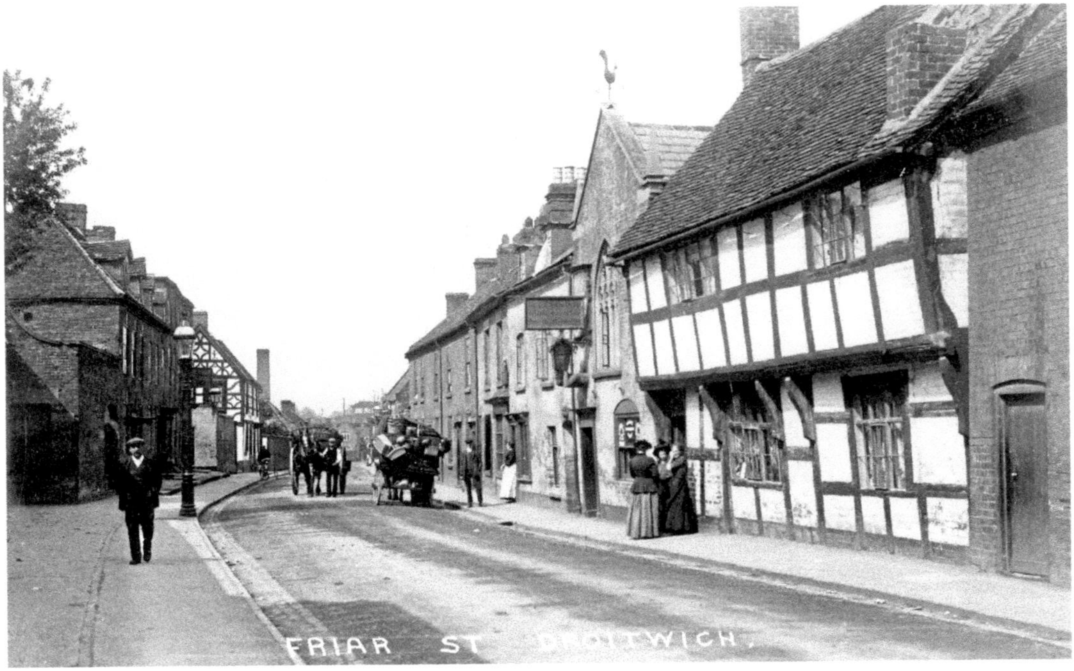

Friar Street

In this charming *c.* 1900 view of Friar Street above, Priory House can again be seen left of centre. The Old Cock Inn, with its familiar weathervane (right of centre), contains some interesting portions of the lost St Nicholas' Church of Friar Street; the remains of which were cleared in the early nineteenth century and the replacement built in Newtown in the late 1860s. Chantry Cottage (further right) was quite a ruin before being fully restored in the late 1970s. A close-up of the high-status Priory House is shown below, and the roofline of the 1890s fire station can be seen just beyond it to the right.

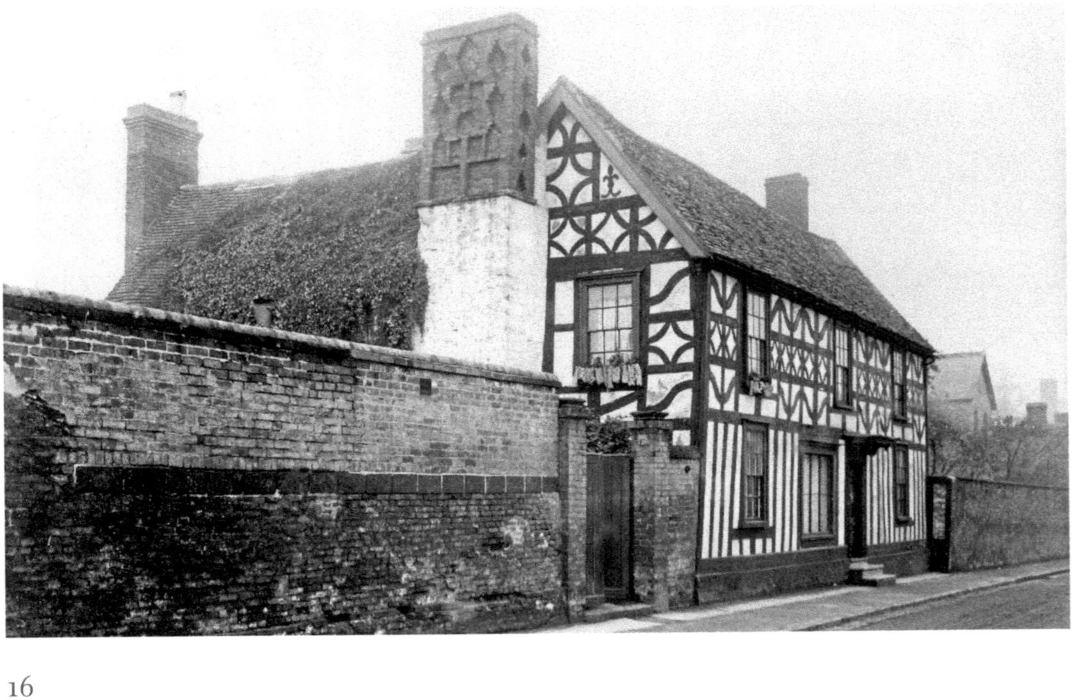

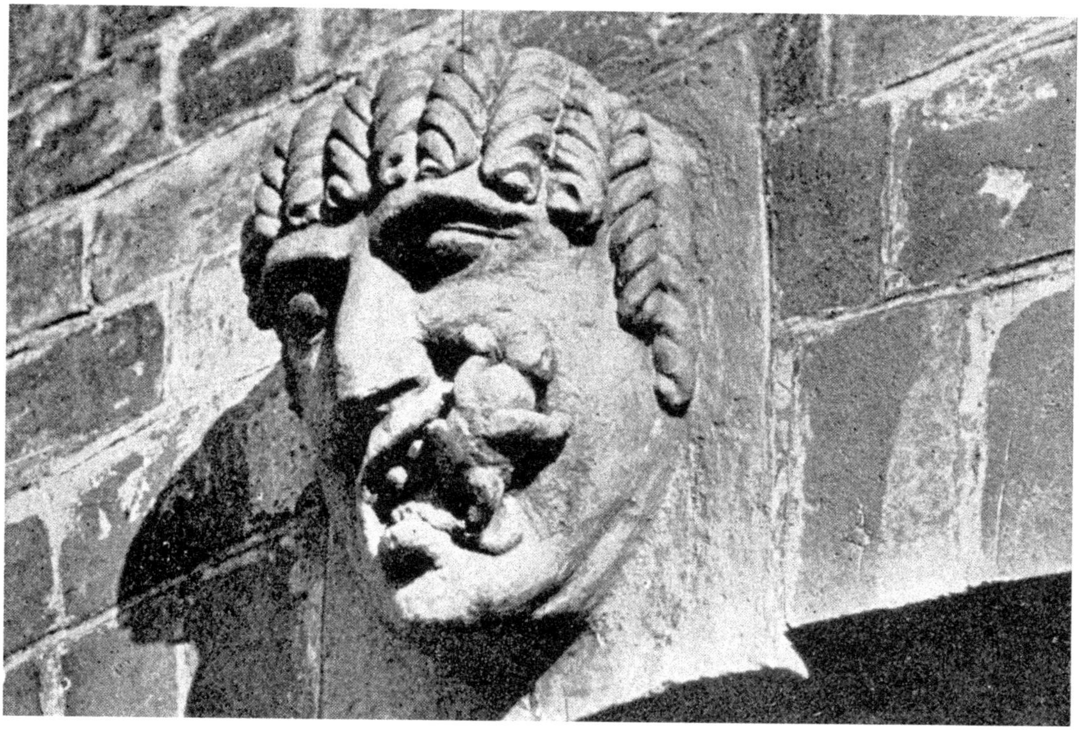

St Nicholas' Church

In these two shots, the salvaged portions of the old St Nicholas' Church can be seen in more detail. The so-called Judge Jeffreys's head is shown above in a photograph taken prior to the terrible erosion that has caused the toad emerging from this individual's mouth to be barely discernible. In the second image, the stone head of a king can be seen, complete with its arms and a lamp. This was knocked to pieces in April 1932 by a large vehicle, and only the head now remains. There are some more fascinating features on the first floor of the pub, including various symbols in the plasterwork.

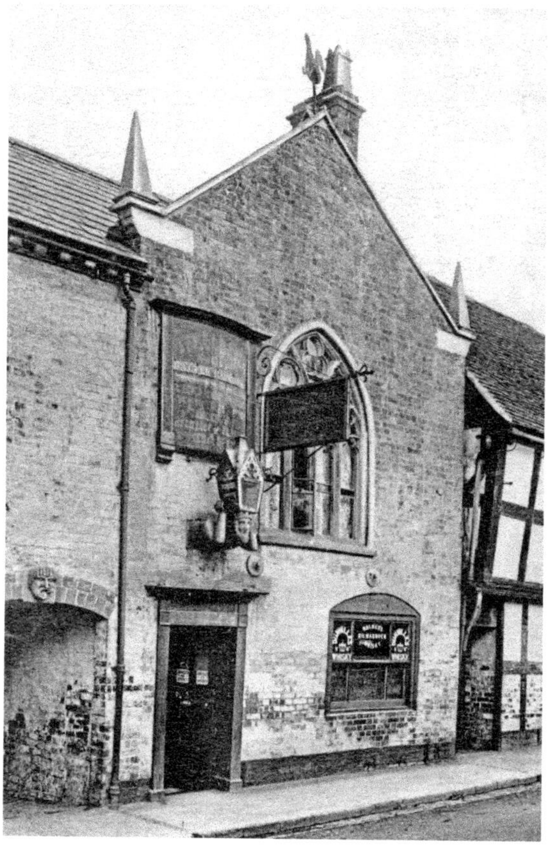

CHAPTER 2

THE VINES, DODDERHILL AND THE SALT INDUSTRY

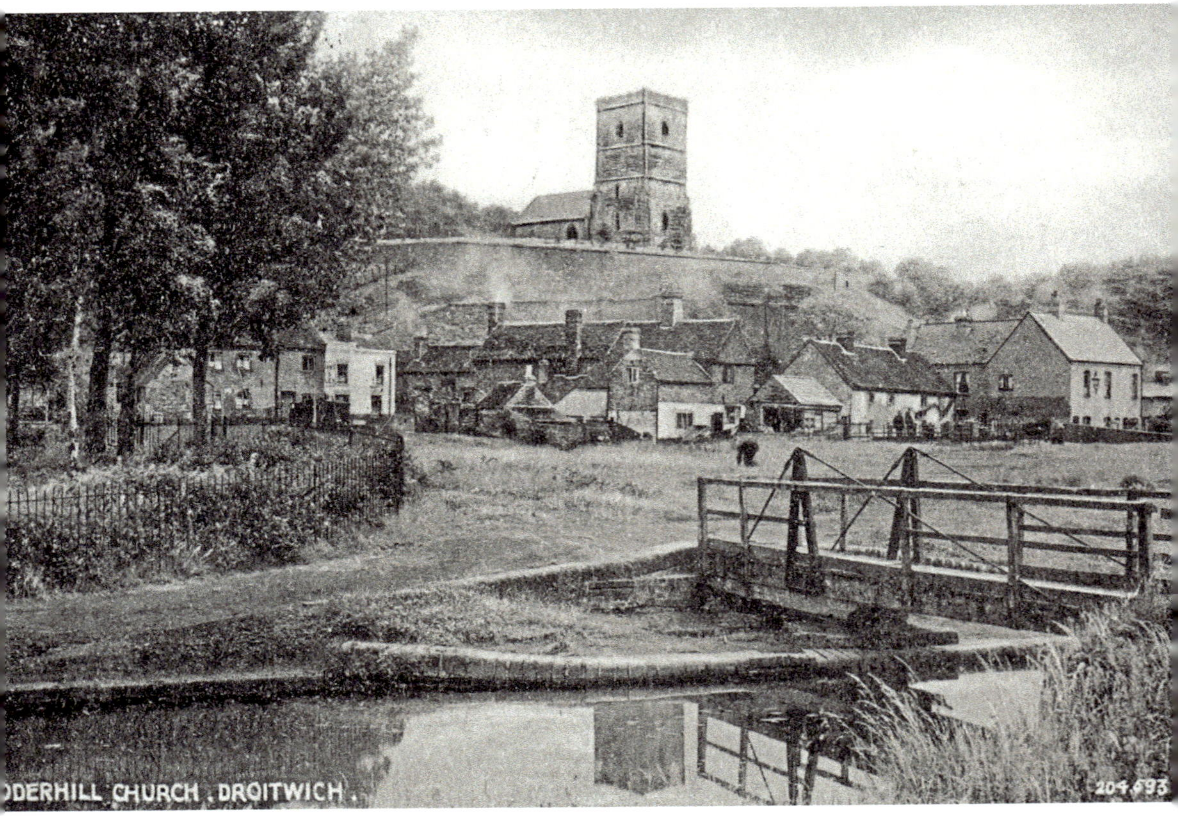

The Vines

The above image of the Vines area in Droitwich was taken in around 1928, from the area now occupied by the Saltway. The canal and one of its swing bridges can be seen in the foreground, which, thanks to the canal's restorers, looks very much the same today. Of all of the buildings in the background, only St Augustine's Church and the Gardener's Arms Pub (the white building left of centre) now remain.

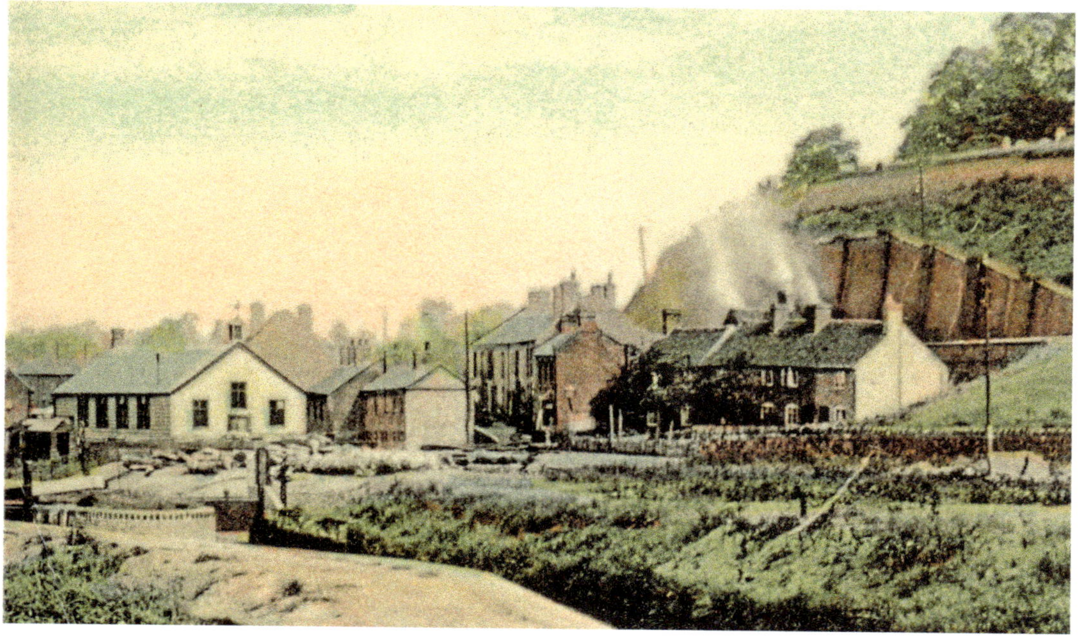

Vines Park

In the above image, taken *c.* 1900 from the canal towpath next to Chapel Bridge, the Vines Park lock can be seen (far left). Many of these cottages were not demolished until the 1960s and '70s, and the Dodderhill Mission Room (far left) survived until the 1980s. The image below is taken from a card posted in 1913, and shows the same cottages in more detail. Many people can still remember Ada Wood's sweetshop, which was situated in one of the cottages in the row on the far left. Dodderhill Mission Room was a popular venue and many functions were held there, including wedding receptions.

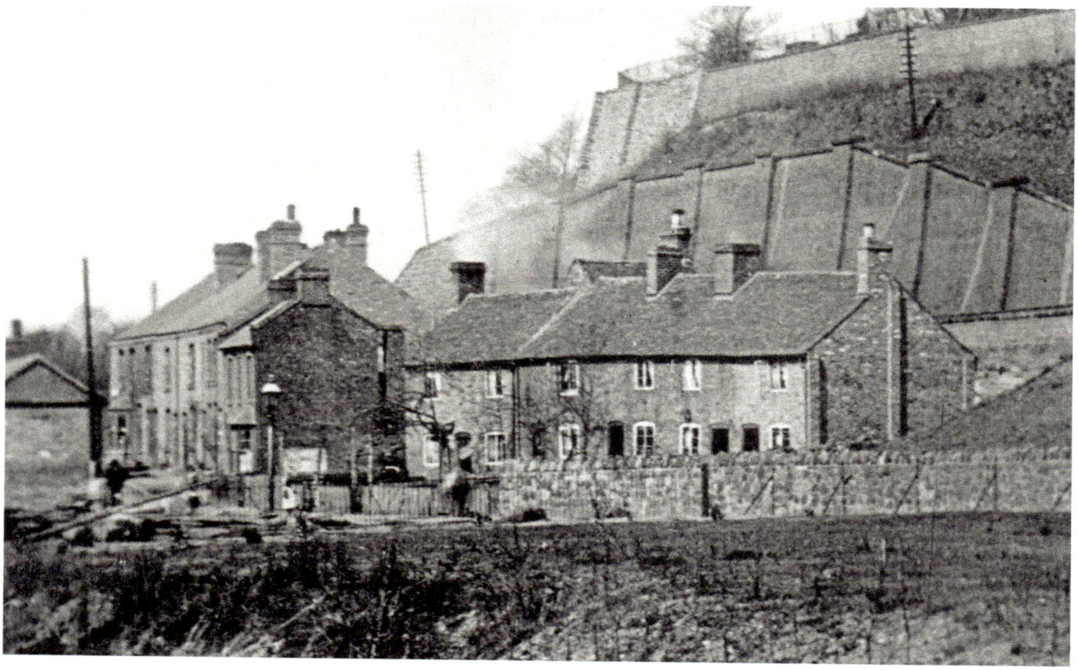

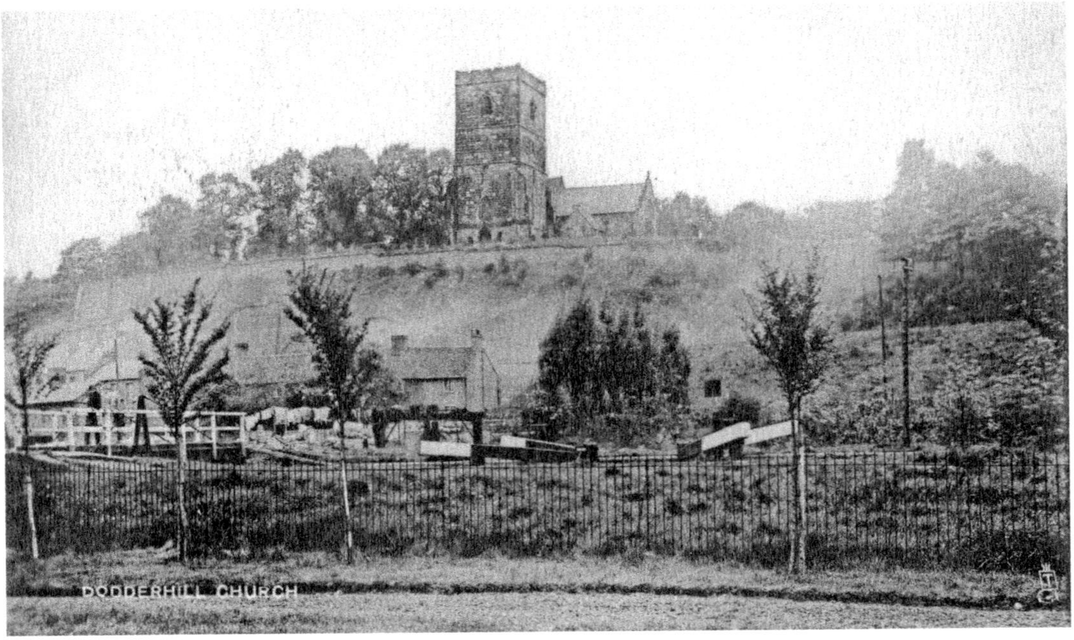

St Augustine's Church

In the above shot of St Augustine's Church and Dodderhill from the Vines, the same lock as featured on page 19 can be seen in the foreground. Note that the configuration of the lock gates has changed since this picture was taken, though the current swing bridges are very similar in appearance to the one seen here and on page 18. The below interior shot of St Augustine's Church dates from around 1905, and shows the church's original layout with the altar to the east. The altar was moved to the west in recent times in order to allow all present to see, as well as hear, the service.

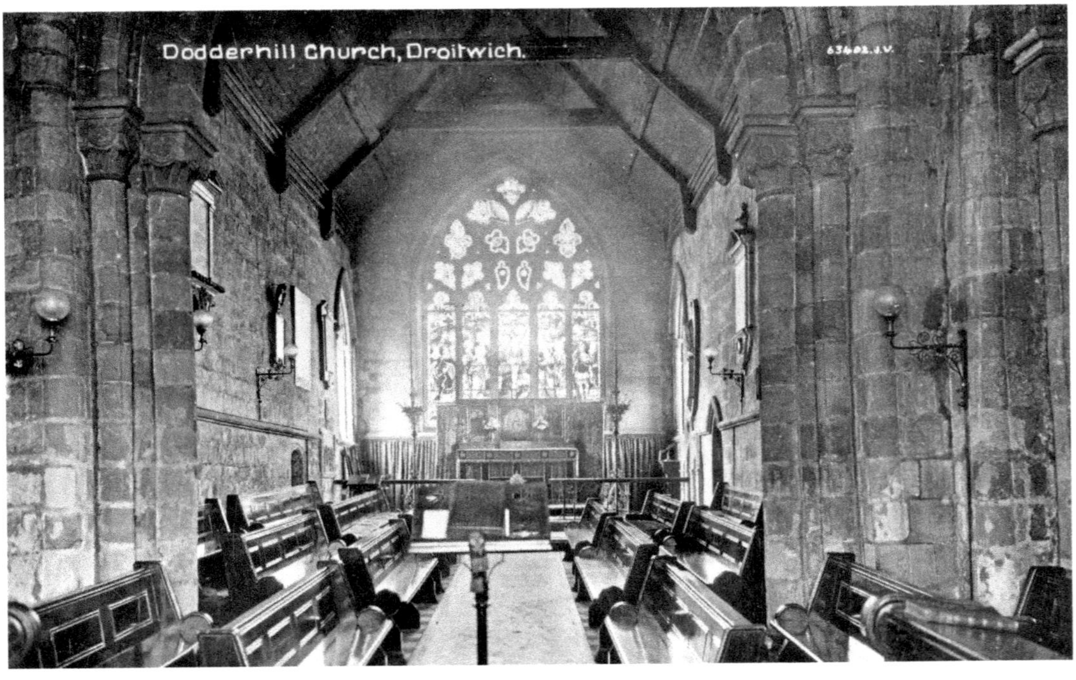

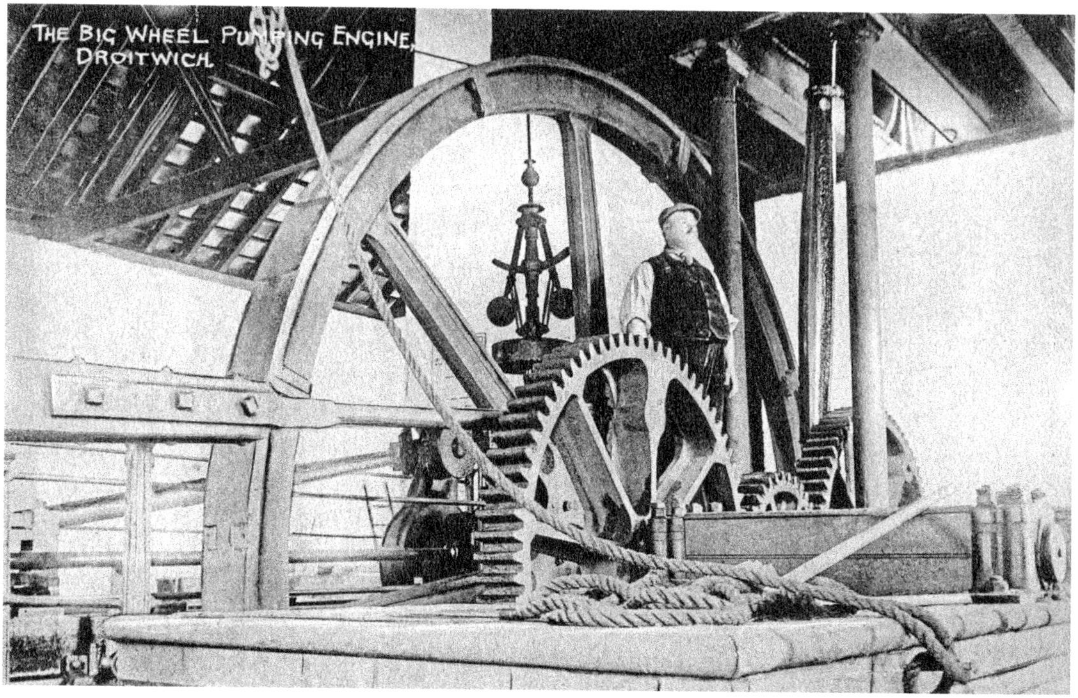

Brine Pits

The 'Big Wheel' brine pumping engine in the early 1900s is shown above, with Bill 'Boner' Evans at the flywheel. The brine pit in question was known as the Mitre Pit, and Bill worked for twelve hours a day with no breaks, even when eating. The covered market hall was built on the site of the pit in the 1980s, and was in turn was demolished in around 2004. The second picture reproduced here also dates from the early 1900s, and shows one of the brine pits with its accompanying pump. These were once a common sight in Droitwich, and this one is thought to have been at Covercroft.

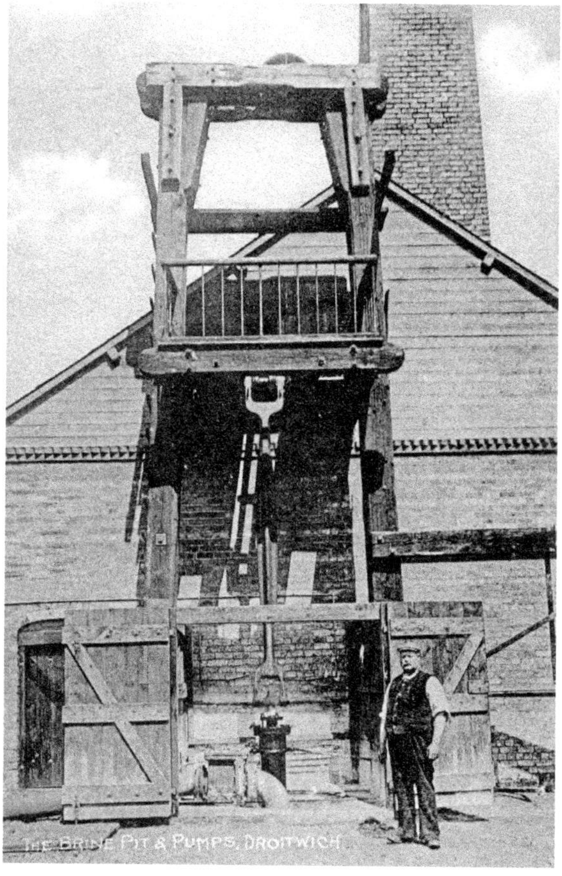

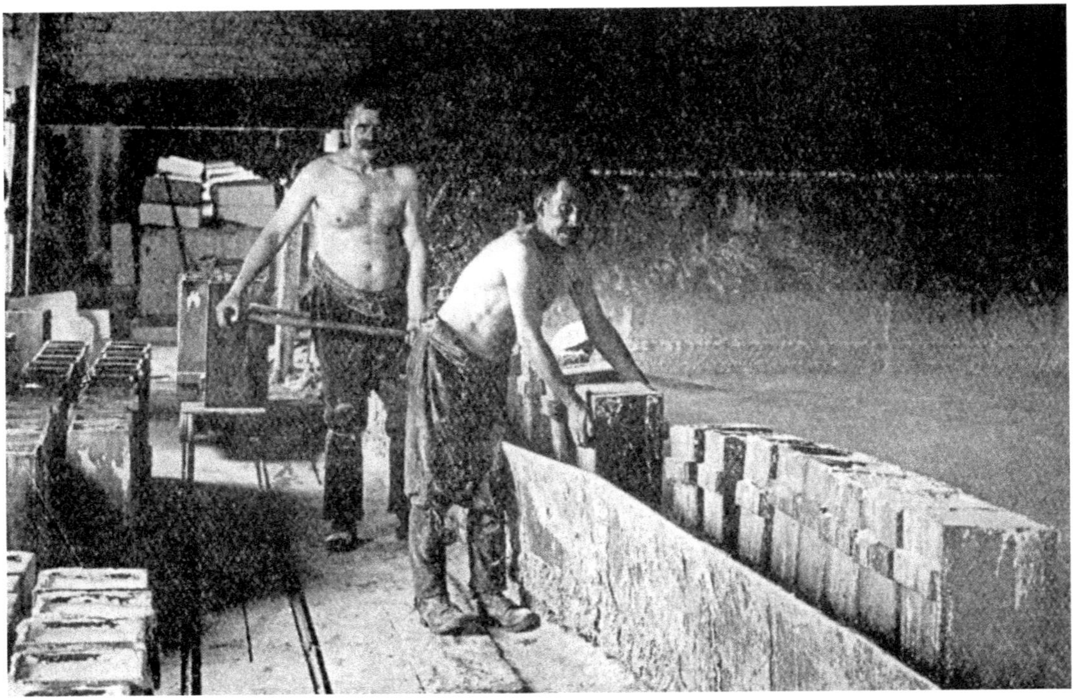

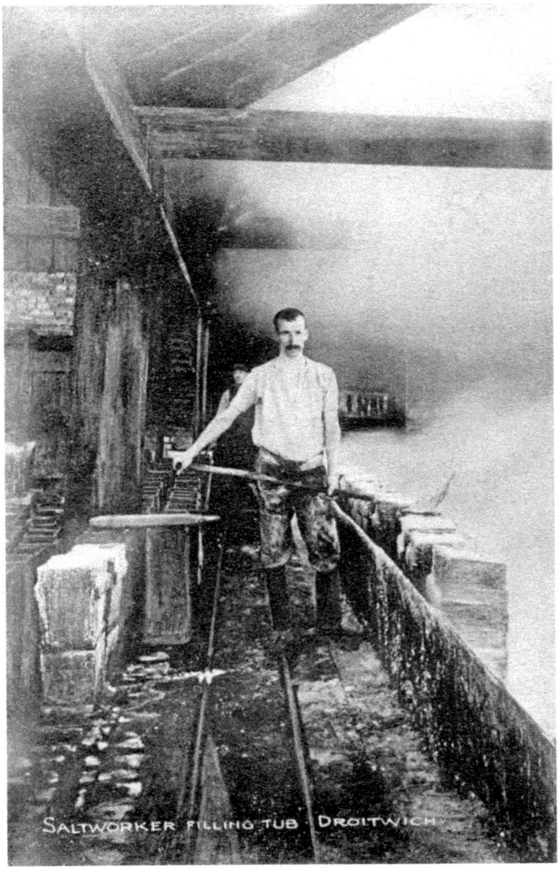

Salt Works

Another early 1900s image of Covercroft Salt Works is shown above, with Mr Jim Bourne on the right and Joe Farr on the left. After the closure of Covercroft in around 1918, Jim Bourne went to work at Stoke Works, and apparently used to walk there from his Droitwich home. The image was taken by F. G. W. Sage of Droitwich, a photographer responsible for many fine images of Droitwich and the surrounding villages, which he reached by bicycle. Mr Sage is interred in St Peter's Churchyard Droitwich. In the second salt works scene shown here, we see James 'Jimmy Fake' Sparkes hard at work at one of the pans.

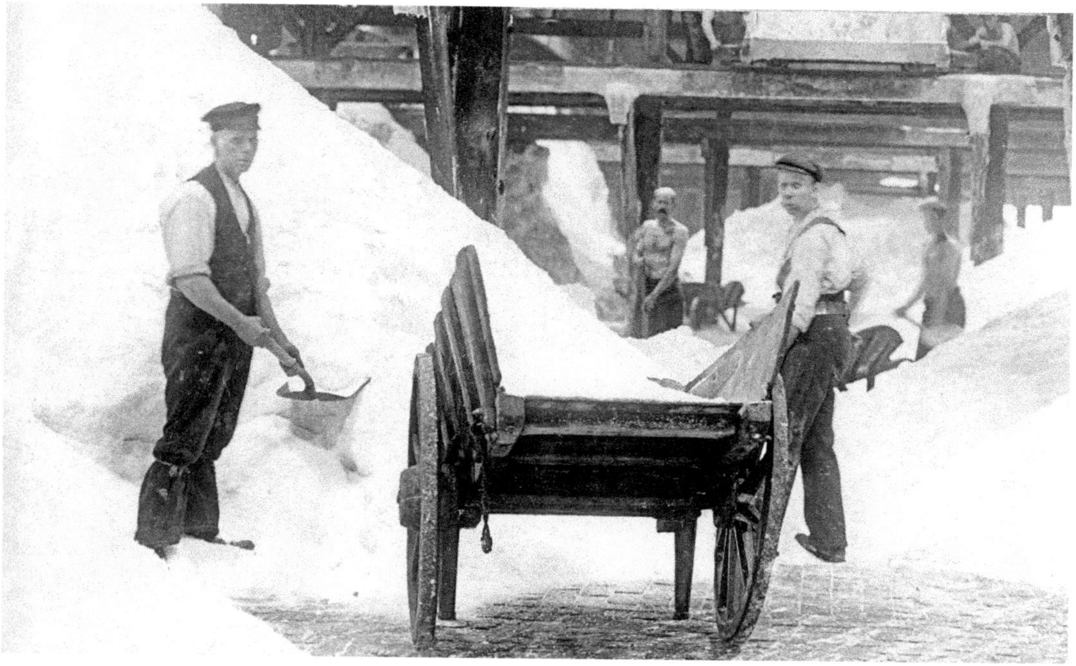

Salt Workers

The scene reproduced above was also taken by Mr Sage of Droitwich, the message on the back of the card reading: 'These are salt workers shovelling the salt out of the vats. But the works are all closed down as the men have struck! Kind regards to Mr & Mrs Godfrey and with love to you all A. J. Harvey Droitwich.' This message was penned in July 1914, and the card posted from Droitwich to 'The Misses Godfrey London'. More salt workers at one of the pans are shown below, with around eighteen blocks of Droitwich salt in the foreground.

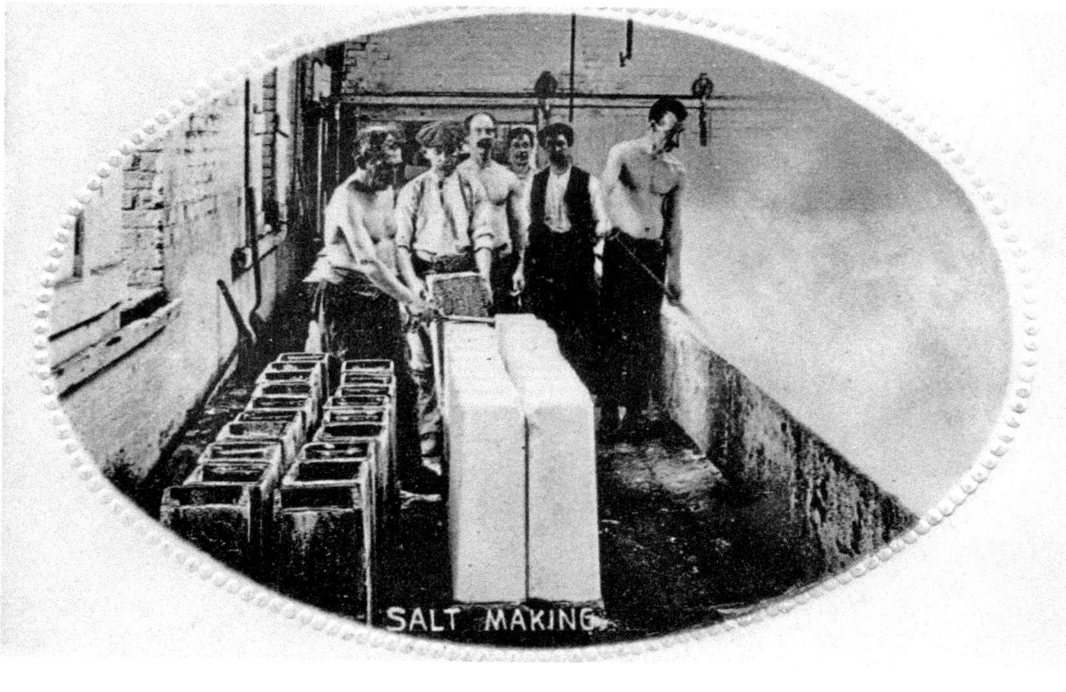

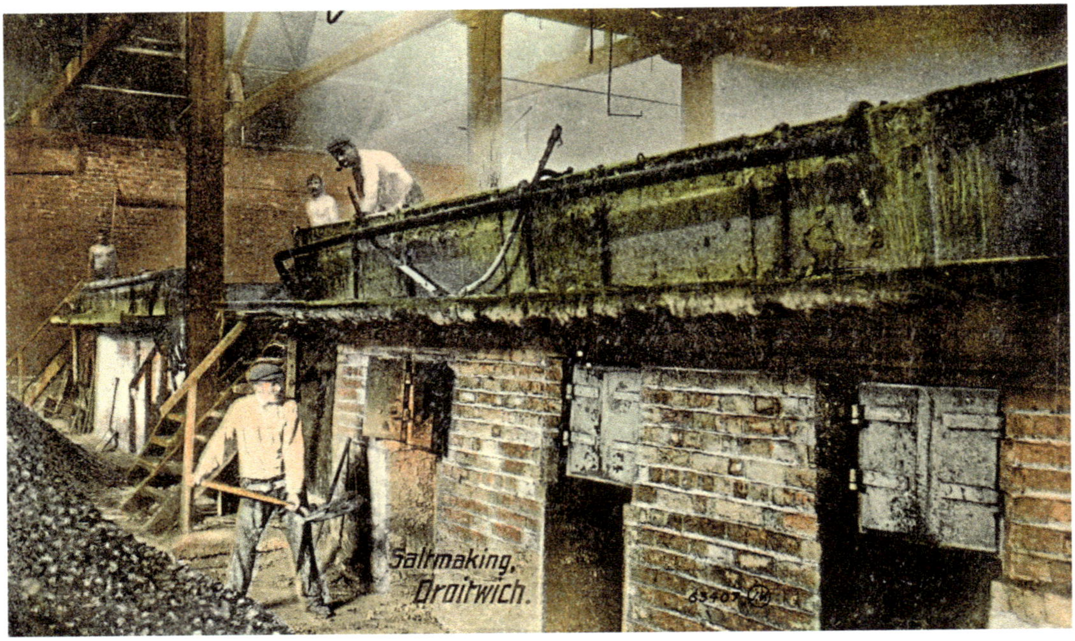

Covercroft Salt Works

Two interior shots of Covercroft Salt Works are reproduced here, with a stoker at one of the fireholes shown above. Each salt pan had three fireholes, and measured around 80 feet by 22 feet. Sometimes, they could be as long as 100 feet, and were usually around a foot and a half or so in depth. Covercroft Salt Works was founded by John and Walter Noak, who in 1847 discovered 'A bountiful source of excellent quality brine beneath Covercroft Field', and went on to exhibit their products at the Great Exhibition of 1851. Coleman Road and a row of shops in Ombersley Street now cover the site.

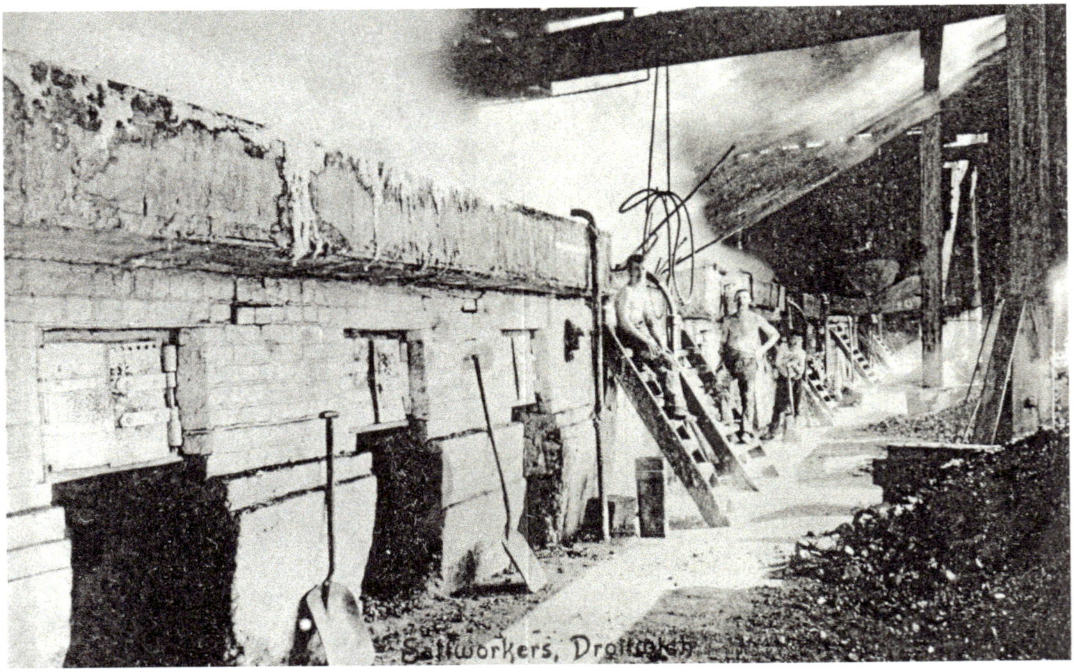

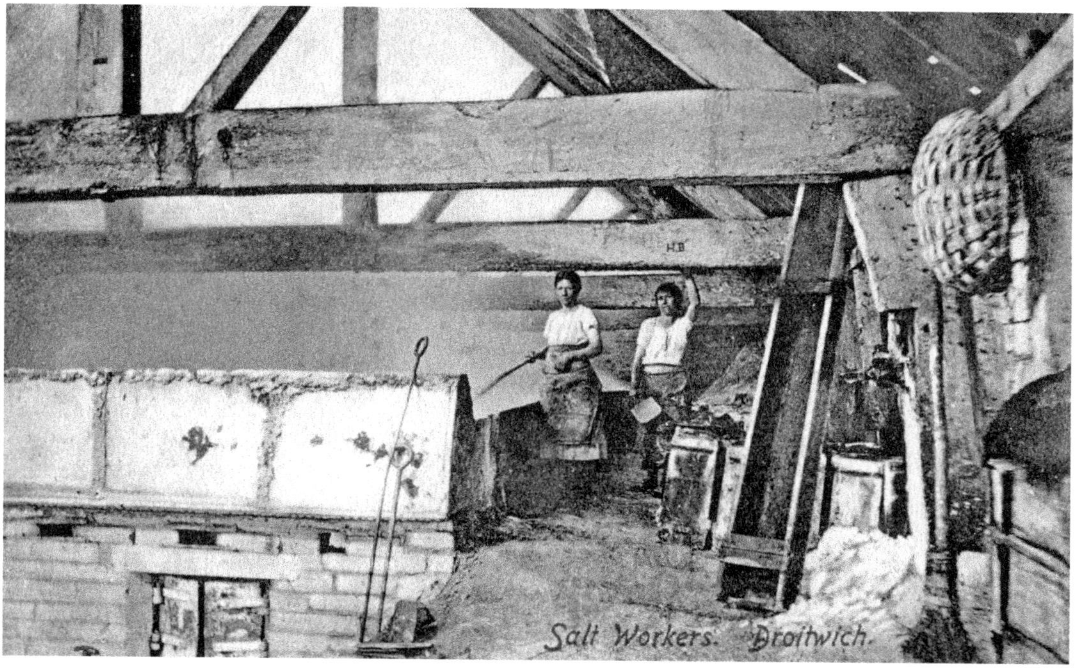

Salt Workers and Vines Park

In the above image taken in 1899, we see two female salt workers at Boucher and Giles Salt Works. The two ladies in question are Elizabeth Goddard of Covercroft and Mary Harris of Woodfield Road. Boucher and Giles Salt Works was situated on the corner of Friar Street and Union Lane, opposite the town's gasworks. At this time, female salt workers had to work for twelve hours a day, but by the early 1920s all of the salt works in Droitwich had closed and the former heart of this industry gradually became Vines Park. The image below shows St Richard's Statue in Vines Park, which was officially unveiled in 1935.

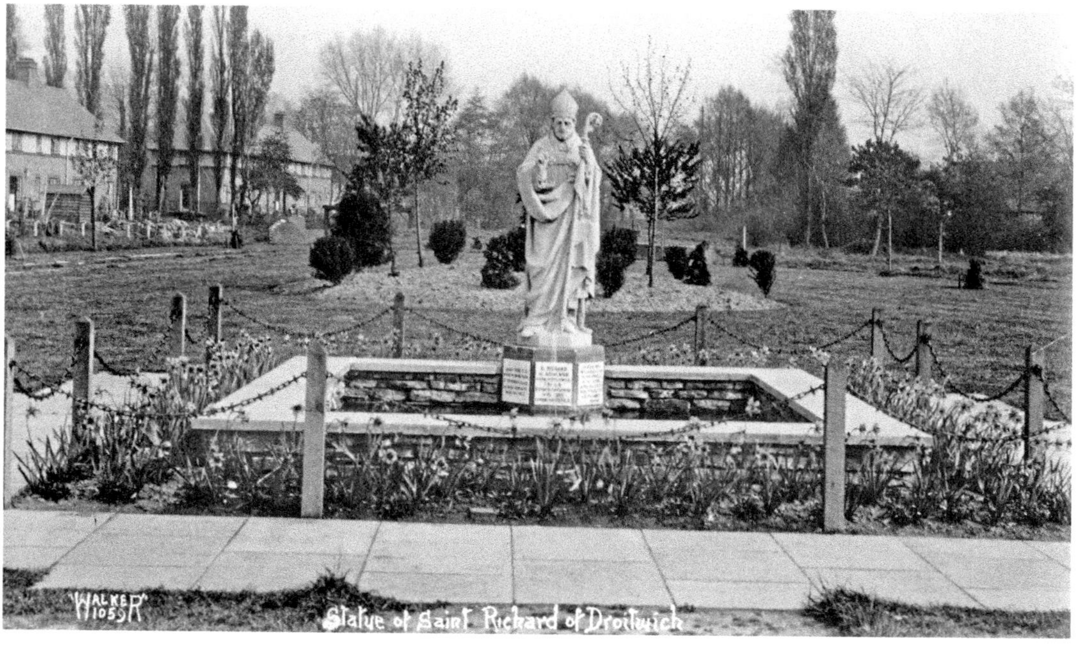

CHAPTER 3

QUEEN STREET, ST GEORGE'S SQUARE AND THE ROYAL BRINE BATHS

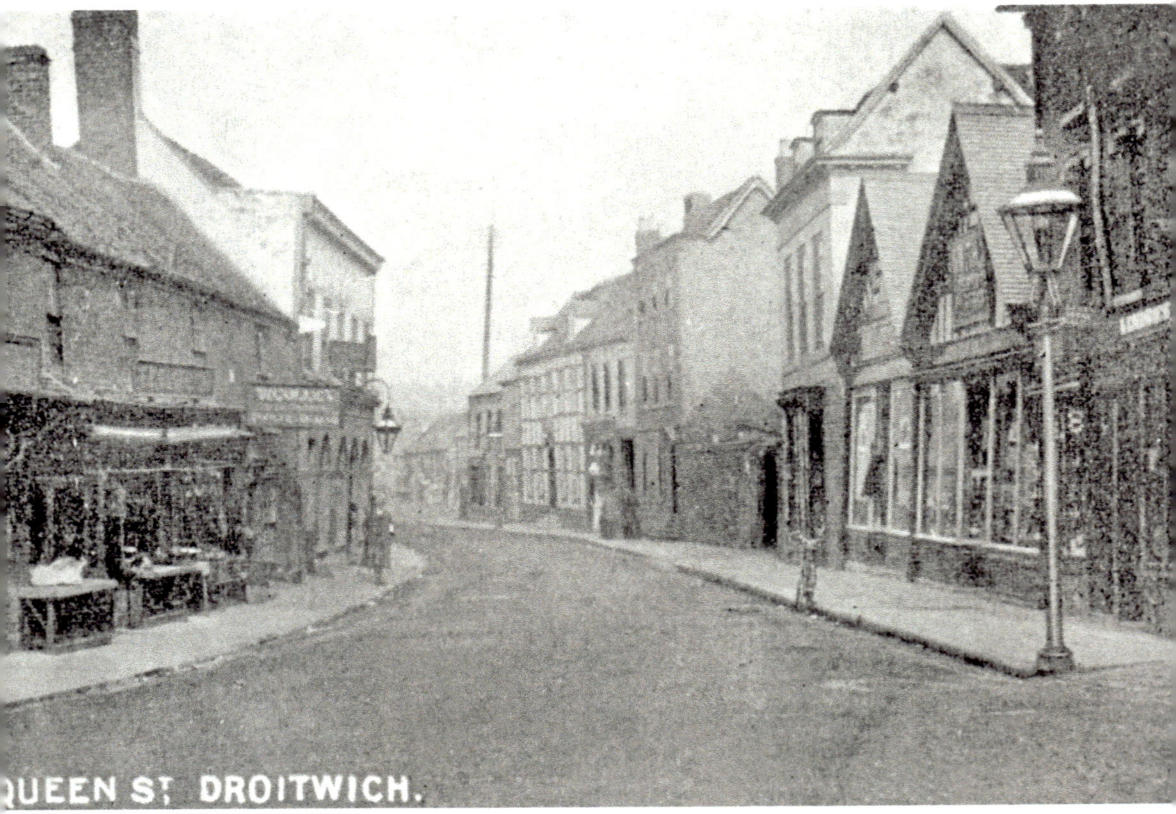

Queen Street

In the *c.* 1905 picture of Queen Street above, Smith's the printers in their new premises can be seen just to the left of the lamp post. This shot also shows T. F. Cooke the butcher's on the far left, with goods displayed on tables on the pavement. Left of centre stands the Royal Exchange Hotel and the light-coloured building in the centre was once known as Oxford House.

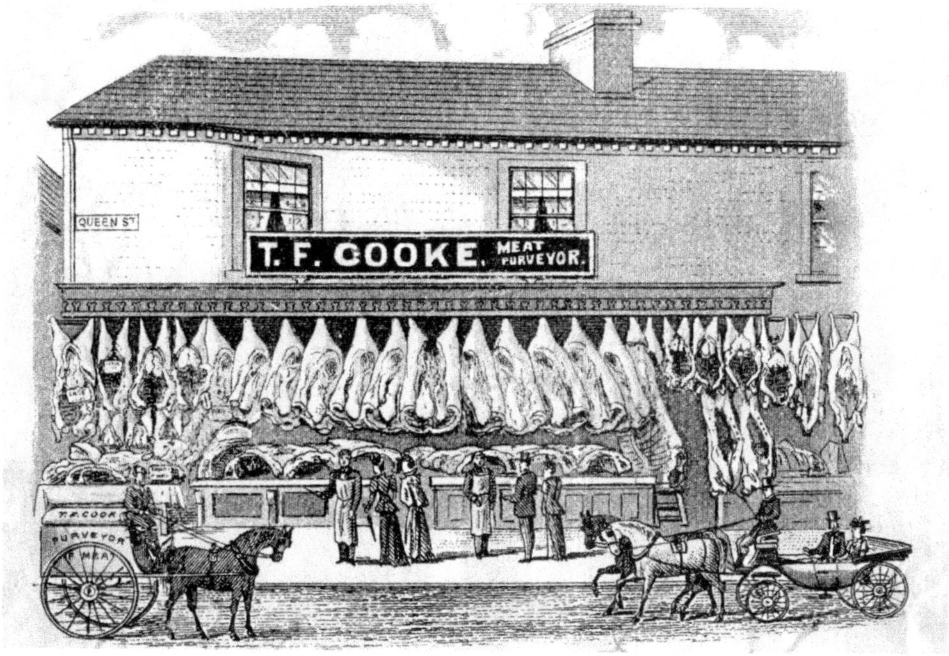

T. F. Cooke

Both of these images of T. F. Cooke's business have been taken from billheads dating from the 1890s. T. F. Cooke's premises were located at what is now No. 5 Queen Street and not at the butcher's shop further along Queen Street as is sometimes stated (note the Queen Street sign attached to the left of the building). Tom Cooke, as he was known to his customers, was a generous man who often gave the poor more than their monies worth. Female salt workers queued at his shop on Sunday mornings for scraps at twopence each. He later retired to the Coventry Homes in the Holloway, where he passed away.

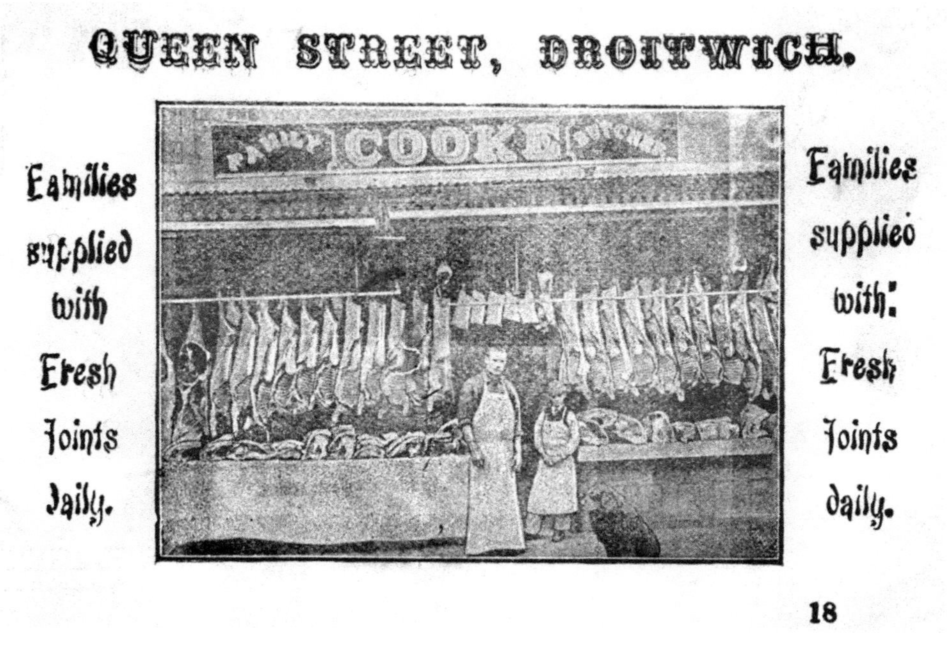

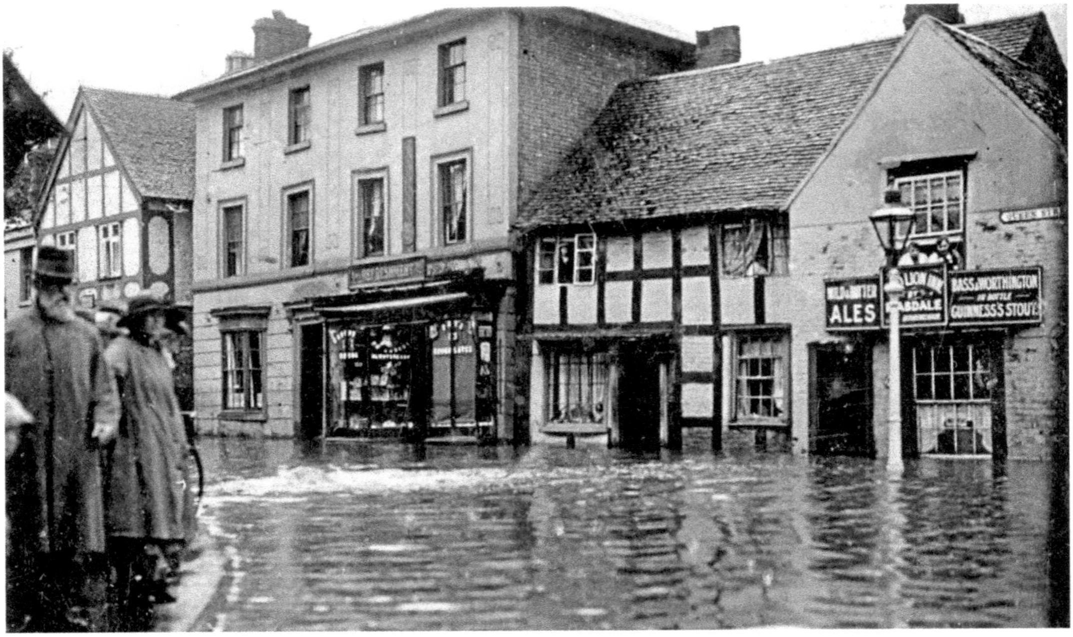

Queen Street

The above image of Queen Street dates from the time of the 1924 flood, and was taken from the corner of Queen Street and Hanbury Street. Two individuals can be seen looking out of the first-floor window of the Red Lion Inn to the right of the lamp post. The Red Lion Inn was later rebuilt, and is now a florist's shop. Further up from Queen Street at Hill End stands Raven Cottage, and this – as illustrated below – was known in the early twentieth century as Ye Olde Curositie Shoppe. This building, which dates from 1878, bears John Corbett's raven and was originally the Corbett Estate Offices.

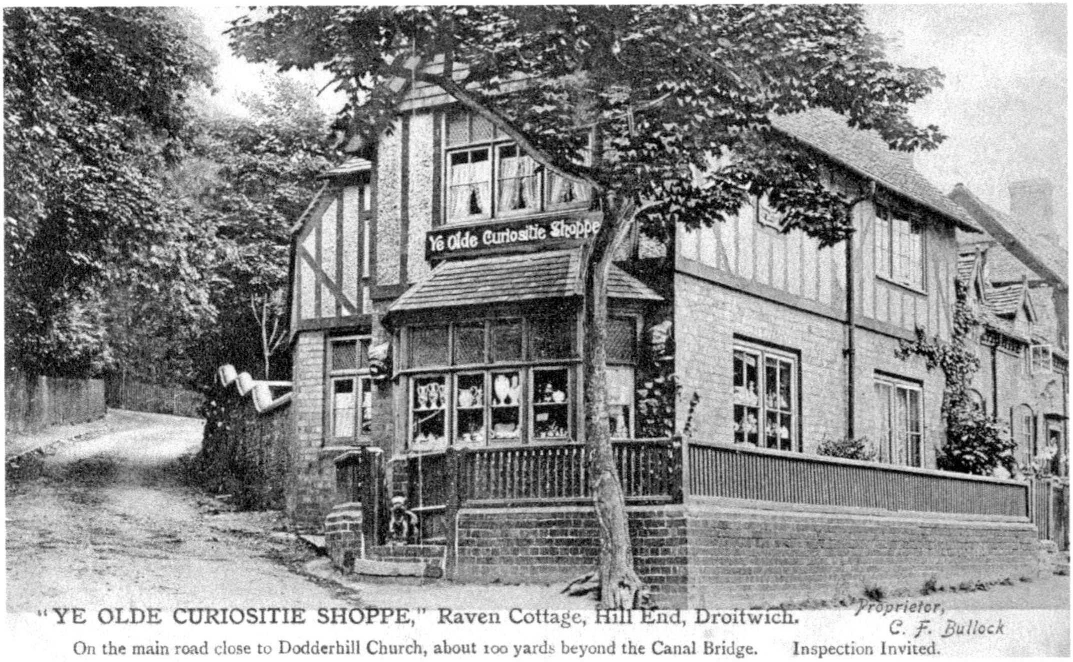

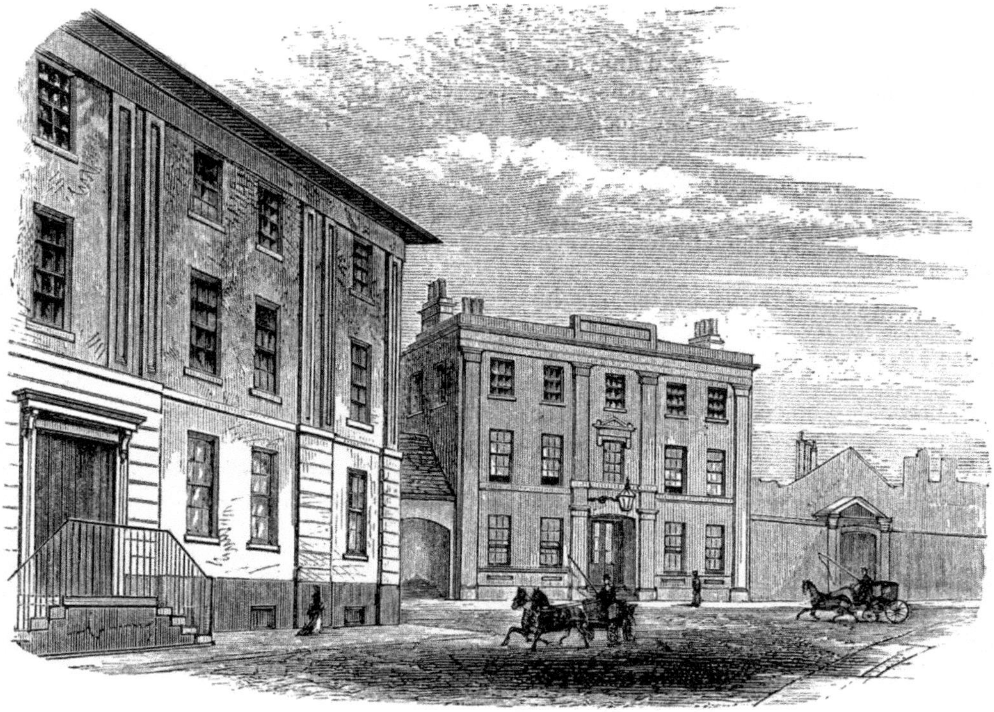

The Royal Hotel

The above print from 1875 looks back towards Droitwich from Hill End, and shows the Royal Hotel and George Inn (centre) and the Ellis Hotel (left). David Neville's furniture store now stands on the site of the rather elegant Ellis Hotel. The Royal Hotel was demolished at the end of the nineteenth century and replaced by a new Royal Hotel set back from the road up a sweeping driveway. The image below, which also dates from 1875, shows the Royal Brine Baths with a person in a bath chair approaching its east entrance. It was to this entrance that the replacement Royal Hotel was later attached.

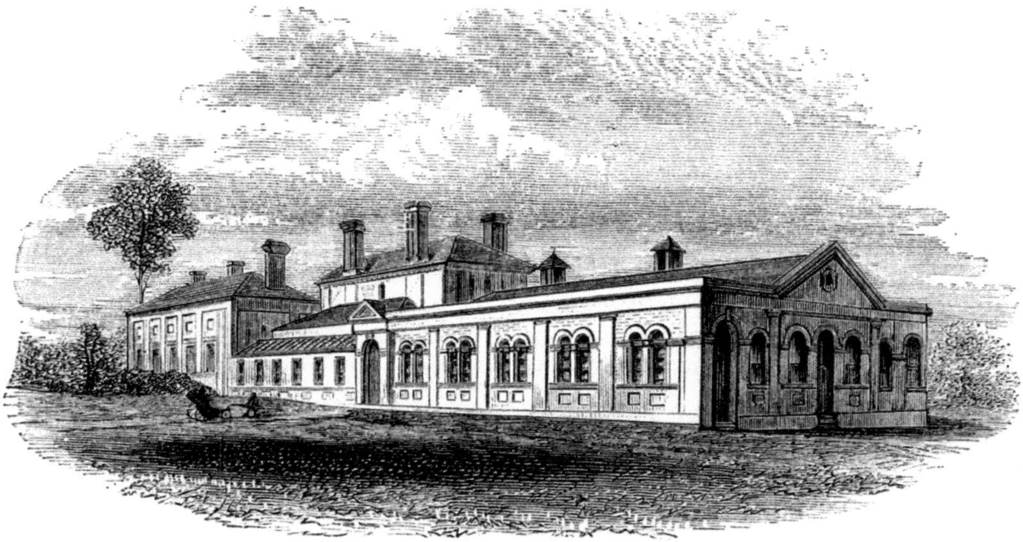

The Brine Baths, Droitwich.

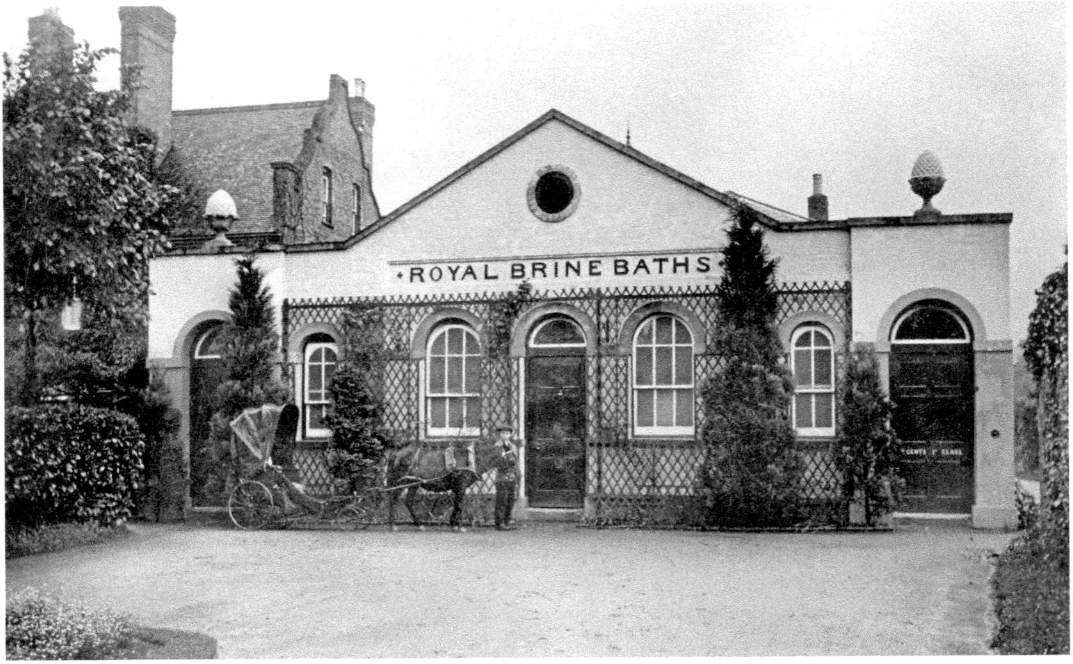

Royal Brine Baths

The above image, which is thought to have been taken during the 1920s, shows the north façade of the Royal Brine Baths, with a pony-driven bath chair parked in front. Part of the replacement Royal Hotel can also be seen on the far left. The Royal Brine Baths were established in 1836, and originally known as the Saline Baths. The image below, which is also thought to date from the 1920s, shows the west face of the Royal Brine Baths (right), and the wooden pavilion-like ticket office and weighing room (left). St Augustine's Church is just visible between the trees in the centre of the image.

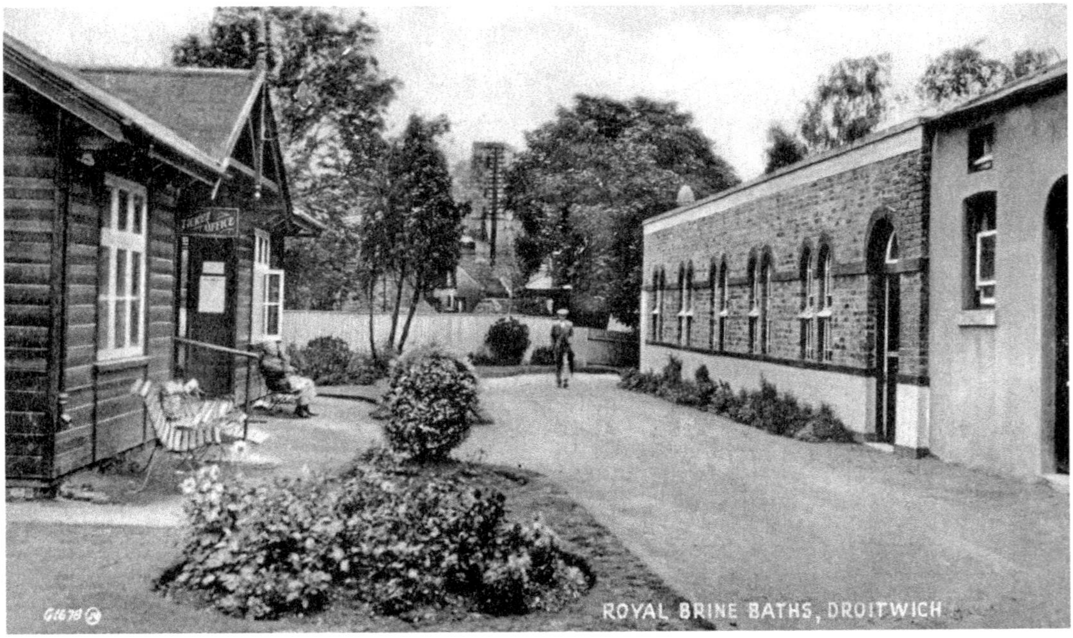

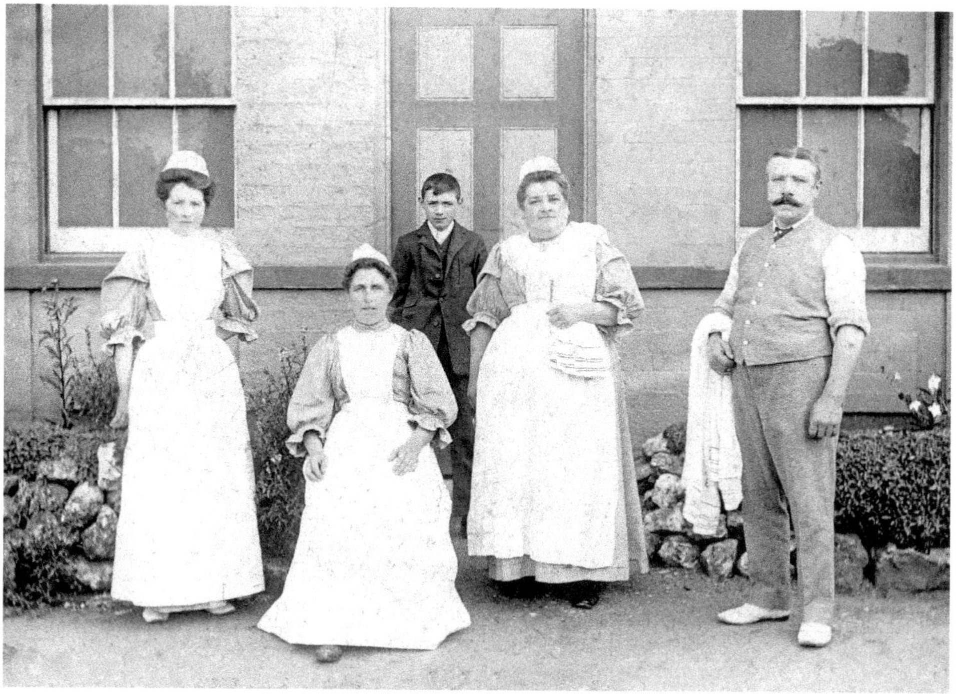

Royal Brine Baths

In the image above, the staff of the Royal Brine Baths are shown standing outside the north entrance in 1899. The names of these individuals have, in the past, been given in the wrong order. The correct order is (left to right): May Morton, Miss Deddicott, Rupert Bourne, Eliza Skerrett and Eliza's brother-in-law Charles Skerrett. This photograph is something of a family heirloom, as Eliza was my great-great-grandmother. The rarely photographed 70-foot by 30-foot swimming pool at the Royal Brine Baths is shown below in *c.* 1910 with an attendant standing next to one of the cubicles.

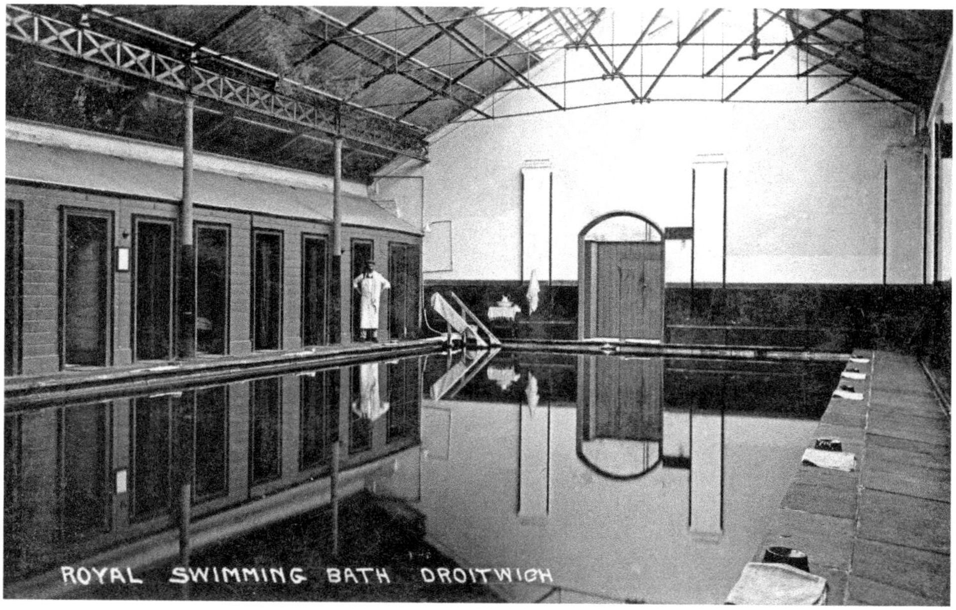

CHAPTER 4

ST PETER'S AND THE HOLLOWAY

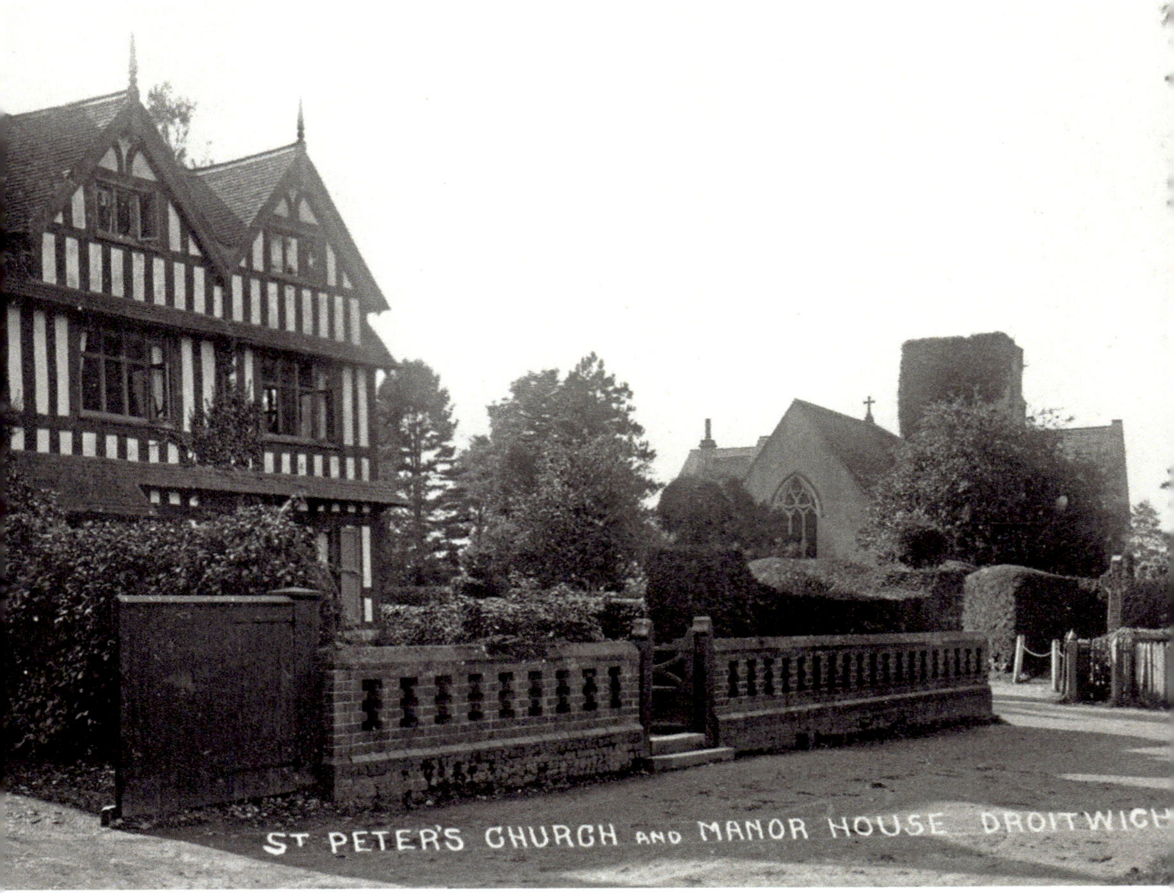

St Peter's Church

Along with Himbleton, St Peter's Church remains one of my favourites among the local churches, and many of our family services have taken place here over the last few centuries. This shot was taken in the early 1900s and shows both the manor house with its fine close-studded timber-framed structure to the left, and the church with its ivy-clad tower to the right. The church is famous for being the christening place of Pilgrim Father Edward Winslow in 1595.

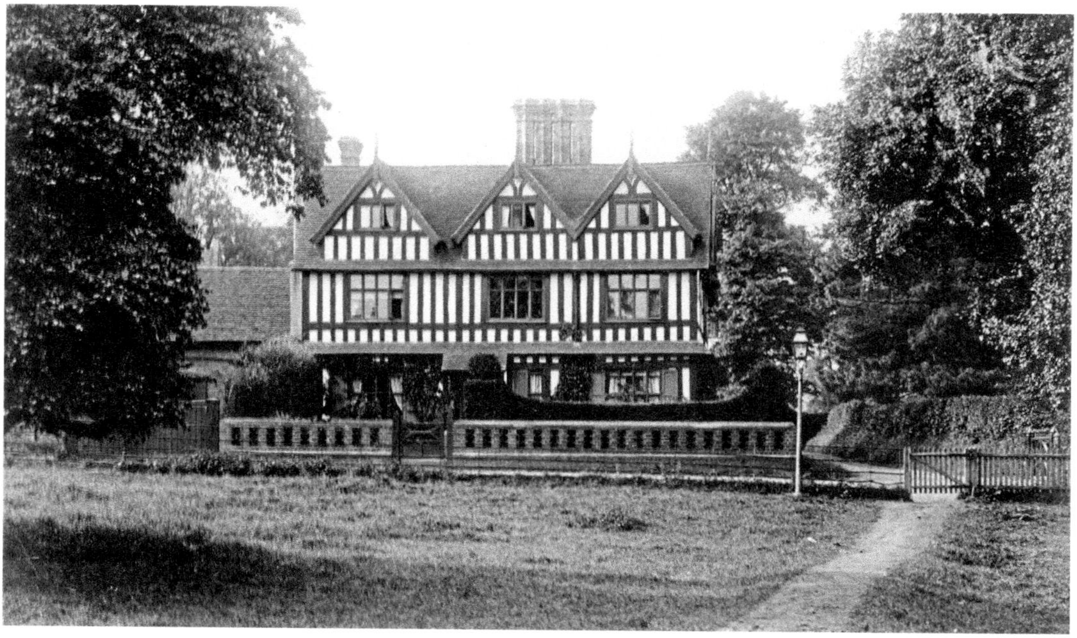

St Peter's Manor House

Two early twentieth-century shots of St Peter's Manor House are shown here, which is believed to have been constructed in 1618. The shot above was taken by F. G. W. Sage and posted in 1914. The Worcestershire historian Dr Treadway Russell Nash presented himself to St Peter's vicarage in 1761, but did not live at the manor house, choosing instead to reside at Bevere near Worcester where he died in 1811. He was, however, interred in the family vault at St Peter's on 4 February 1811 at the age of eighty-five, and there are a number of fine monuments to members of the Nash family inside the church.

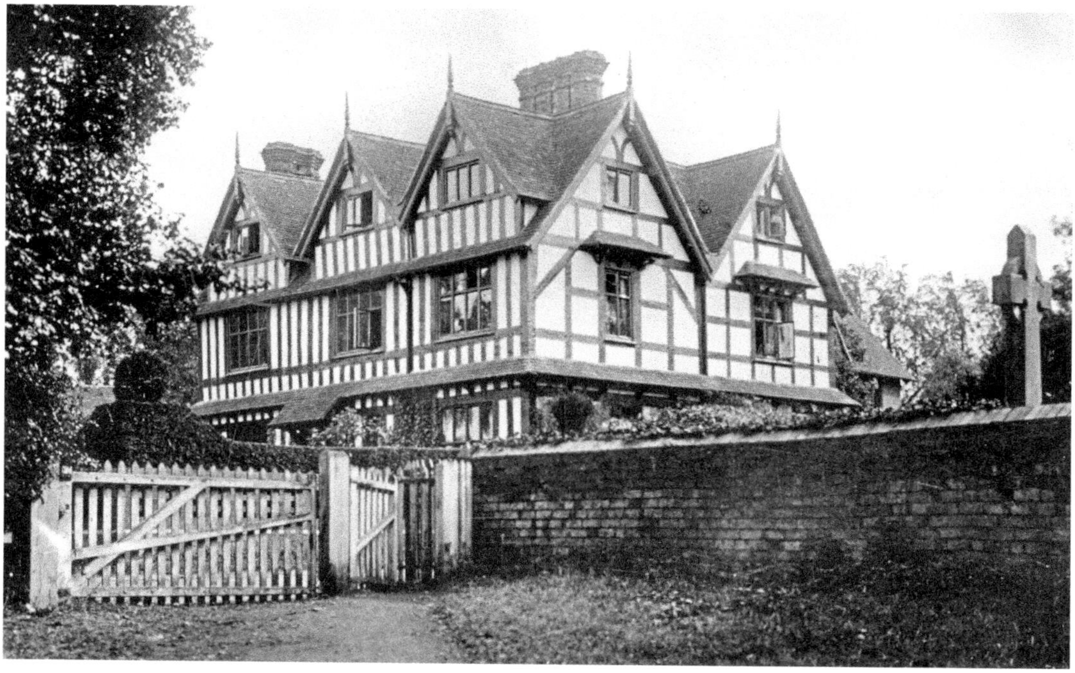

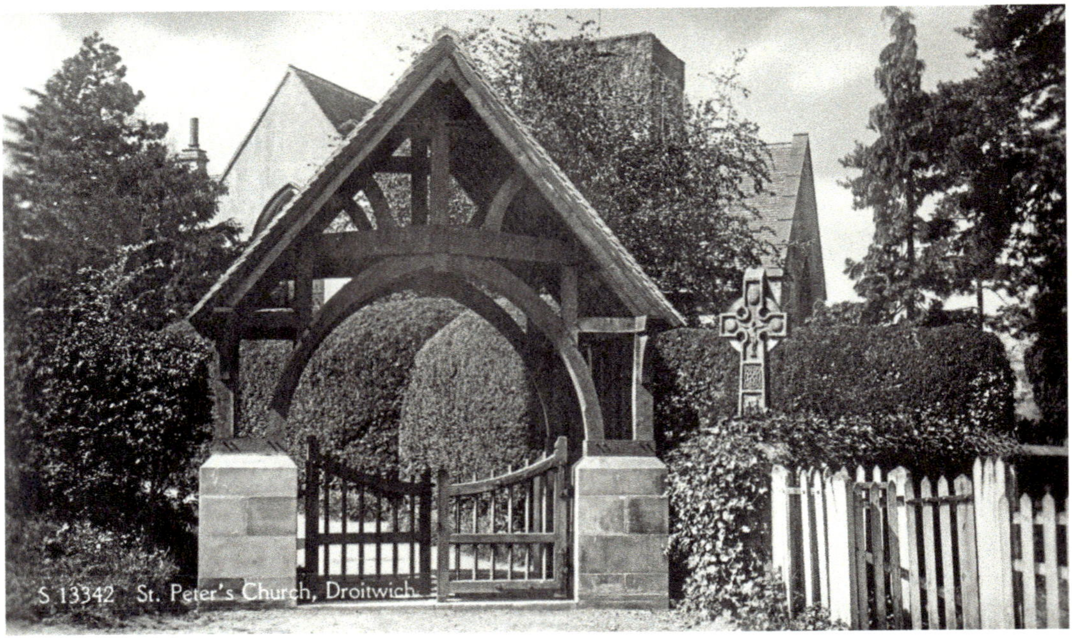

St Peter's Church

Now you see it, and now you don't. It is sometimes assumed that the lychgate at St Peter's Church (above) is rather ancient, whereas it was in fact erected in 1911 as a memorial to salt works proprietor William Young. Inscriptions on the lychgate read: 'Pitifully behold the sorrows of our hearts', 'A. M. D. G. and in memory of William Young of St Peter's Manor 1911, by his wife and children' and 'Mercifully forgive the sins of thy people'. A. M. D. G. refers to *AD Majorem Dei Gloriam,* which translates as 'To the greater glory of God'. The image below shows the same scene prior to the construction of the lychgate.

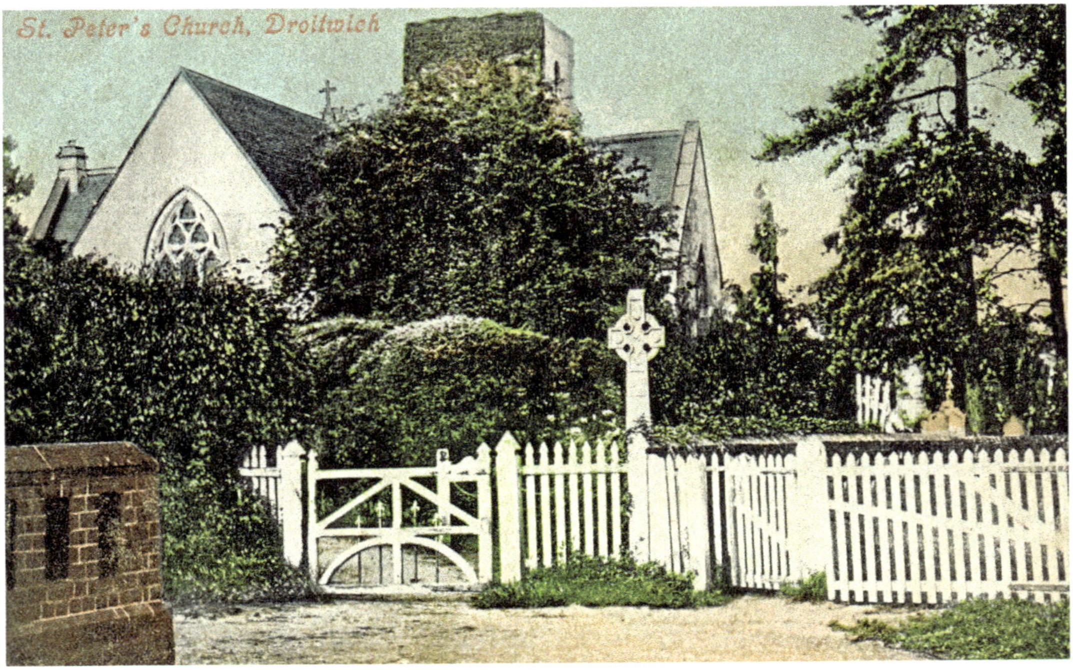

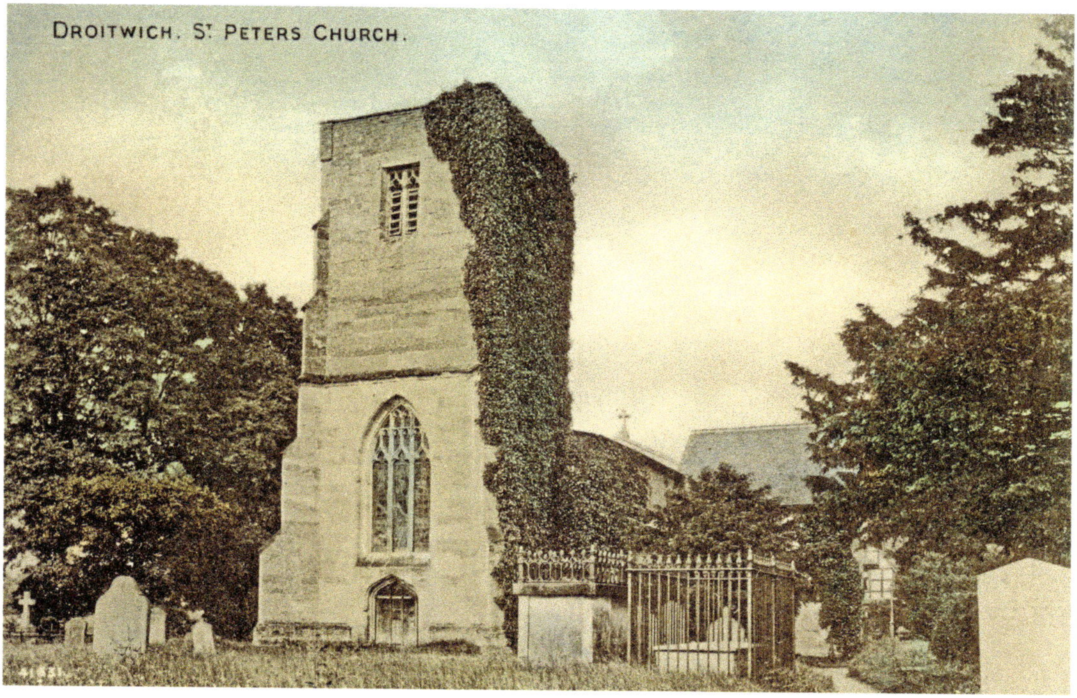

St Peter's Church

Two more shots of St Peter's Church are shown here, both of which date from the early twentieth century. Iron railing around monuments can be seen in the image above, with St Peter's Manor House just visible through the trees on the right. Part of the message on the back of the card below reads: 'The best I could get of the dear old place where I worshipped so many years. I cannot go now, it is too far … I miss the walk to St Peter's very much. Those lovely fields all so peaceful … 27/6/07.' Sadly, the writer of this message neglected to give their name, though their address is given as 'Queen Street, Droitwich, England'.

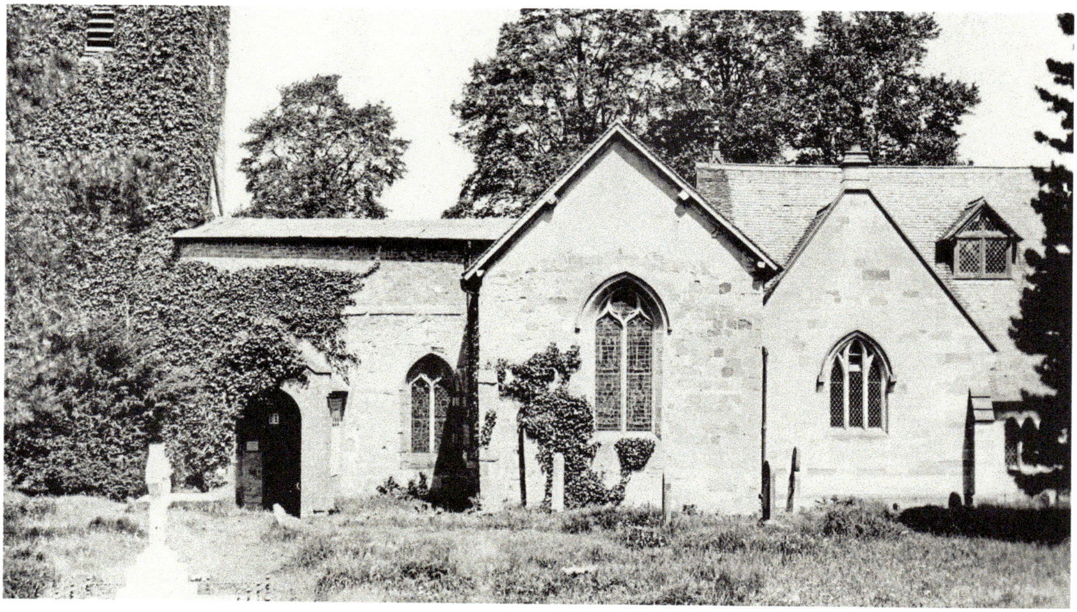

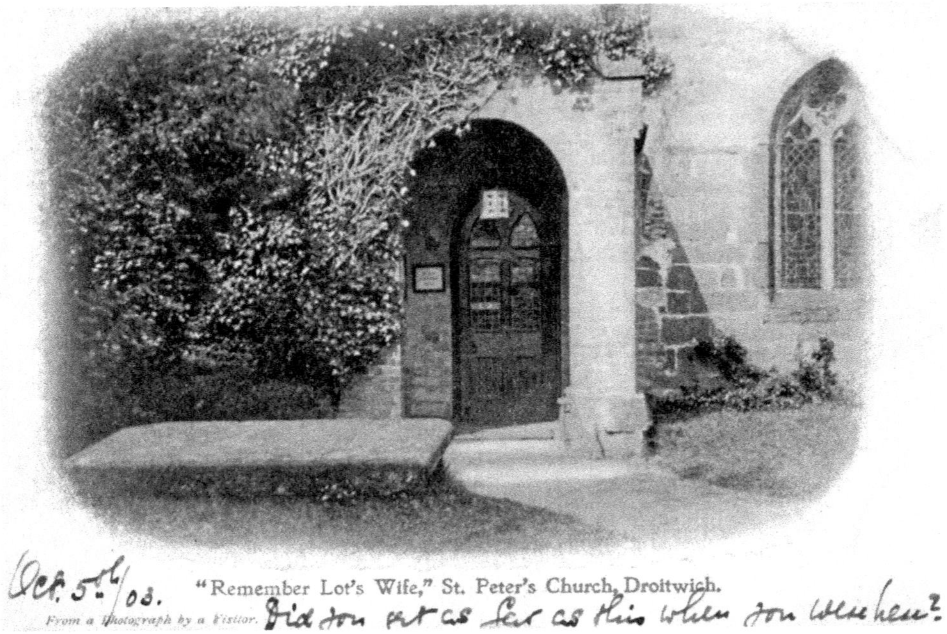

St Peter's Church

The Broseley brick porch at St Peter's Church (above) was constructed in 1825, replacing a much earlier timber-framed structure. In the late nineteenth century, Archdeacon Lea had 'Remember Lot's Wife' (who, the Bible tells us, was turned into a pillar of salt) painted inside the porch above the south entrance. The image below shows the nave of St Peter's Church with numerous paraffin lamps hanging from the roof. Electric light was installed in the church in 1927, in memory of carpenter John Elijah Guise and his wife Emma, of Fern Villa Oakley Street (now Corbett Avenue) Witton.

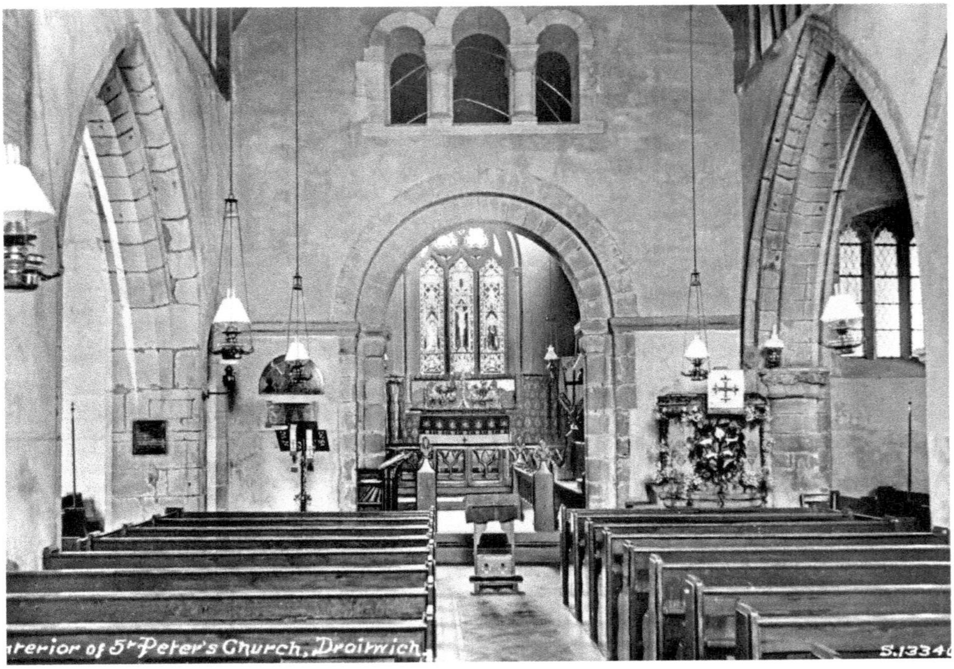

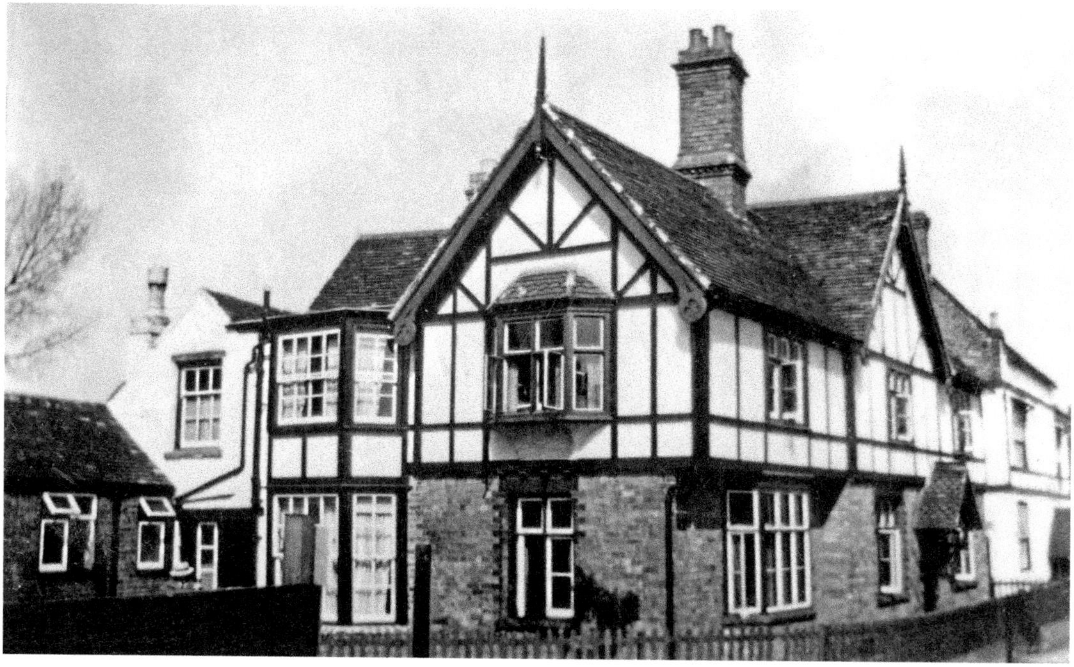

Gable House

The Gable House (above) was a home for patients of the brine baths and was situated on St Peter's Walk, just above the Holloway. This was owned for many years by Nancy Hawkes and her sister Hilda Cook. The Gable House itself was the family residence, and 'the Annex' (the white house on the far right) was for female guests. The modern portion (left) was known as 'the Men's End' and was of course for male guests. Sadly, the Gable House was demolished in the 1970s due to structural problems. The photograph below shows the gardens to the rear of the Gable House and the Annex.

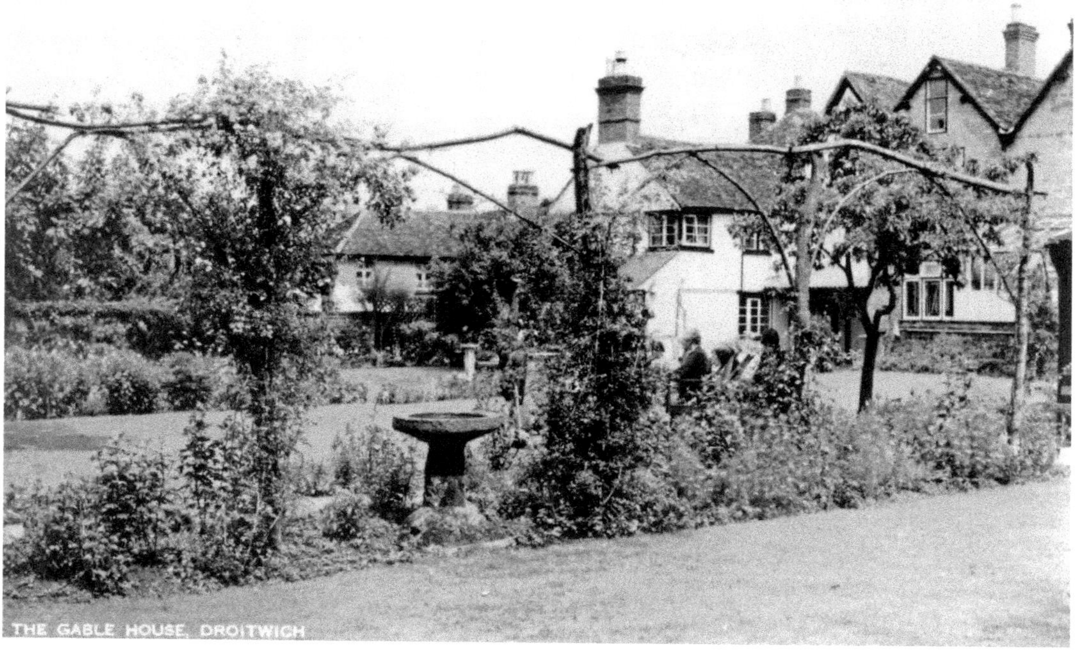

CHAPTER 5

VICTORIA SQUARE AND ST ANDREW'S BRINE BATHS

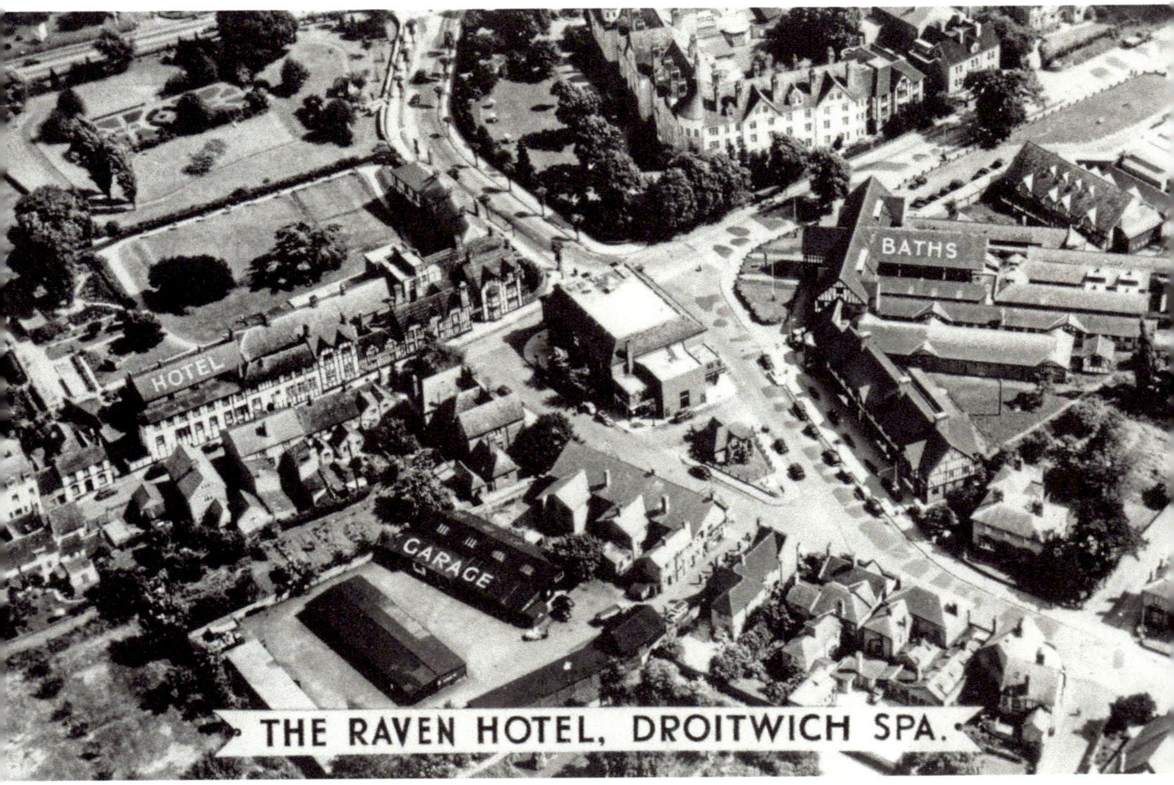

Victoria Square

An aerial shot of Victoria Square is shown above, with the present Salters' Hall (now the library) in the centre. All of the buildings to the left of Victoria Square in the bottom left portion of this image were cleared in the mid-1970s in order to make way for St Andrew's Square Shopping Precinct. This also involved the demolition of most of the western side of St Andrew's Street.

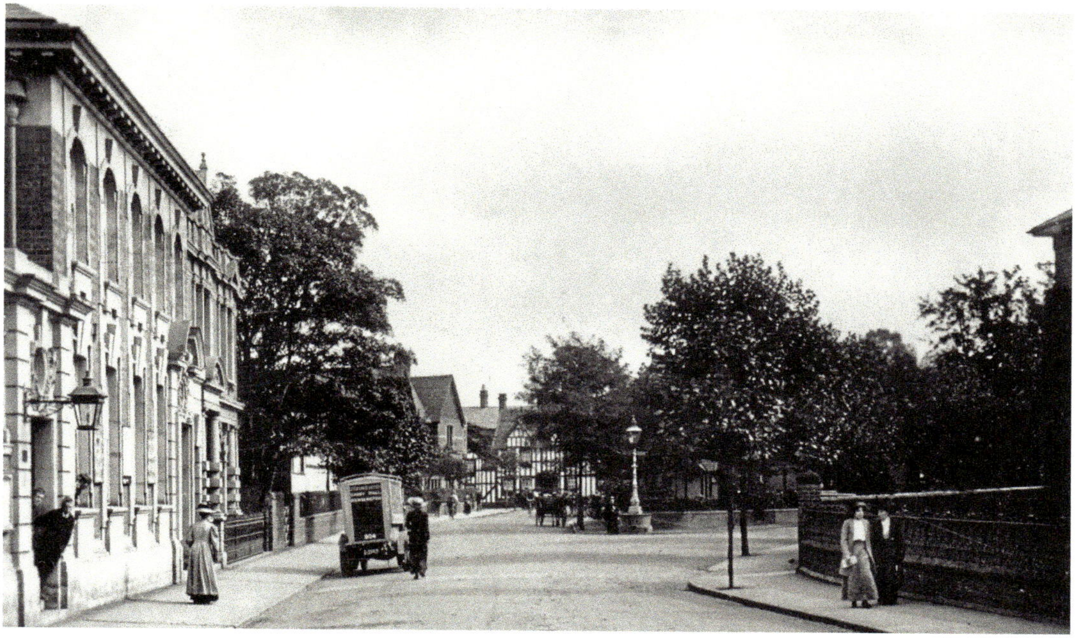

Victoria Square

The above *c.* 1910 image of Victoria Square looks east towards a tree-obscured Salters' Hall. Just behind the tree on the left stands the original stables for the Raven Hotel, and further along the Lloyd's Bank and the Raven Hotel itself can be seen. On the far left stands the 'new' post office, which is also illustrated in the *c.* 1908 image below. The post office had previously been in St Andrew's Street and moved to this location in 1907. The vacant post office in St Andrew's Street then became an annex of the Randolph Boarding Establishment, which stood opposite, and later part of the Clarendon Hotel.

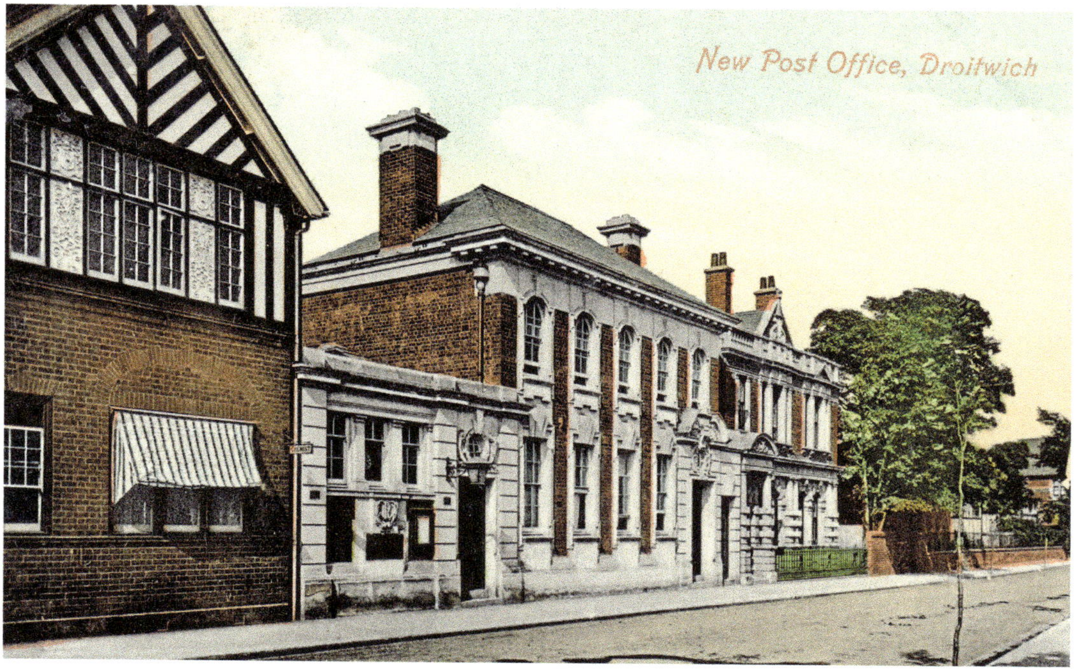

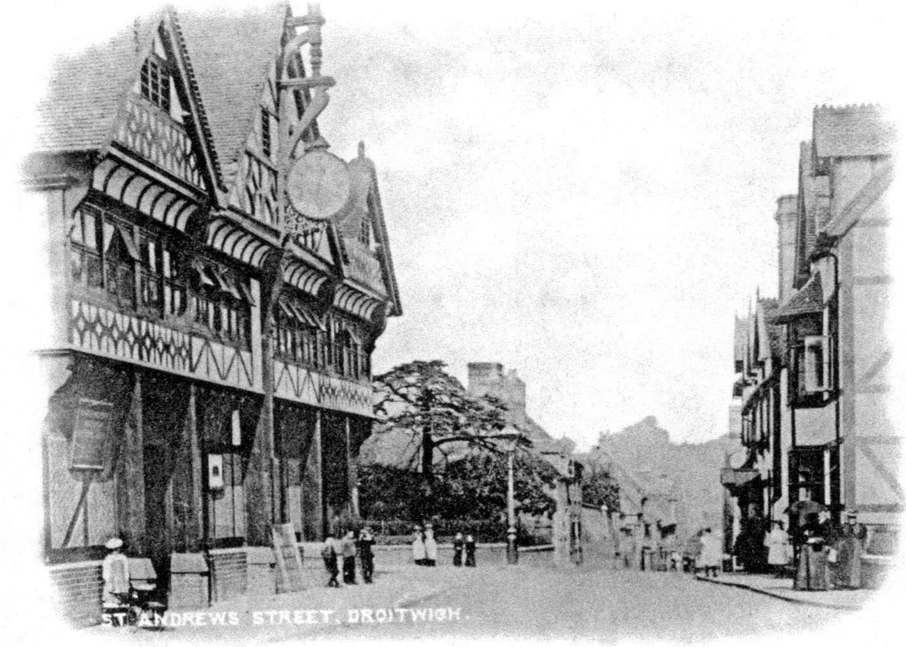

St Andrew's Street

Two shots looking down St Andrew's Street from Victoria Square are shown here. In the image above, which may date from the 1890s, the original Salters' Hall can be seen on the far left. Its large chiming clock was added in 1887 to celebrate Queen Victoria's Golden Jubilee. With the exception of the Spinning Wheel Café building, the buildings seen in the centre and right of centre were all demolished to make way for the shopping precinct in the mid-1970s. The image below dates from the early 1900s and shows the buildings on the opposite side of St Andrew's Street, including the Raven Hotel in the foreground.

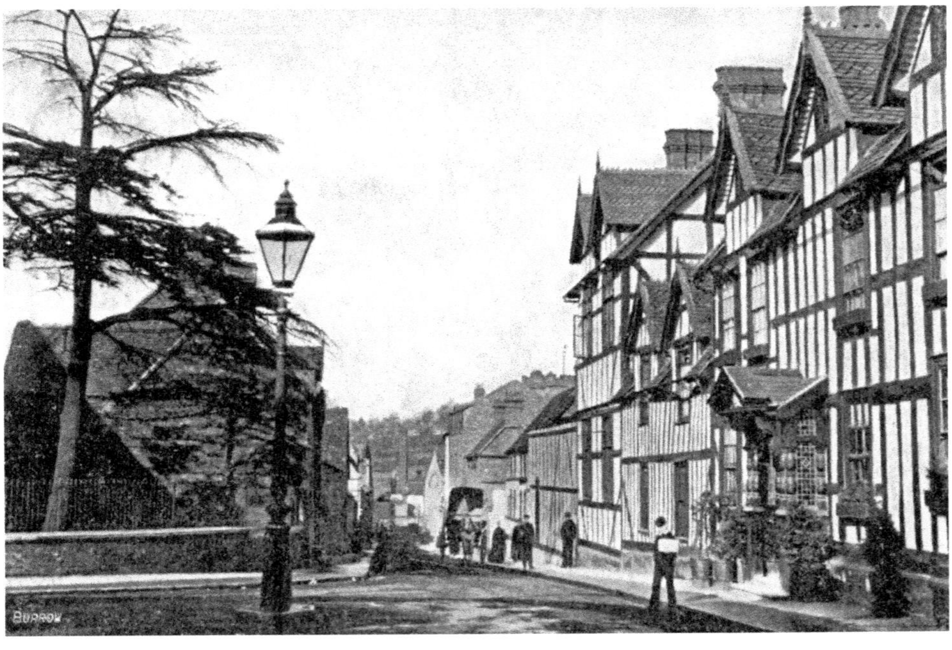

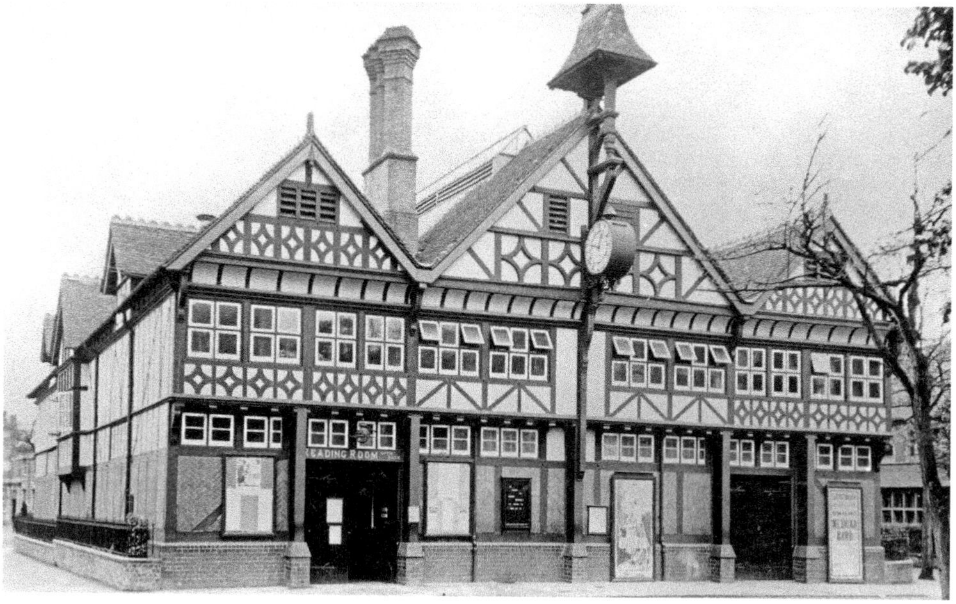

Salters' Hall and the Raven Hotel

The east façade of the Salters' Hall can be seen in more detail in the image above, with its entrance for the reading room ('open daily') on the left. The poster on the far right advertises the 'Don Pedro Mexican Band'. After standing empty for some years, the current Salters' Hall was rather appropriately converted into a library in 1983. The shot below dates from the early 1900s, and shows the Raven Hotel from the east façade of the Salters' Hall. Though the Raven Hotel is currently closed, it is hoped that the historic core of the complex seen here will reopen at some point as a restaurant.

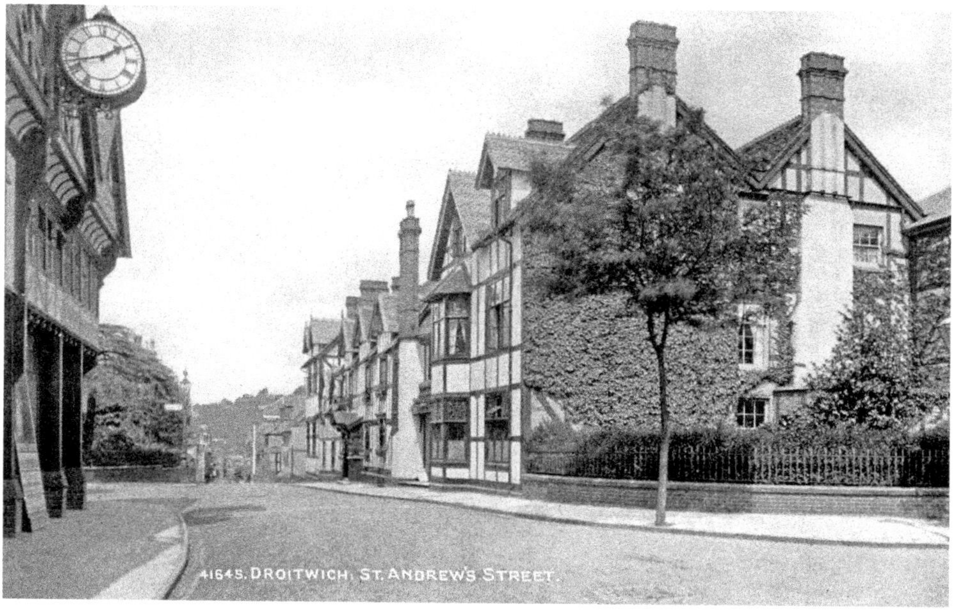

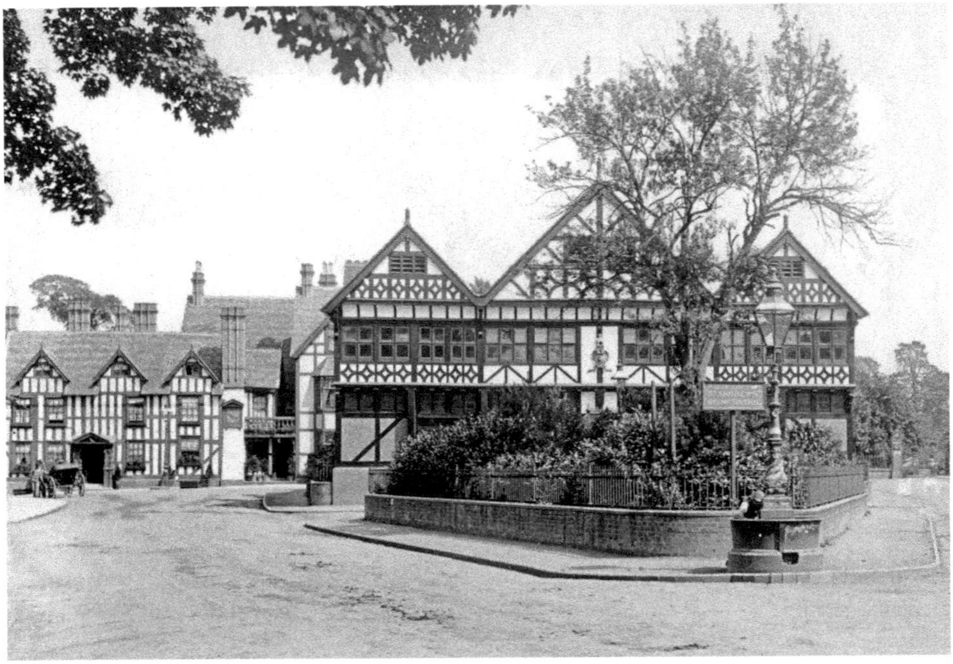

Salters' Hall

This wonderful early photograph of the Salters' Hall from the west probably dates from the mid-1890s. The Raven Hotel (far left) is shown in detail below. The Salters' Hall and the Raven Hotel were both projects of John Corbett, and first opened to the public in 1879. The Raven was originally intended to house those attending the refurbished Royal Brine Baths in St George's Square, though the construction of the St Andrew's Brine Baths opposite the Salters' Hall followed less than a decade later in 1887. The sign to the left of the lamp post in the full image above reads 'To the St Andrew's Brine Baths'.

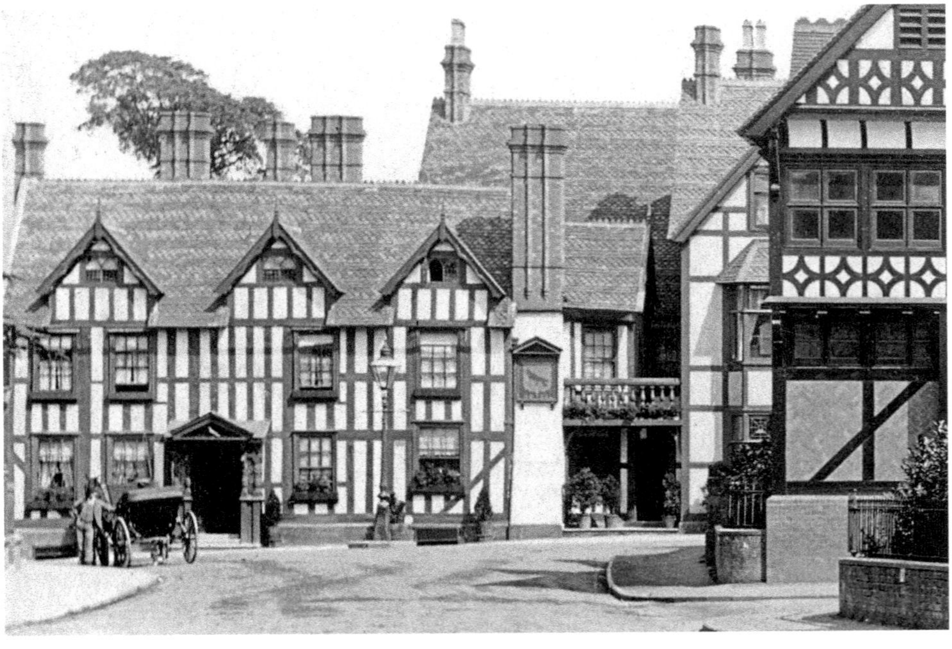

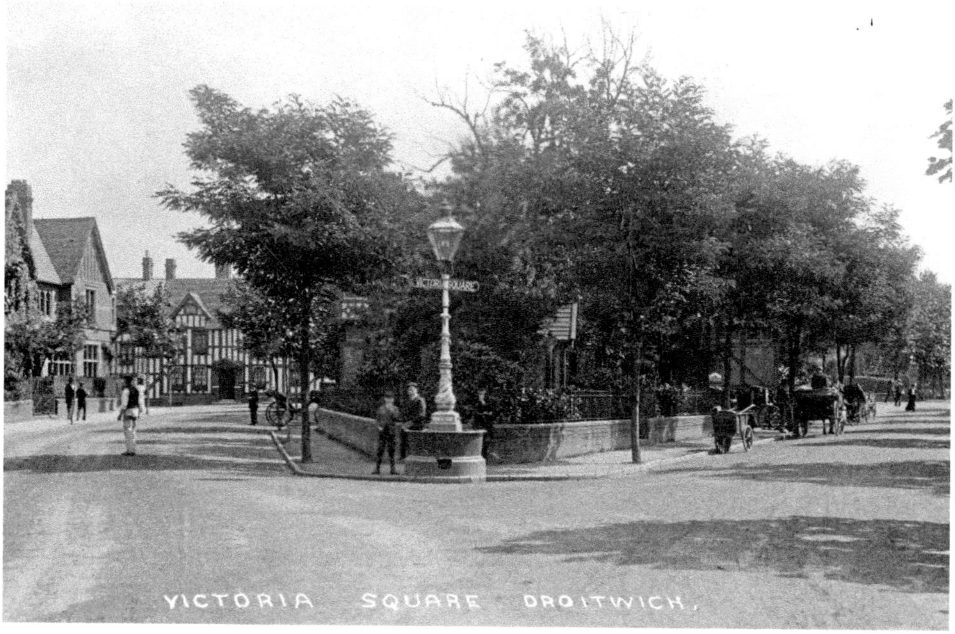

Salters' Hall

The shot above dates from around 1910 and was taken from almost the same angle as the image opposite. Since the shot opposite was taken, the Salters' Hall has become obscured by trees planted on the pavements. Lloyd's Bank can be seen on the left, with its western gable end covered in ivy, and various vehicles – including a road sweeper's cart – line the road on the right. A similar view taken in the 1930s is shown below, with the replacement Salters' Hall of 1933 on the left and the row of shops dating from the same period on the right. A telephone box stands on the site that was soon to be occupied by the war memorial.

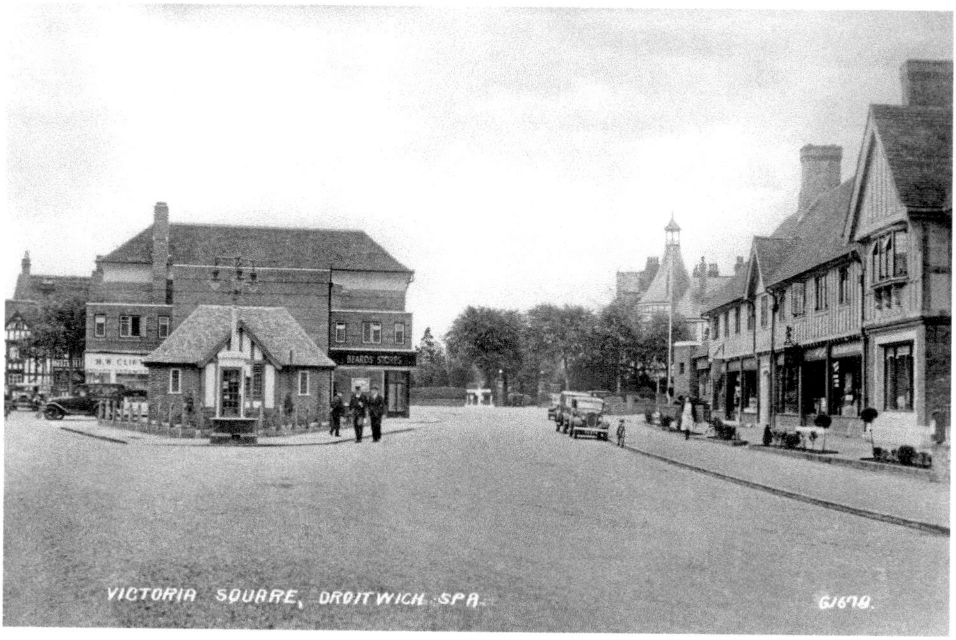

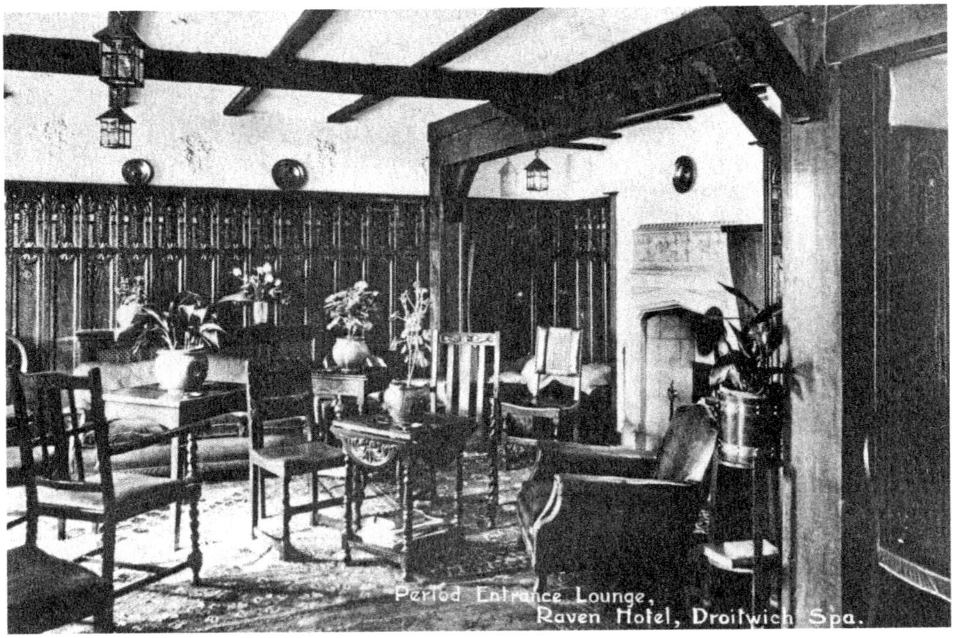

Raven Hotel

The 'period entrance lounge' of the Raven Hotel is shown above, with what appears to be Jacobean wainscoting. It was recently discovered, however, that some of the wainscoting was in fact moulded asbestos! It had previously been thought that this very convincing panelling was cast iron. The Bromsgrove architect John Cotton restyled the hotel in 1883 and designed many of its features – including the fireplace as seen to the right. The picture below was taken from the Raven Hotel entrance in *c.* 1910 and looks towards the Raven Hotel Stables (right of centre). WHSmith has occupied this site since the late 1920s.

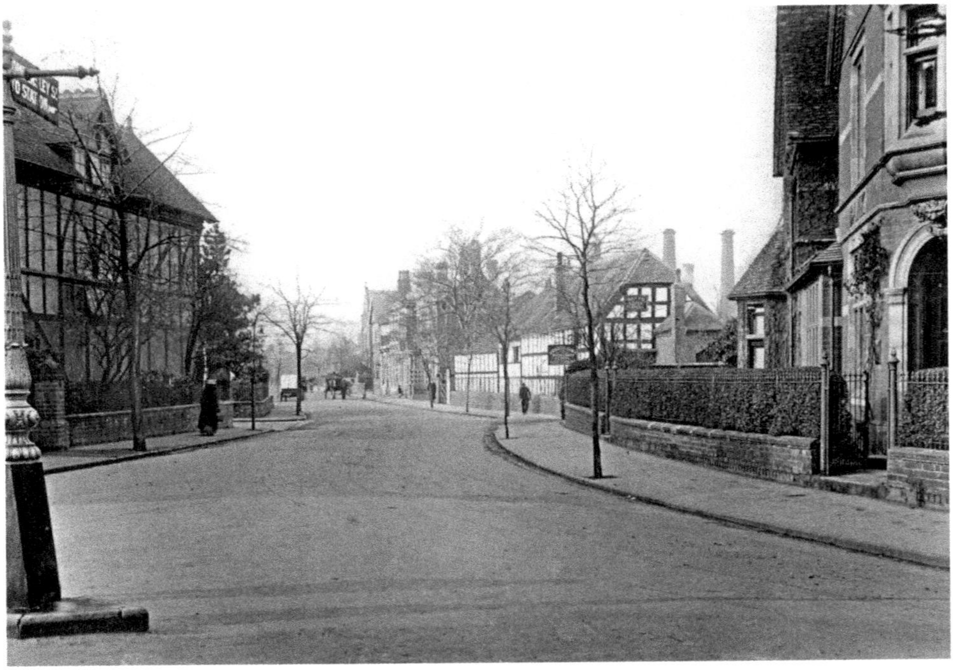

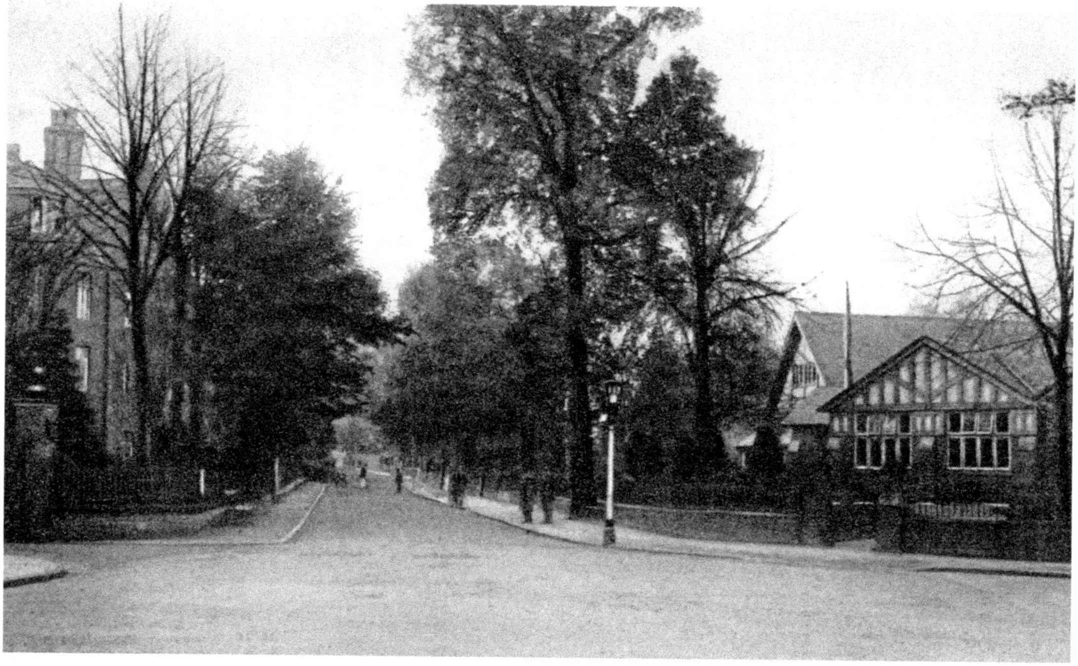

St Andrew's Road

The above shot looks south from the Salters' Hall along a very leafy St Andrew's Road, and was probably taken shortly after the First World War. St Andrew's Brine Baths can be seen on the right, and the Worcestershire Brine Baths Hotel on the left. In 1933, the Winter Gardens (below) opened in St Andrew's Road on land just south of the St Andrew's Brine Baths. This building was a very popular venue – particularly in the 1960s – and many famous pop groups performed there. It later became a cinema and was again very popular; but despite this it was closed down and demolished in the early 1980s.

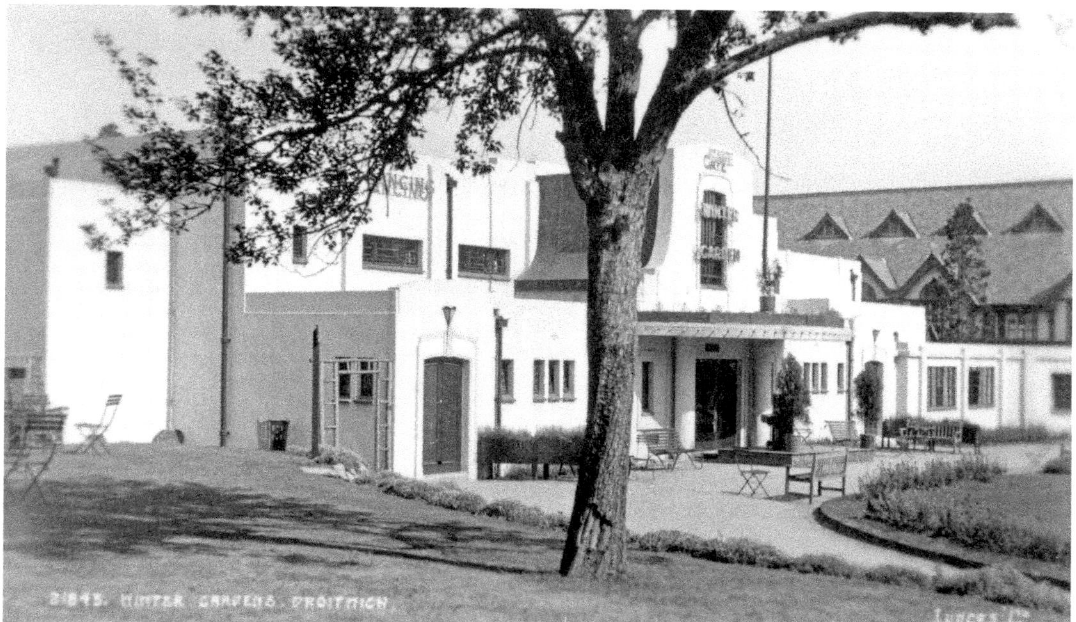

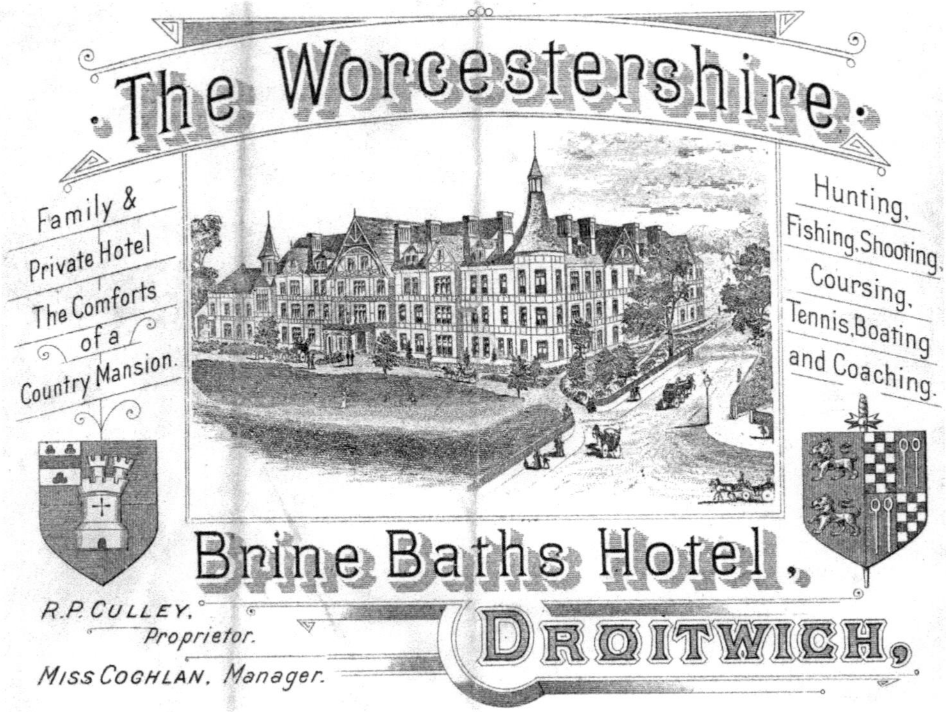

Worcestershire Brine Baths Hotel

The above beautifully illustrated billhead for the Worcestershire Brine Baths Hotel dates from 1892 – just one year after the grand opening of the hotel in 1891. The hotel was another Corbett venture and was managed at this time by a Miss Coghlan – the proprietor of the business being R. P. Culley. The illustration shows the hotel from a viewpoint above the Salters' Hall, and to the left and right the arms of Worcester and Droitwich are shown. In the below image from the early 1900s, a morning band performance is taking place in front of the Worcestershire Brine Baths Hotel.

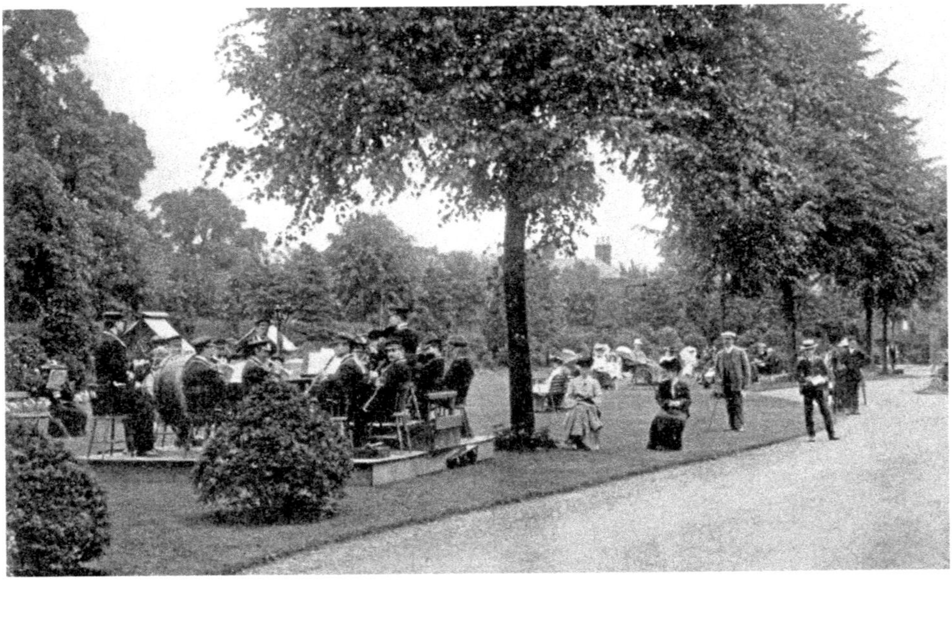

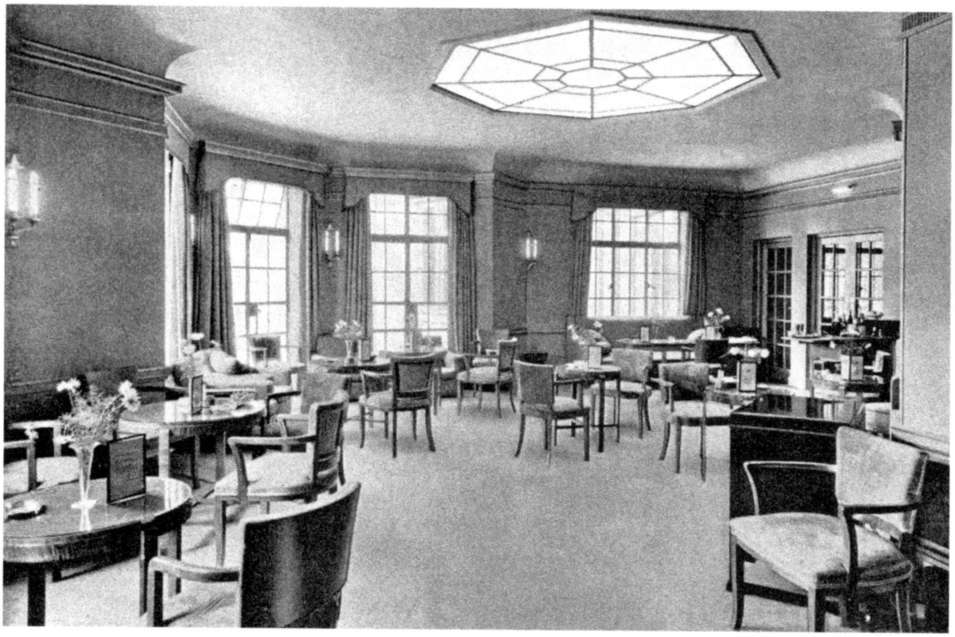

Worcestershire Brine Baths Hotel

Two 1930s interior shots of the Worcestershire Brine Baths Hotel are reproduced here – the rather deco sun lounge (above) and the sumptuous dining room (below). The construction of the hotel took nearly two years and cost almost £15,000. Over 130 attended a meal held in the hotel's coffee room; but this was not attended by John Corbett, who was also unable to attend the hotel's inaugural dinner held at the Salters' Hall due to ill health caused by insomnia. The hotel closed in the early 1980s, and both it and its separate Vaults Bar on the Worcester Road were finally demolished in 2003.

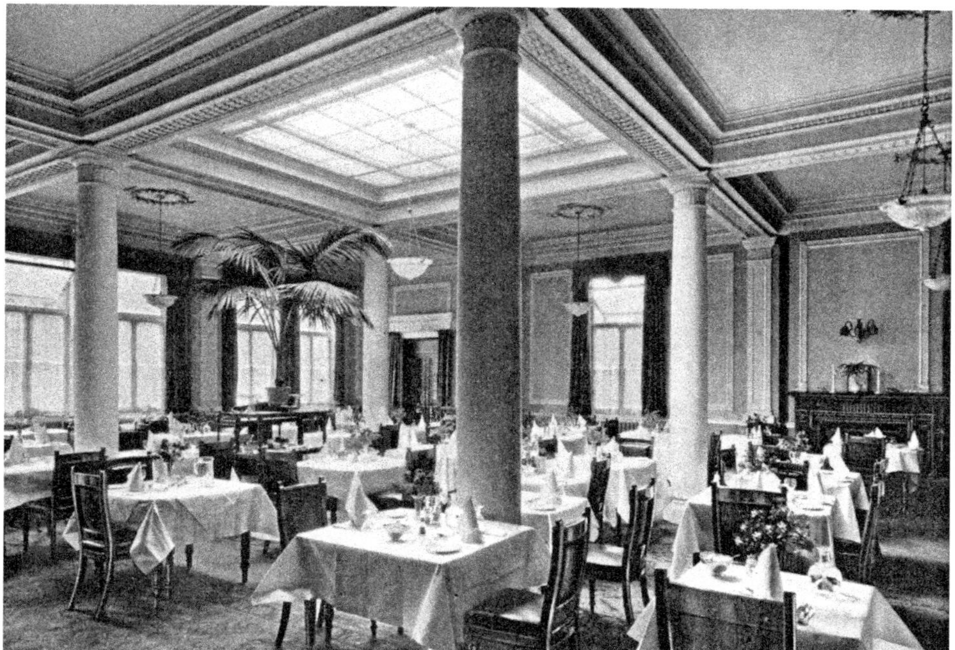

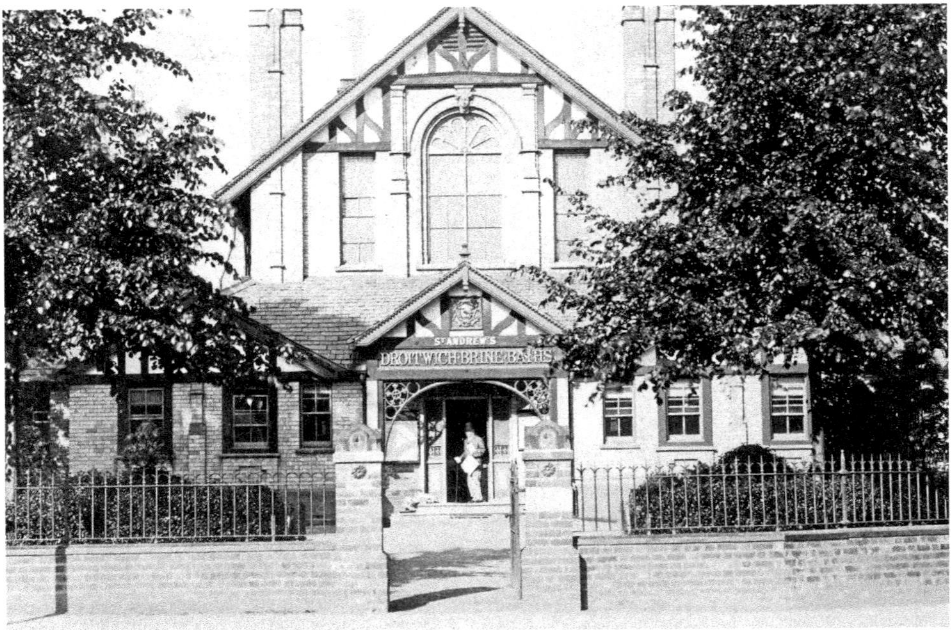

St Andrew's Brine Baths

The above shot of St Andrew's Brine Baths was taken in around 1900 and shows the building as it originally looked when constructed in 1887. This was another of Corbett's projects and was designed by one of his favourite architects – John Cotton of Bromsgrove. Cotton was also responsible for work at the Raven Hotel and Elephant and Castle at Witton (*see* page 61). The opening of the extensions to the baths by Lord Coventry on 1 June 1907 is shown below. The mayor of Droitwich at this time was the proprietor of the Raven Hotel – Percy Pond – and he can be seen in the mayoral robes and chain left of centre.

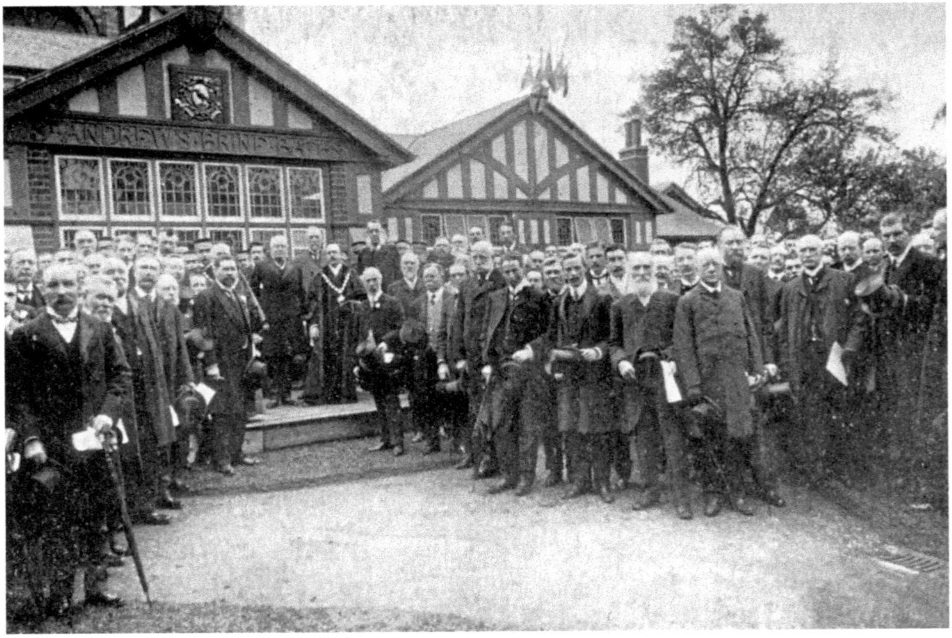

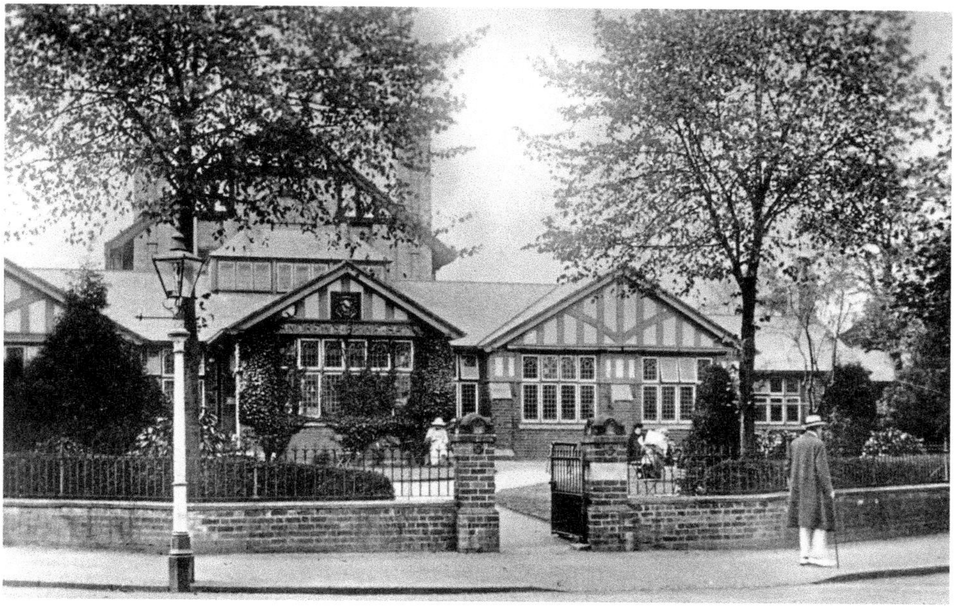

St Andrew's Brine Baths

The above shot of St Andrew's Brine Baths was taken in around 1910 and shows the later façade of 1907, which differs only slightly in style from the original one of 1887 opposite. In the early 1930s, the baths' main entrance building was again rebuilt, and today houses the Droitwich Heritage Centre and mayor's parlour on its ground floor. A 1930s guidebook describes the new building as a 'triumph of period architecture'. The image below, which probably dates from around 1930, shows the St Andrew's Brine Baths reception lounge. A weighing machine can be seen right of centre behind the wicker furniture.

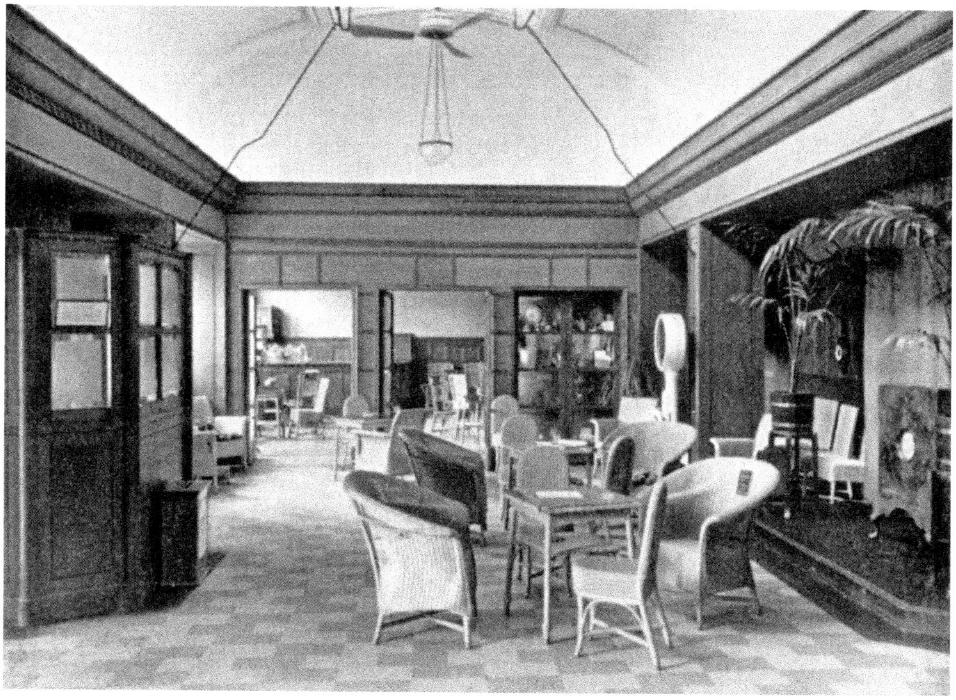

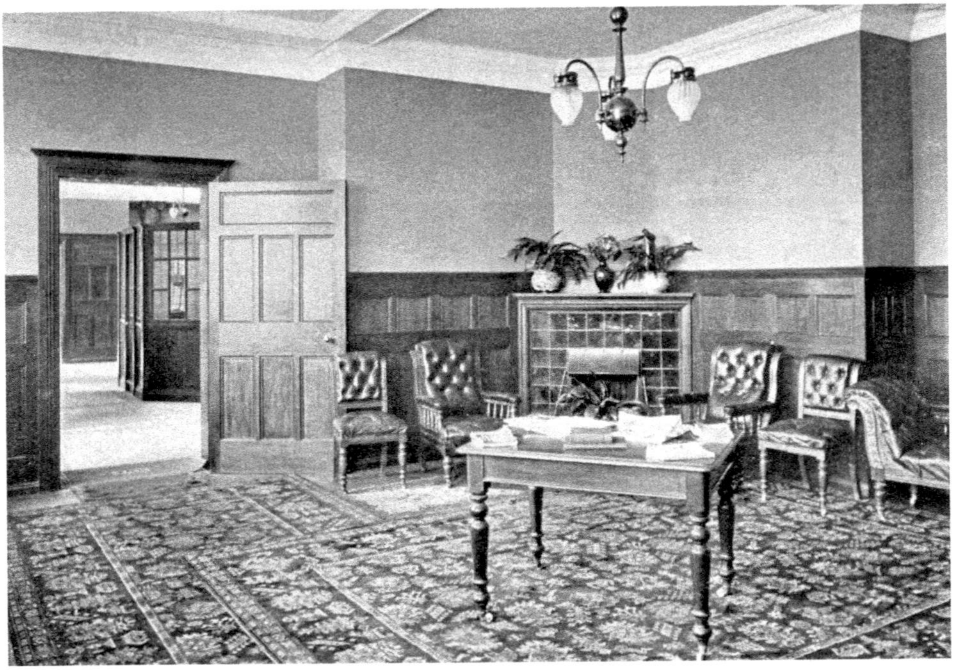

St Andrew's Brine Baths

Two more interior shots of St Andrew's Brine Baths are reproduced here, with the above F. G. W. Sage image of *c.* 1908 showing one of the waiting rooms. The table appears to be strewn with local guidebooks and periodicals, and part of the reception lounge can be seen through the open doorway. The photograph below shows the aeration baths, which were an adaptation of the French whirlpool system and were first installed at St Andrew's Brine Baths during the First World War. This treatment was particularly good for wounded limbs and numerous painful conditions. For brine, the fittings had to be of very sturdy construction.

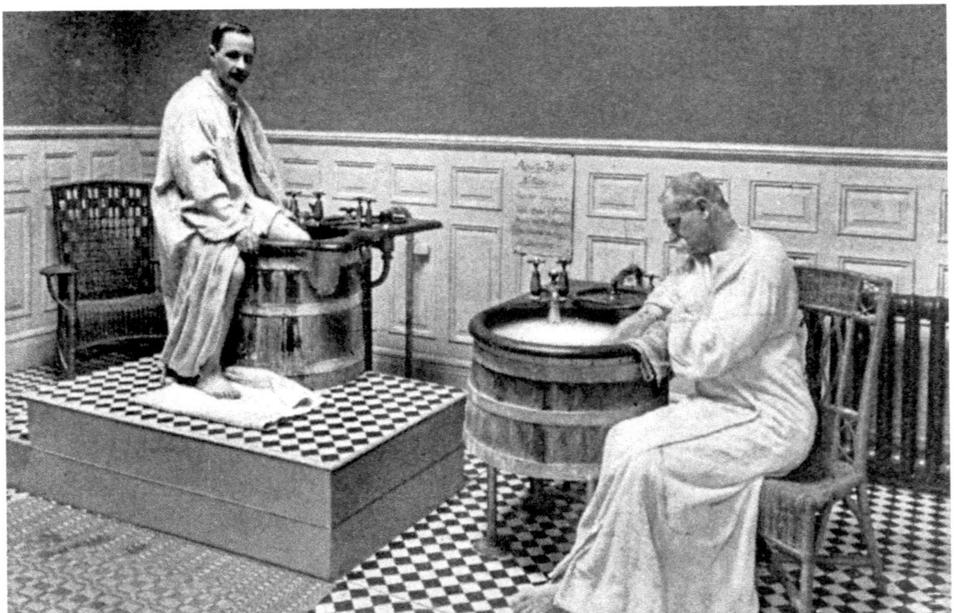

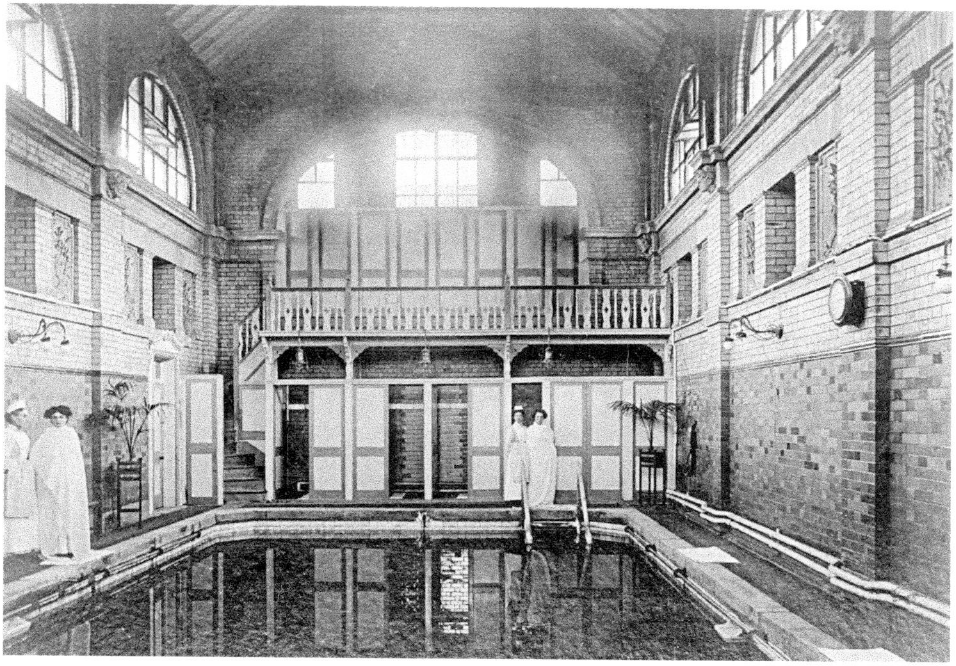

St Andrew's Brine Baths

The above image, showing the ladies' pool as it appeared in around 1910, is another fine example of Mr Sage's work. Originally known as the plunge pool, it was soon to become the ladies' pool, as a separate gentlemen's pool was added to the complex in 1888. Cubicles can be seen in the background, and the large archway (centre) still survives in the south wall of the present 1930s entrance building. Though bricked-up and plastered over externally, this arch can still be seen in a first-floor storage room above the Heritage Centre. Bathers in around 1930 are shown in this charming image below.

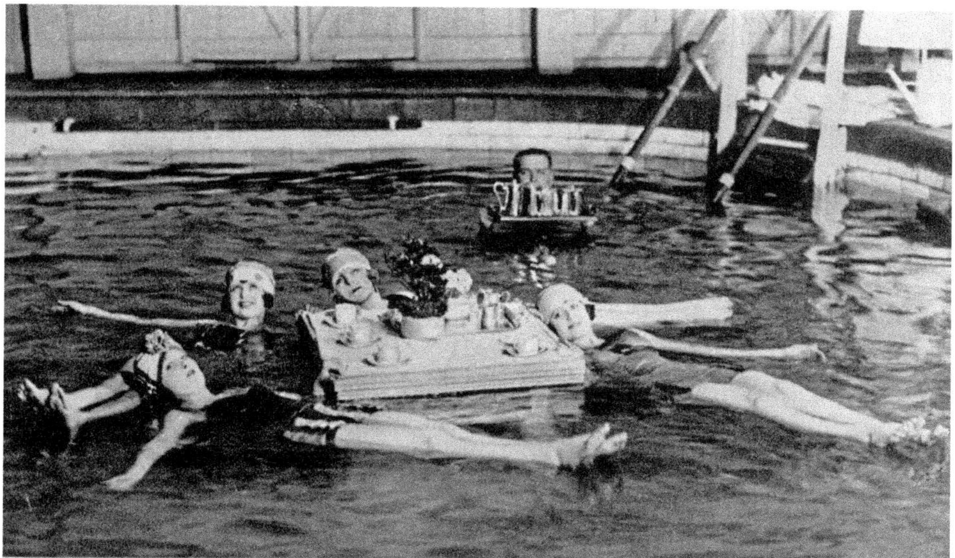

DROITWICH SPA, IN SYLVAN WORCESTERSHIRE FOR TREATMENT OF RHEUMATISM & ALLIED AILMENTS "AFTERNOON TEA IN 6 FEET OF BUOYANT BRINE"

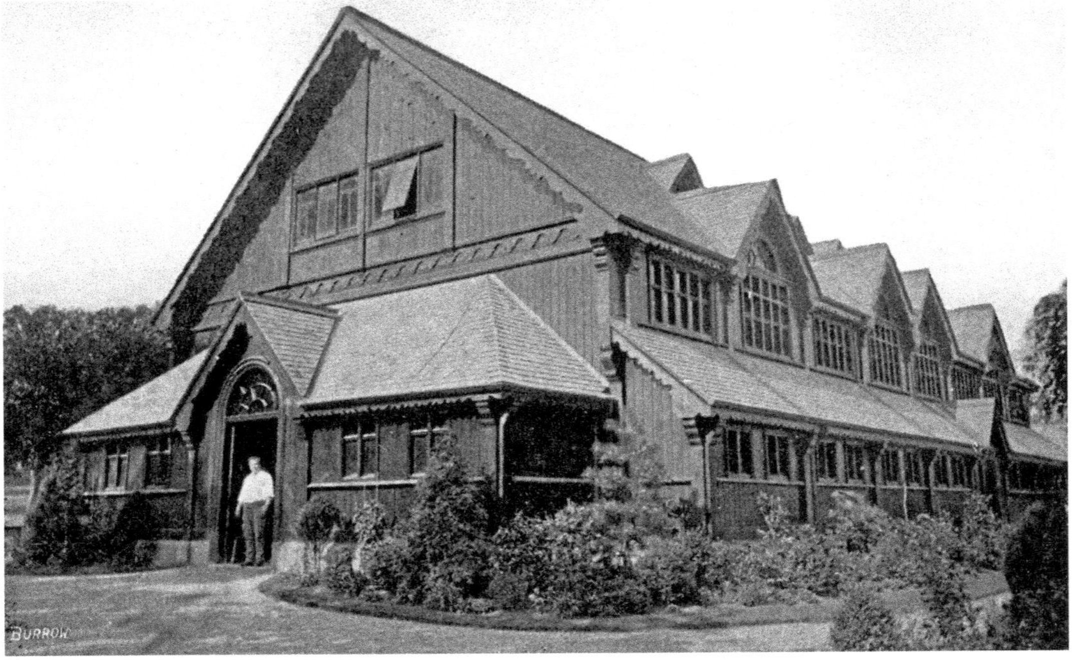

The Gentlemen's Pool

The two shots of the gentlemen's pool shown here both date from the early 1900s. There are many today who fondly recall using this pool, which, as previously mentioned, was constructed in 1888. I can recall seeing this building as a ruin with its pool partly filled with debris, just prior to its demolition in the early 1980s. A new complex was constructed on the site in 1984, but the brine pool was closed some years ago, leaving only the private hospital. Hopes are high for a new pool in Droitwich and the Save Our Brine Baths campaigners are doing all that they can to raise the necessary funding.

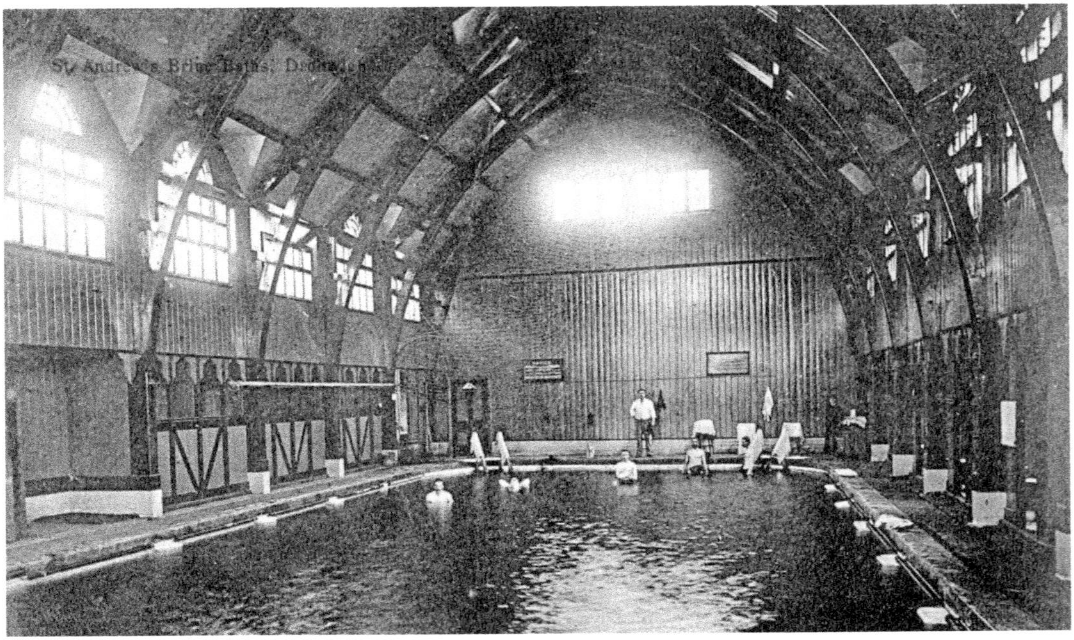

CHAPTER 6

OMBERSLEY STREET AND OMBERSLEY ROAD

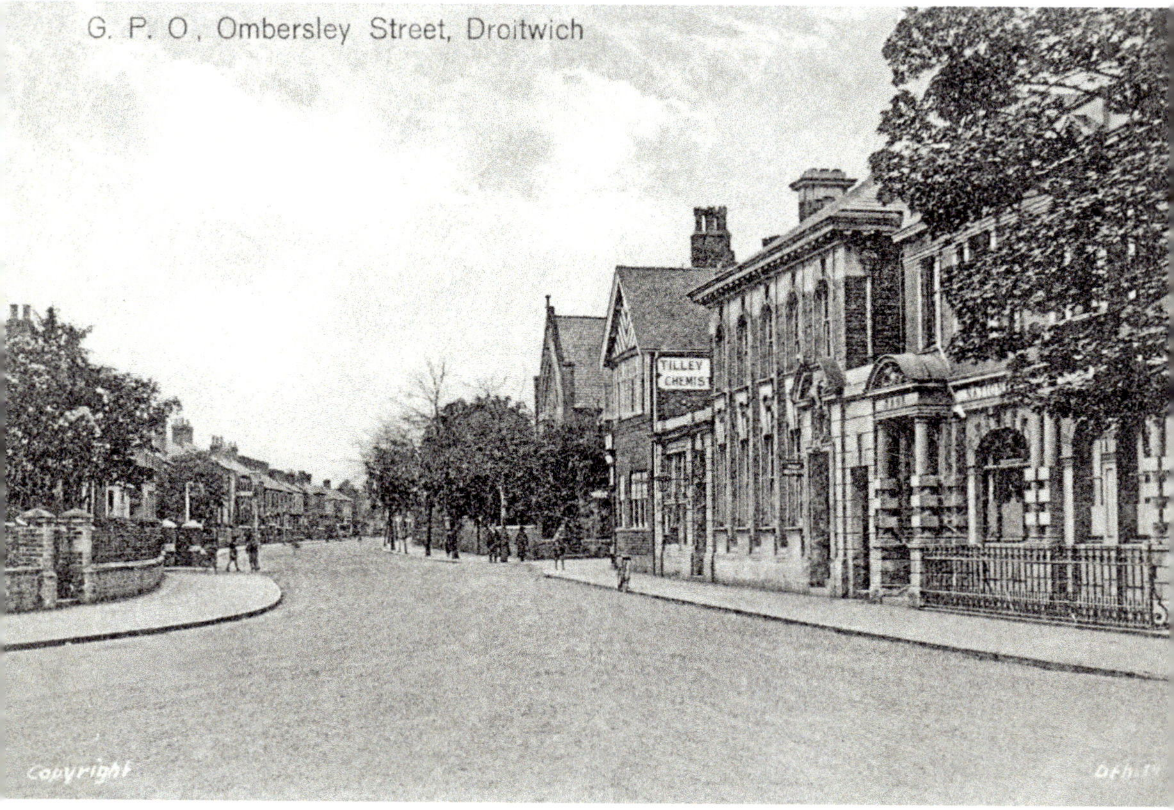

Ombersley Street

Ombersley Street, looking west during the 1930s, is shown above with both the post office and the National Provincial Bank of England Ltd on the right. The bank later became NatWest and finally closed in 2017. All of the premises on the left were demolished during the 1970s in order to make way for a health centre, police station and magistrates' court. Only the police station survived further development in 2008, and the site of the former health centre is now a carpark.

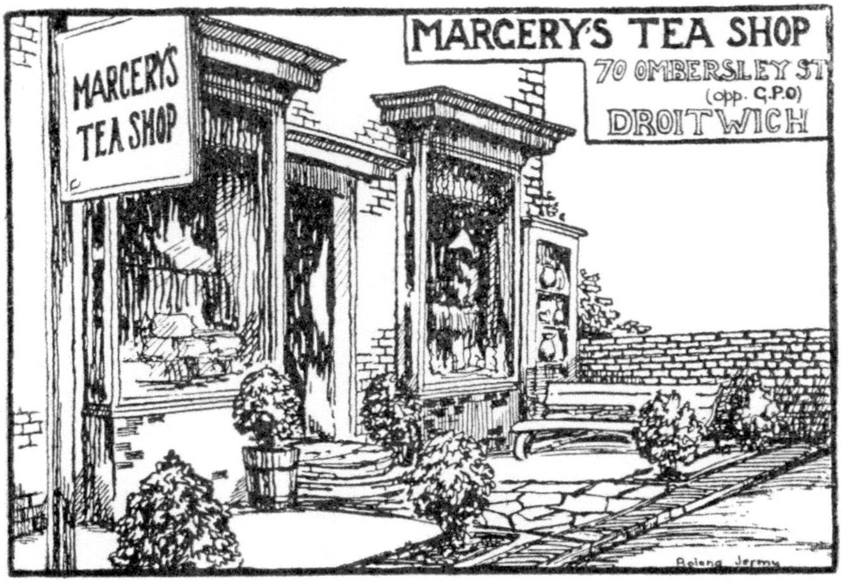

Ombersley Street

Margery's Tea shop (above) was one of the Ombersley Street properties to meet the bulldozer in the 1970s. This was run throughout the 1930s, '40s and '50s by Miss Marjorie Elsie Holt and stood, not opposite the post office as is stated in this 1930s illustration, but directly opposite the Baptist church. Marjorie was born in 1886, and died in 1973. Illustrated below is a fine shot of M. M. Stanton's stores on the corner of Ombersley Street and Burrish Street in *c.* 1905. The store was advertised in the early 1900s as a tobacconist, confectioner, stationer and fancy goods dealer, with pony chaise and bath and wicker chairs for hire.

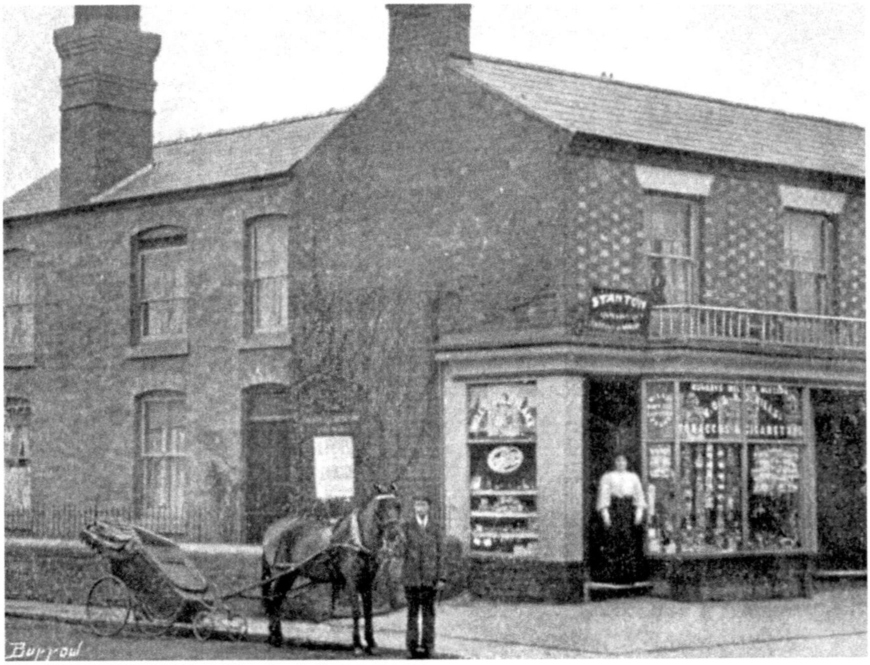

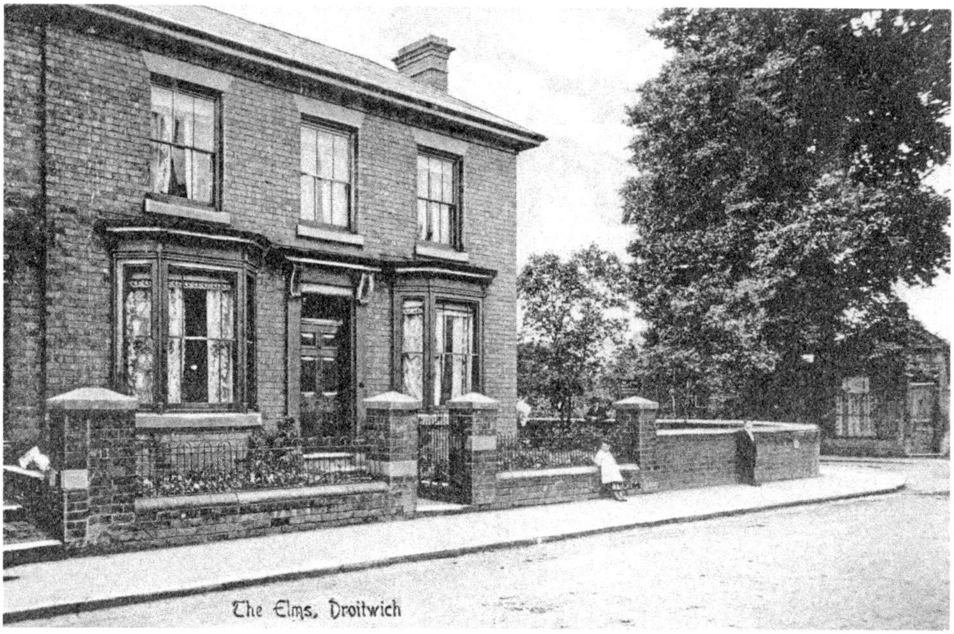

The Elms and Richmond House

The Elms on the corner of Ombersley Street and Albert Street is shown above in around 1900. In the 1930s, the Elms proudly advertised that the property had 'two sitting rooms, five bedrooms, inside sanitation, and hot and cold water'. In the early twentieth century, the workshop of gunsmith Charles Rawlins was located on the far right. On the opposite side of the road stands Richmond Boarding House, as shown below in a shot from the early 1900s. Richmond House boasted at this time of 'special dietary for invalids' and of a 'specially fitted massage room for patients and visitors'. St Nicholas' Church can be seen in the distance.

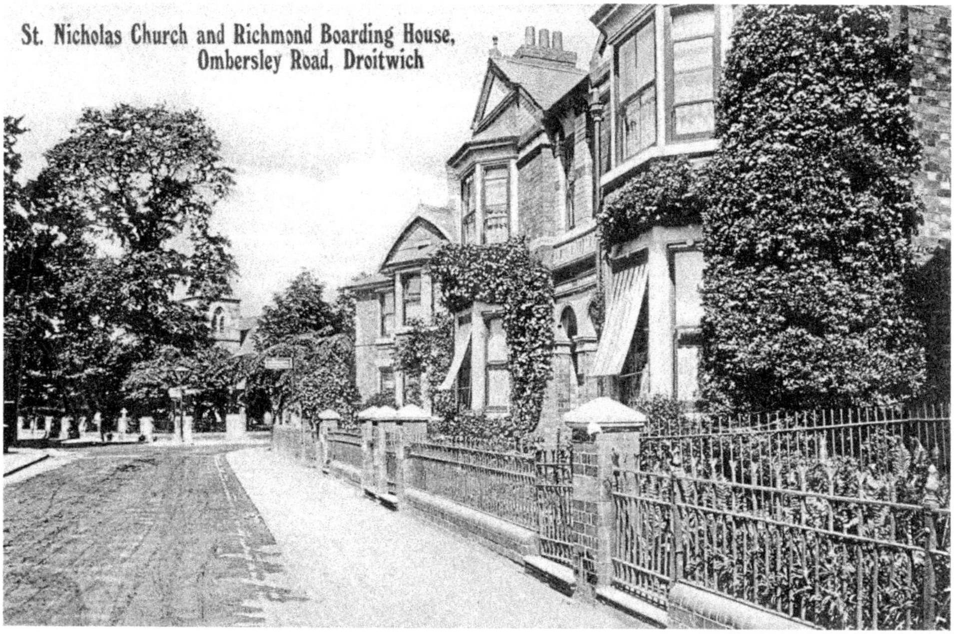

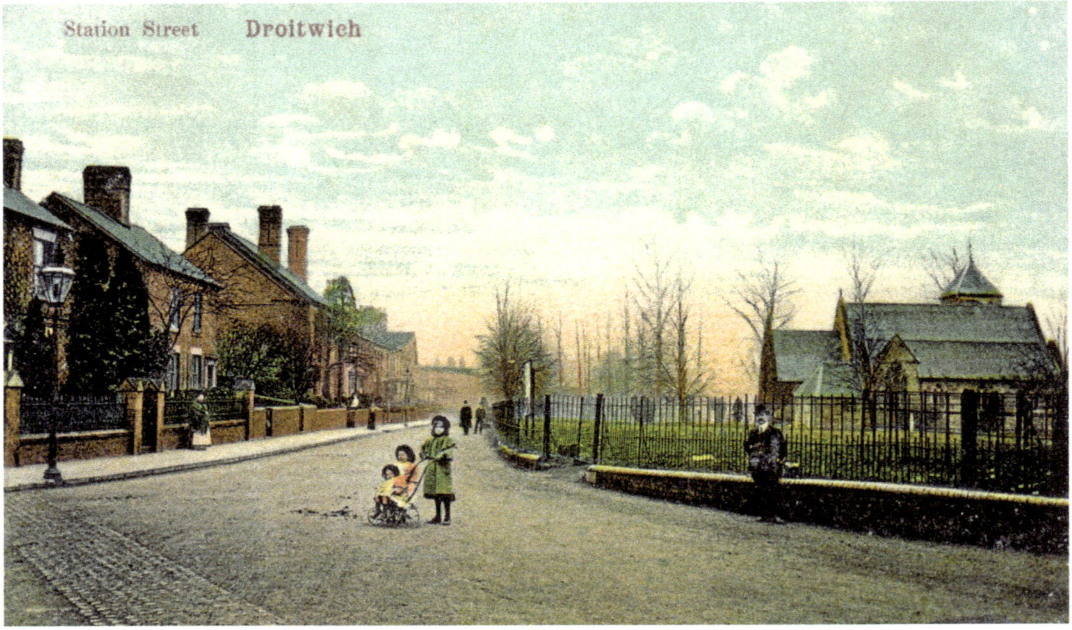

Station Street and Westcroft Street

The two streets shown here were dramatically reduced in size due to the construction of Ombersley Way in the 1970s. In the beautifully colourised early 1900s image of Station Street above, St Nicholas' Church stands on the far right, with properties demolished during the 1970s for the construction Ombersley Way on the far left. A bunting-strewn Westcroft Street is shown below, decorated for the coronation of Elizabeth II in June 1953. Today, Ombersley Way cuts straight through the middle of this scene, leaving only the southern stump of Westcroft Street where a block of flats stand next to an underpass.

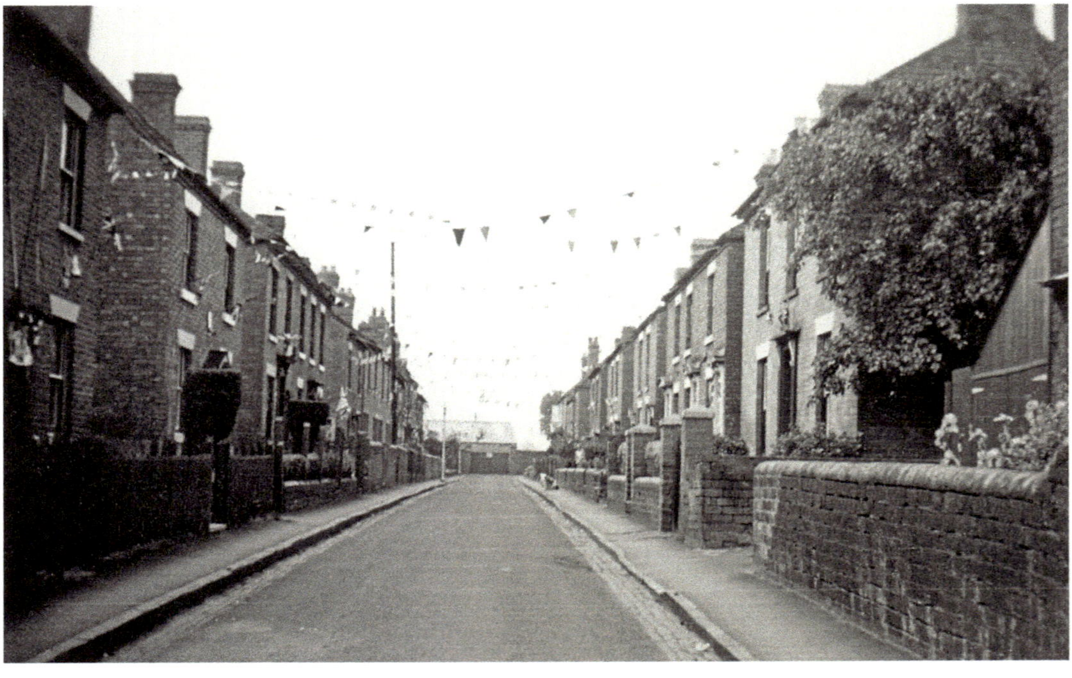

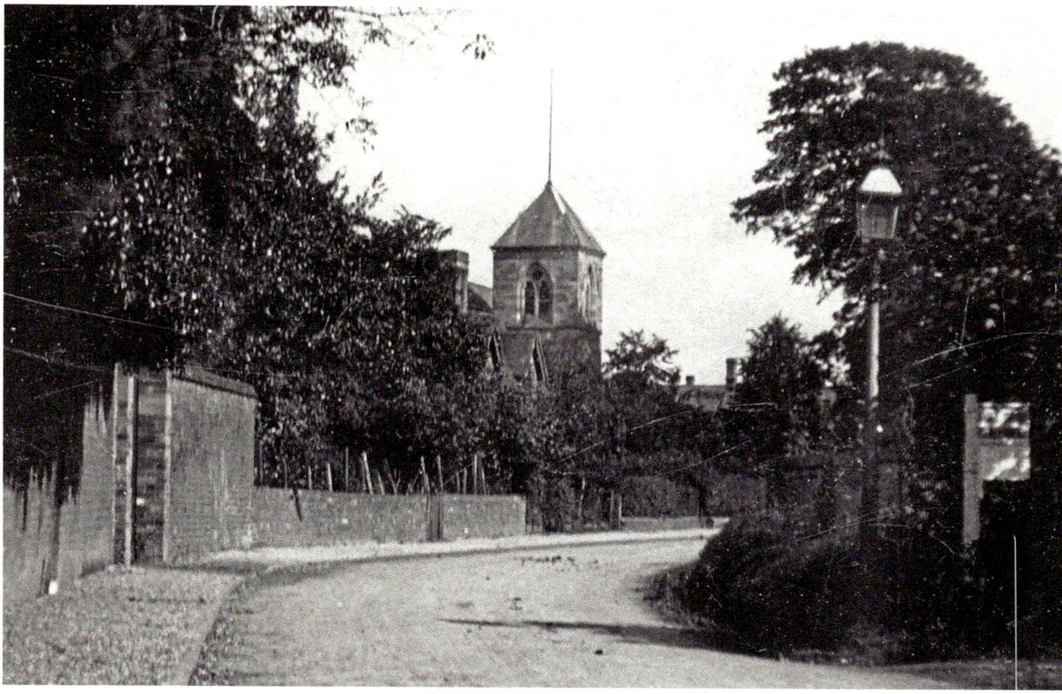

St Nicholas' Church

Moving further along into Ombersley Road, a unique card of St Nicholas' Church is shown here with a detail shot above. It was posted in 1905 to a Mrs Tolley of Hampton Villa in St Peter's Walk Droitwich, and both photograph and verse are by Frank Tolley. The verse reads as follows: 'Jack and Jill went up the hill, A famous view to find there, Jack was mad, For Jill – too bad!, Had left the plates behind her.' St Nicholas' Church was designed by Droitwich architect John Smith and was consecrated in December 1869. John Smith was also responsible for the now lost St Mary's Chapel at Witton.

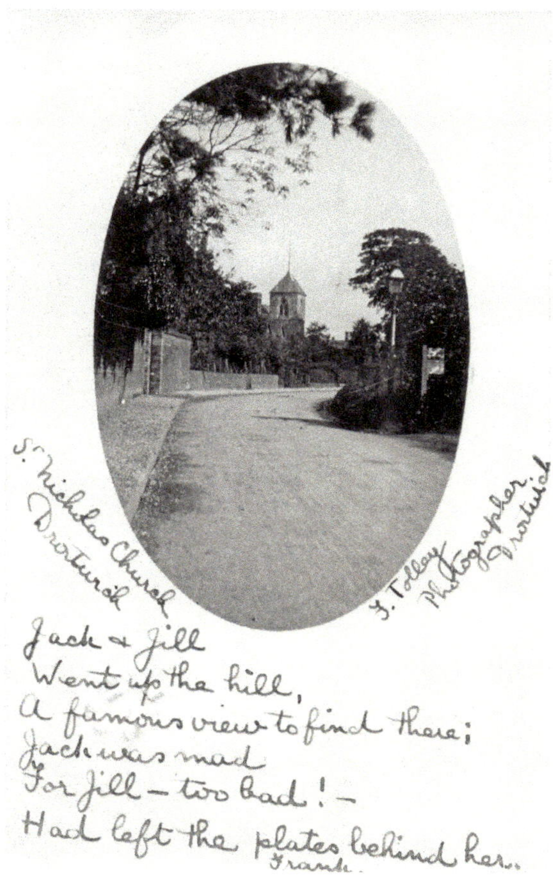

CHAPTER 7

WORCESTER ROAD, THE PARK AND WITTON

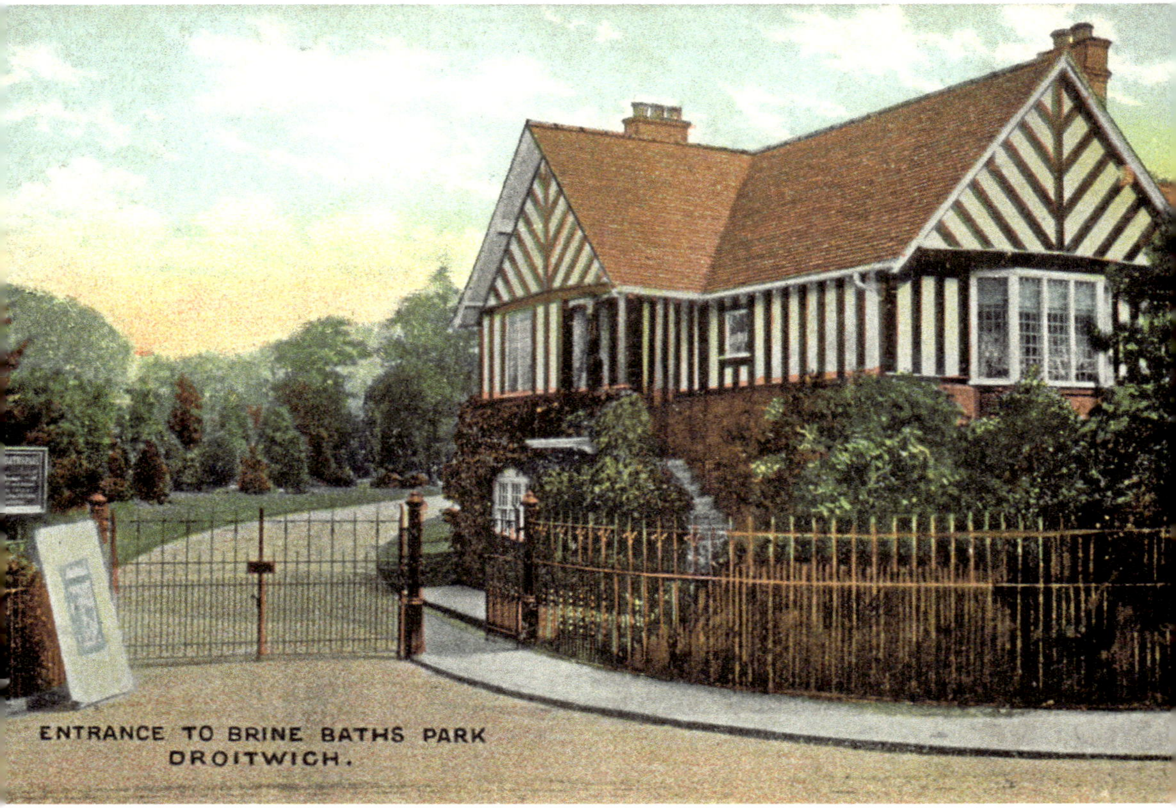

Brine Baths Park

The view above of the Brine Baths Park entrance on the Worcester Road has hardly changed since this postcard was produced in the early 1900s – this particular example was posted in 1907. Long since renamed the Lido Park, numerous events have taken place here, including the Donkey Derby in the 1970s and '80s. This charming open space is as popular as ever, and no doubt many future events will be held here.

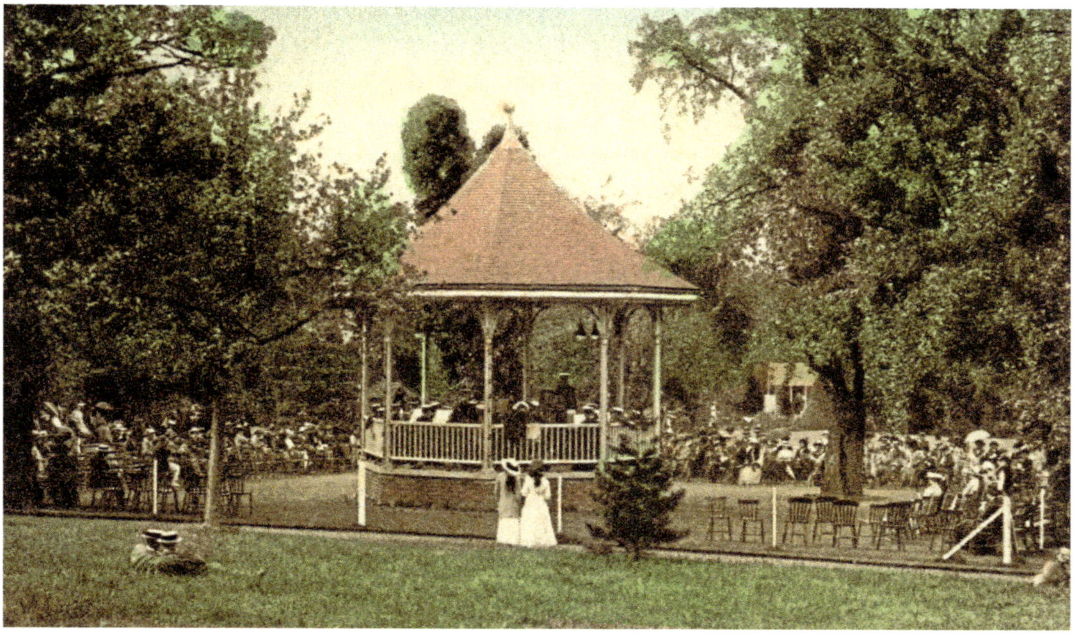

Brine Baths Park

A performance in the Brine Baths Park in the early 1900s is shown in the image above. Quite a crowd gathered for the band's performances in those days, and many still attend the performances at this very same bandstand today. The Lido pool was officially opened by the comedian Ralph Lynn in 1935, who christened the pool by pouring a bottle of champagne into it! The image below would have been taken in 1935 or 1936, as the café on the far left was converted into a two-storey building in 1937. This building can still be seen in its 1937 form at this ever popular pool today.

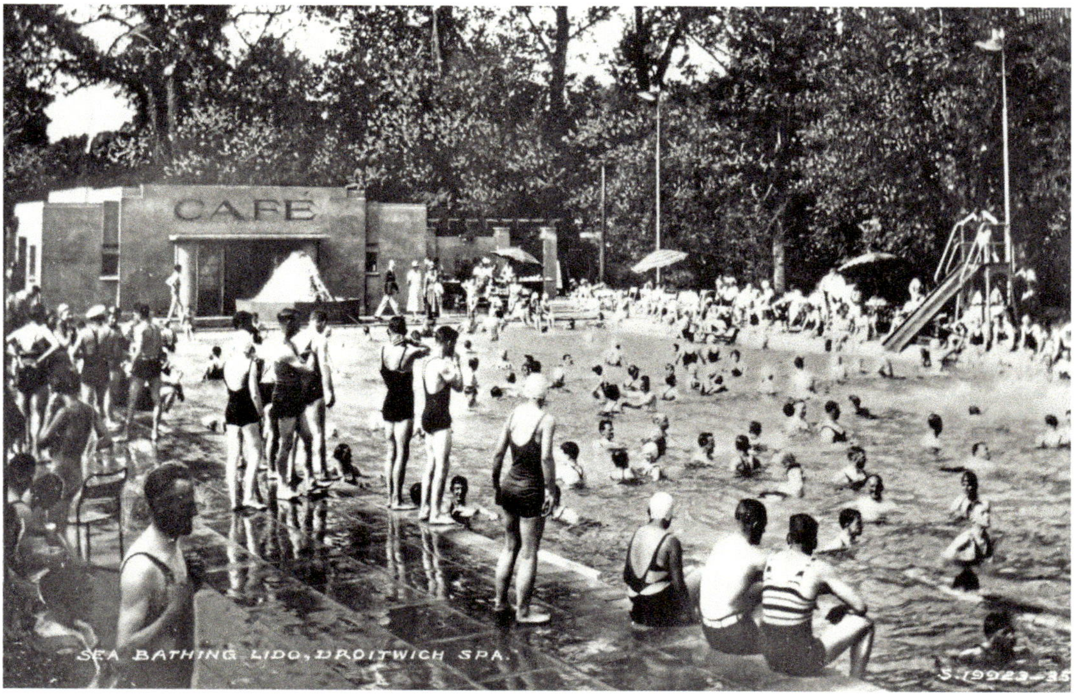

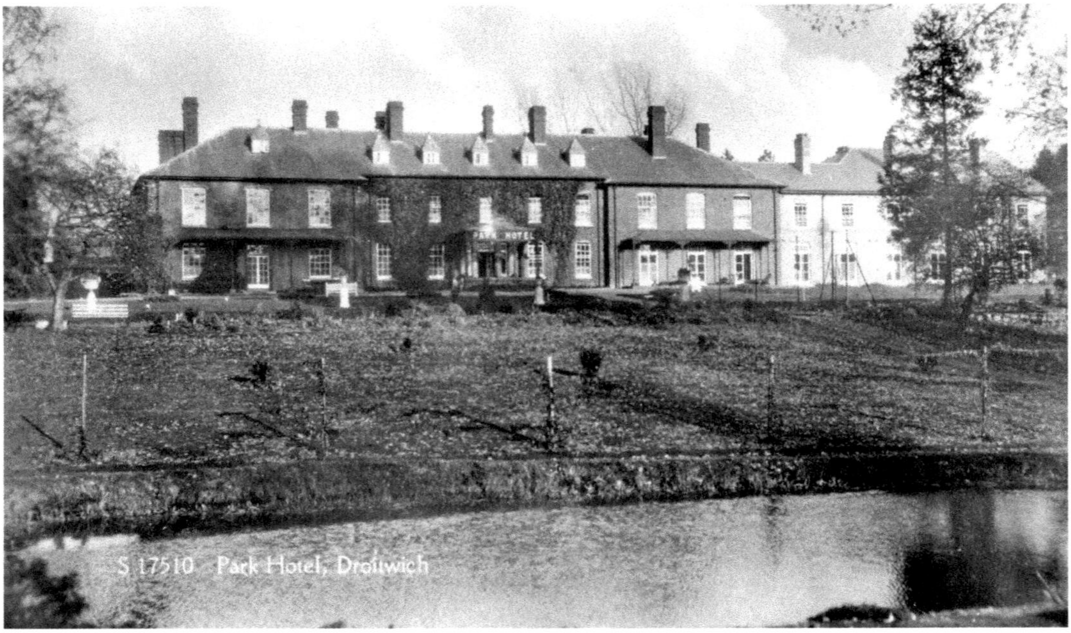

Park Hotel and Albion House

The image reproduced above shows the Park Hotel with the Heriotts Pool in the foreground. The oldest part of the Park Hotel was once known as the Harriotts and later the Heriotts, and was for a large portion of the nineteenth century the home of Revd John Topham. Albion House is pictured below in around 1900, which at this time and during the 1890s consisted of a number of apartments let by Selina Skerrett to those seeking the cure. Selina's husband was Cab Proprietor Philip Skerrett. In the 1870s and 1880s, Albion House was run by the Bowles family, after which they moved to the Larches at Witton.

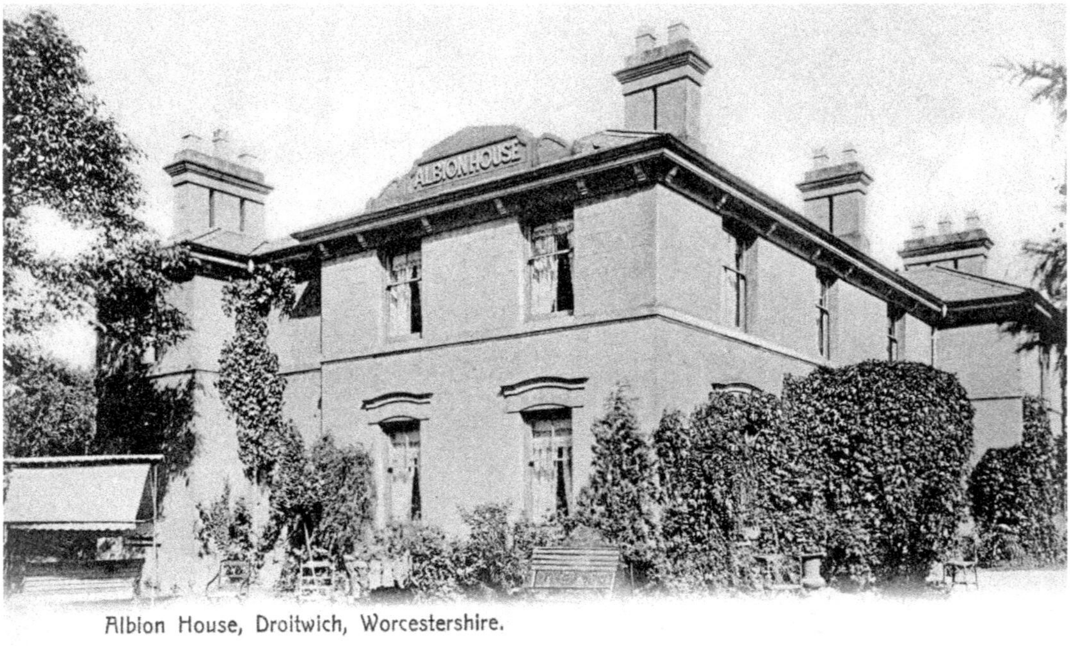

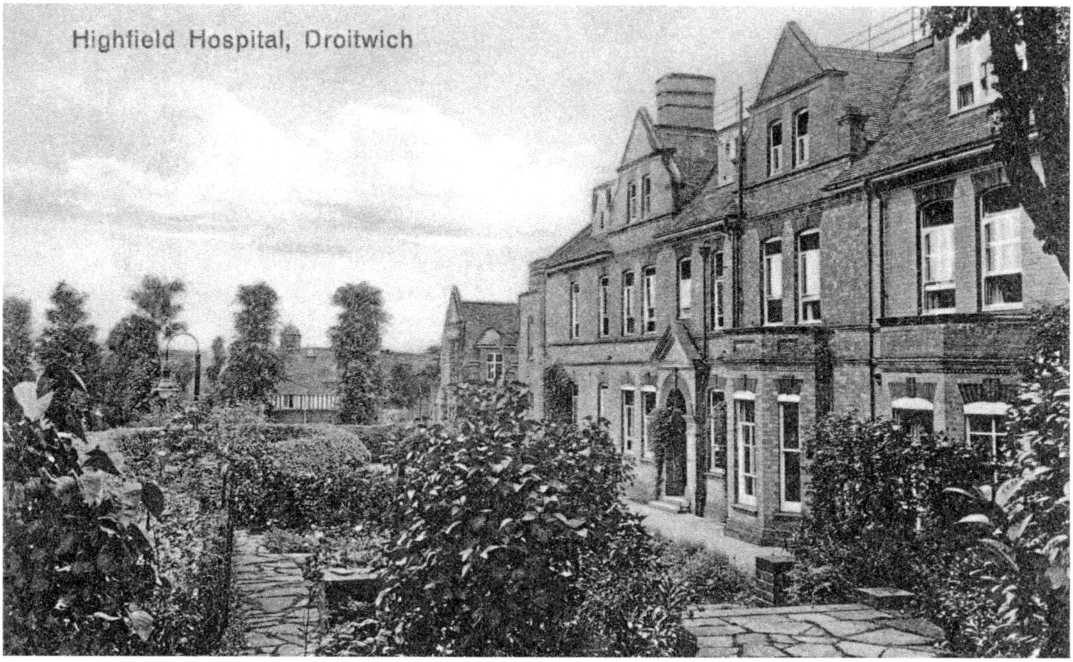

Highfield Hospital and the Castle

Highfield Hospital is shown above, with a property known as Ashlea in the background. Highfield was built by Dr John M. Cuthbertson in around 1894 as a family home and for the reception of patients undergoing treatment for rheumatism. In 1914 it was taken by Lady Georgina Vernon and Sir Harry Vernon and soon became an auxiliary Red Cross hospital. In 1917 it was re-established as a Birmingham Hospital Saturday Fund hospital. It was used again for soldiers during the Second World War, and demolished in 1995. The Elephant and Castle Pub at Witton was renamed the Castle in 1911, and is shown below in *c.* 1930.

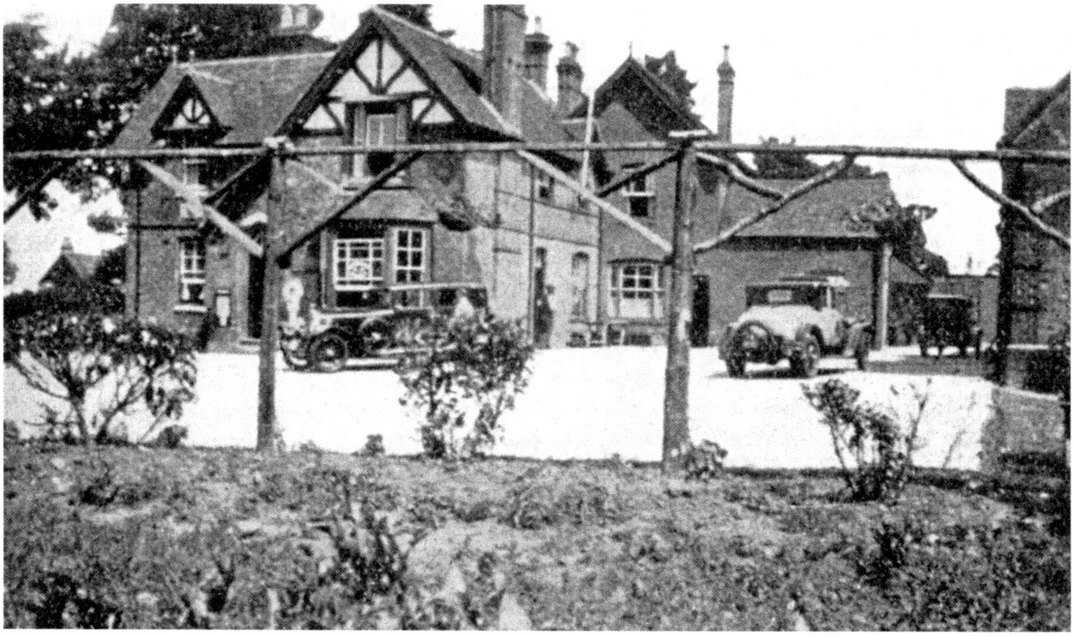

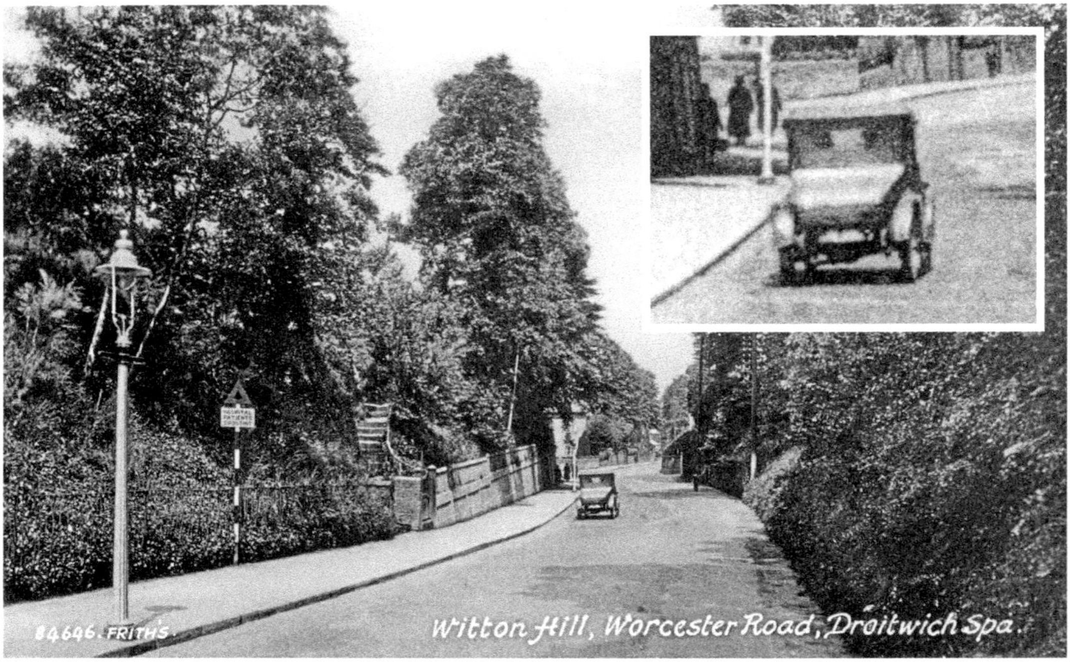

Witton Hill

A very quiet Witton Hill (the A38) in 1931 is shown above, with the car enlarged as an inset. The earlier shot of Witton below looks north towards Droitwich from approximately the site of the current post office. The building on the right stood for many years on an island at the point at which Tagwell Road once forked; this, however, was demolished in the 1930s. The island itself was not removed until much more recent times, when the junction with Tagwell Road and the Worcester Road was improved and parking provided for the shops. These shops now stand on the extreme right of this view.

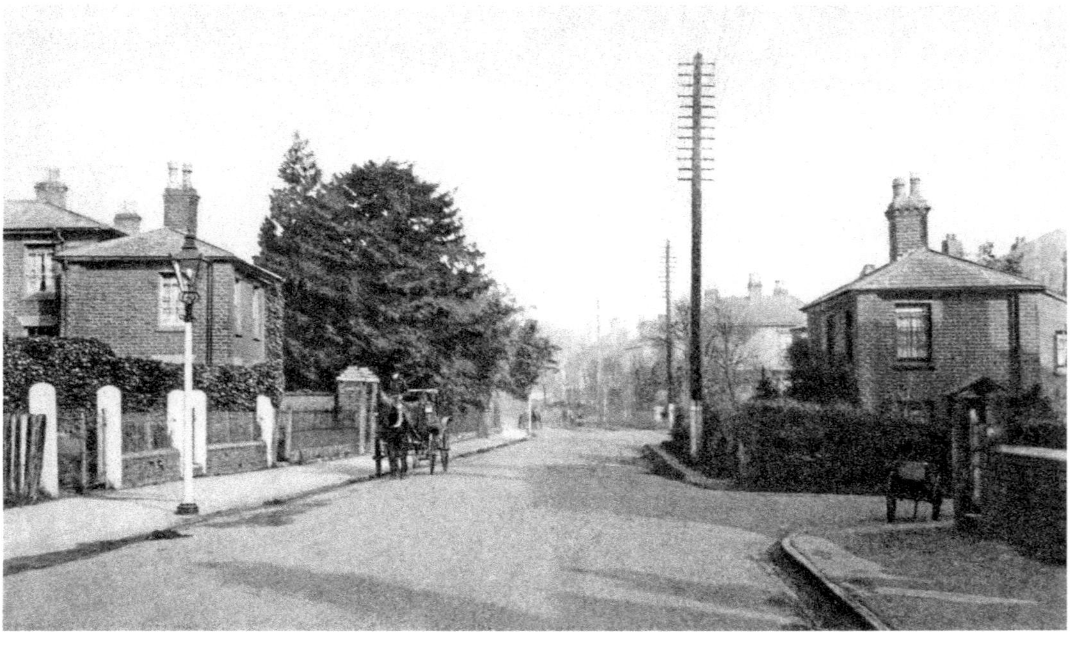

CHAPTER 8

IMPNEY AND WESTWOOD

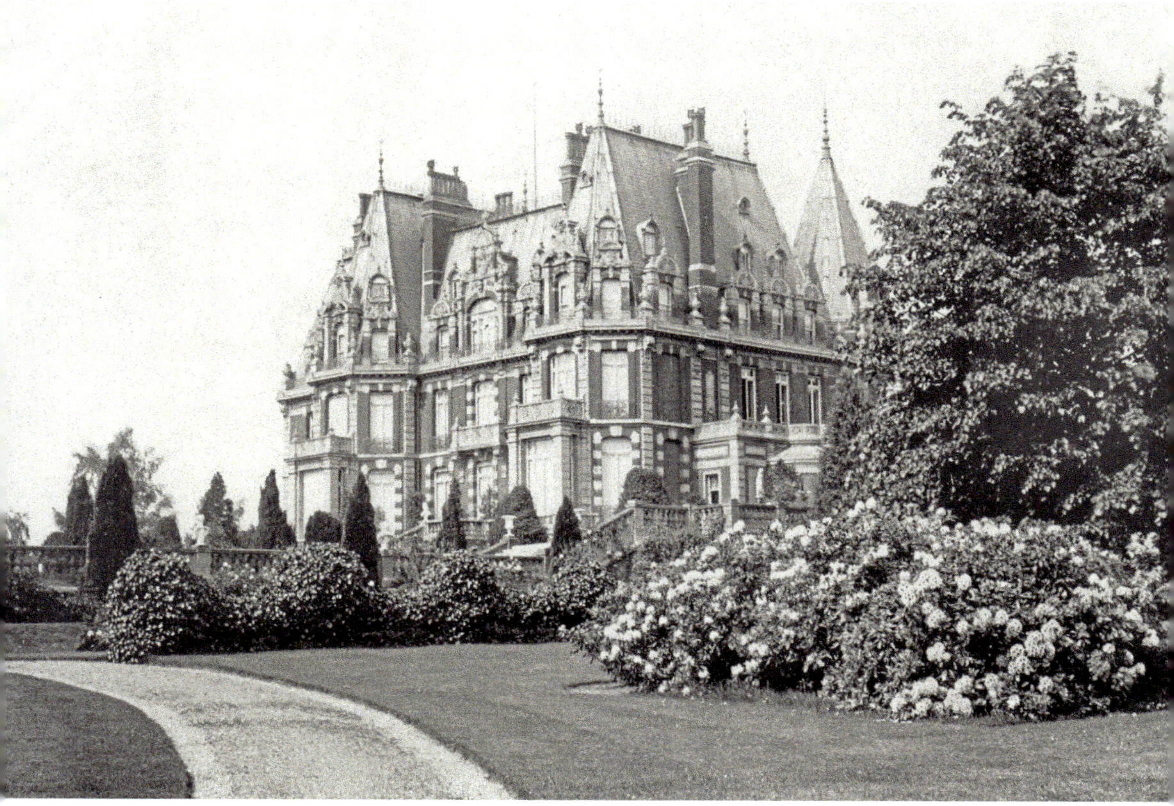

Impney

John Corbett's Impney is shown above from a card posted in 1906 – just five years after Jonn's passing. Impney was designed in 1869 by Auguste Tronquois of Paris and R. P. Spiers in the Louis XIII style and constructed in the early- to mid-1870s. John's animal-loving brother Tom Corbett lived at Impney from 1902, but in 1906 he sold off much of the furniture and effects and died in the same year.

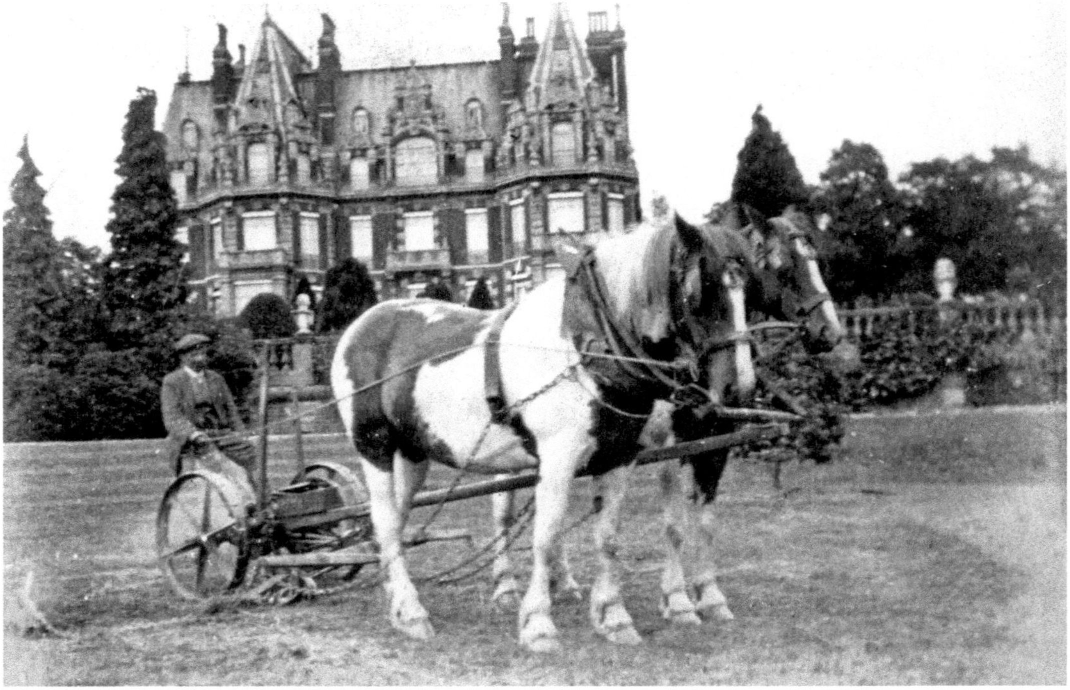

Impney

The shot above shows a lovely pair of horses with a driver seated behind in 1923. Impney is visible in the background and the team has paused for a moment from their ploughing work in order to pose for the photograph. Below, the Impney sluicegates and cascade can be seen in 1917, with a man in a cap watching the whole spectacle from the footbridge. The sluicegates and cascade were to be found to the south of the main house next to Mill Cottage. A monument to John and Tom Corbett's pets and horses was once located at the rear of this property and now stands next to the Lido's carpark.

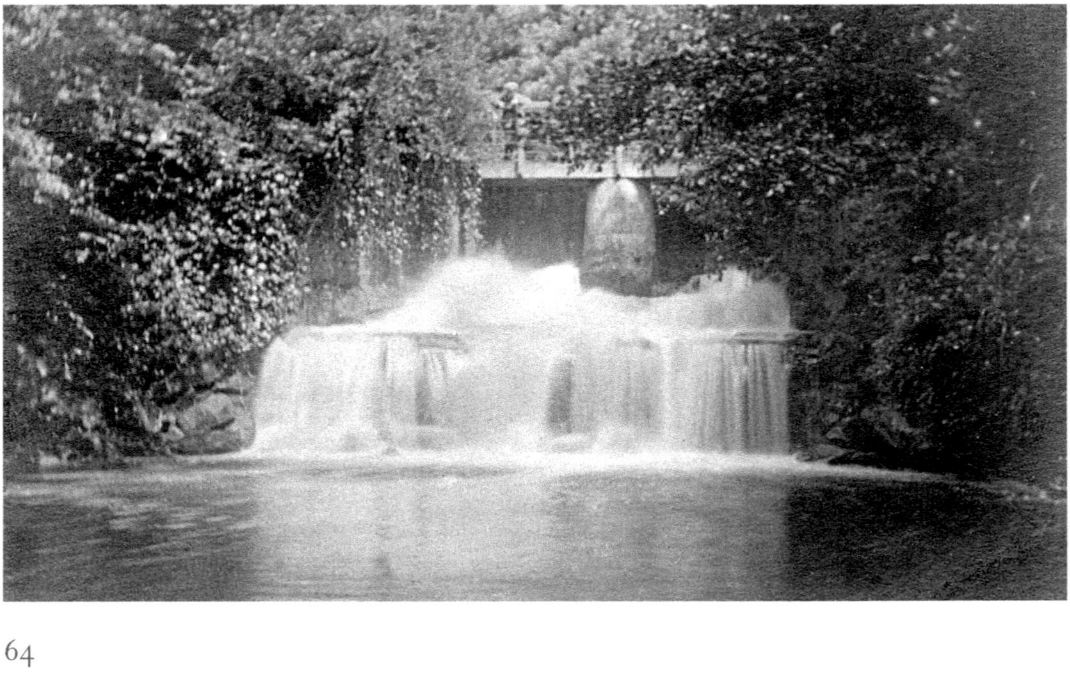

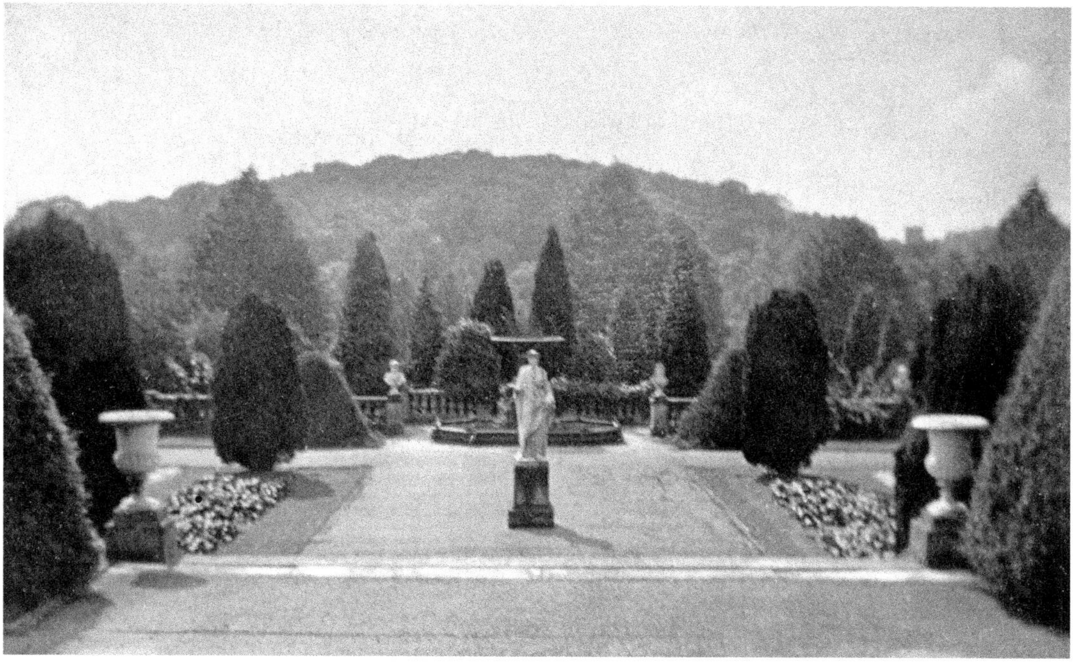

Gardens

The above shot was taken from the terrace at Impney in 1923, and looks south towards Pridzor Wood. The statue in the centre of the image is *Flora*, a figure that remained on site despite an auction of Impney effects – this was perhaps due to a missing hand. *Flora* can still be seen in the grounds of Impney today from the site's south driveway. The image below was taken at a garden party at Westwood Park in 1910 during a presentation to Liberal candidate C. B. Harmsworth by Earl and Countess Beauchamp. Harmsworth, however, did not stand in that year's election due to illness and had intimated so at this event.

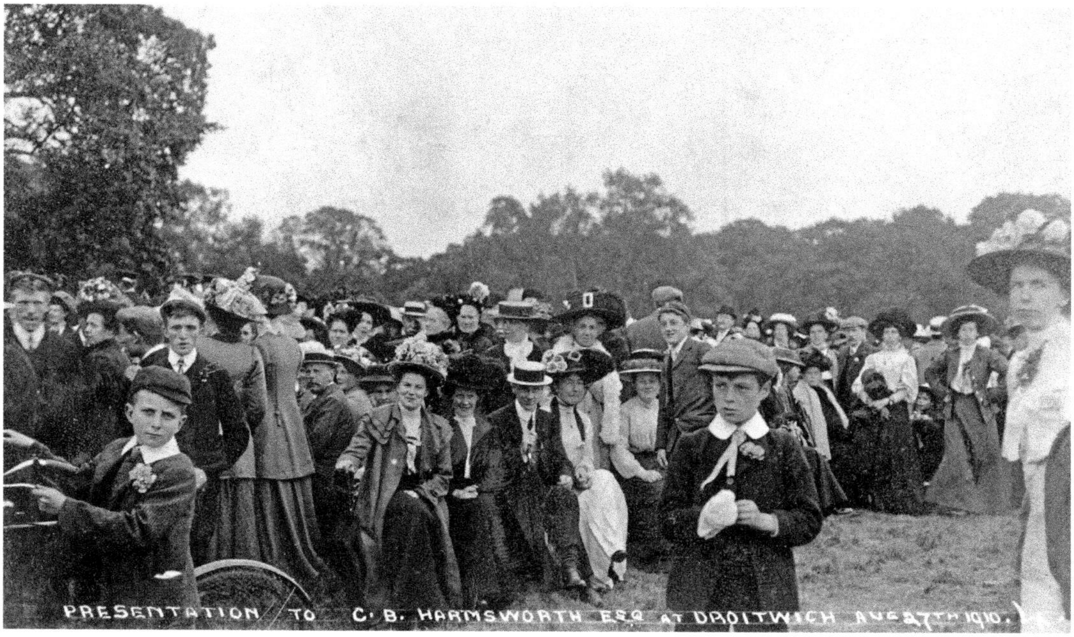

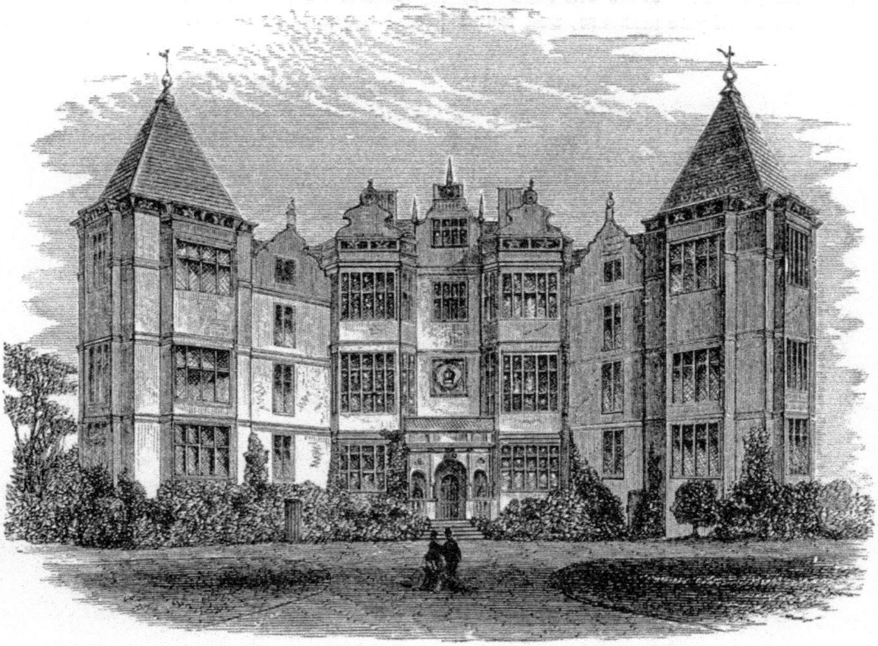

The Principal Front.

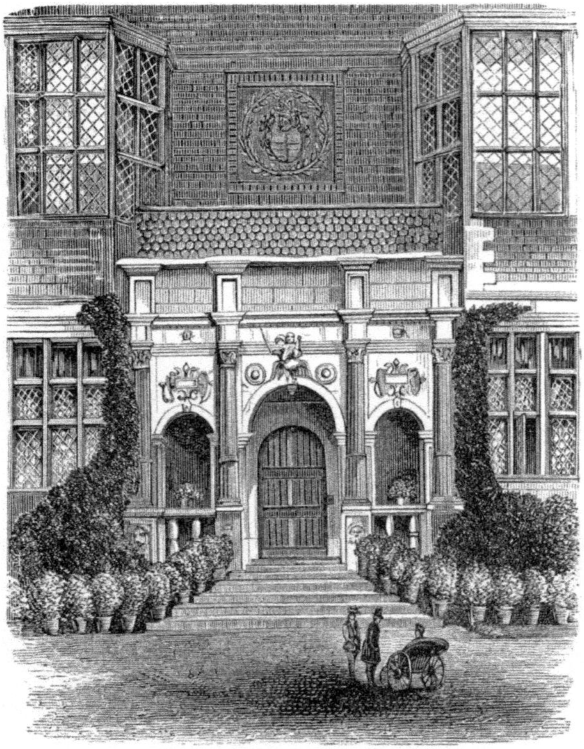

The Entrance Porch.

Westwood

Four images of Westwood are shown here, all of which were published in 1875. The principal front of this property was constructed in around 1612–17, and the wings were added later in around 1625. Westwood was founded in the mid-twelfth century as a priory and later became a Benedictine nunnery, which used the original St Nicholas' Church as its chapel – the current St Nicholas' Church in Droitwich being the third. The Pakingtons acquired the land after the dissolution, and the house built by one of Queen Elizabeth's favourites – Sir John Pakington – nicknamed Lusty, apparently for his athletic achievements!

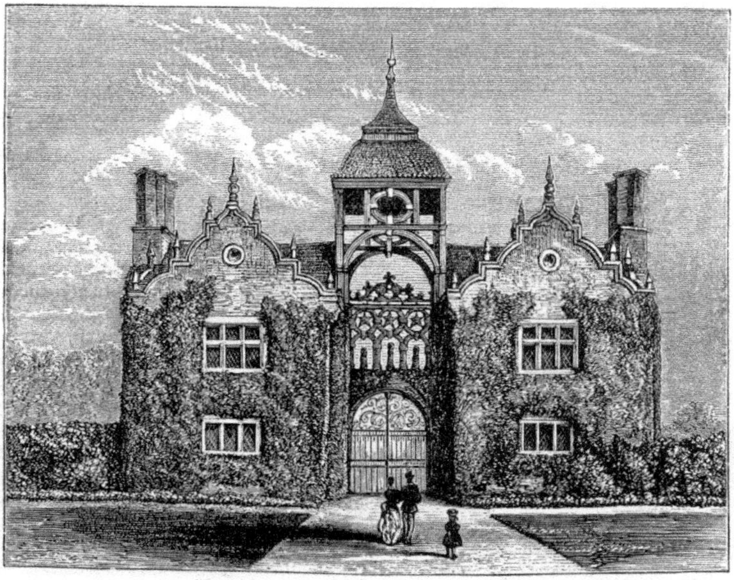

The Gatehouse, as seen from the Mansion.

Westwood House

A fine gatehouse is situated in front of Westwood House and this is shown above. The wings to the house were originally given pyramid roofs (top left), but in the early 1920s they were altered for the second Lord Doverdale and made to match the roofs of the pavilions and the gatehouse's cupola (above). The estate's Gothic lodges probably date from the early 1840s. The lodge shown below is known as Droitwich Lodge and is to be found just east of the Great Pool. It was sold in 1952 for £2,000. Incidentally, 'Lusty John' upset the local inhabitants by creating the Great Pool and thus submerging a right of way!

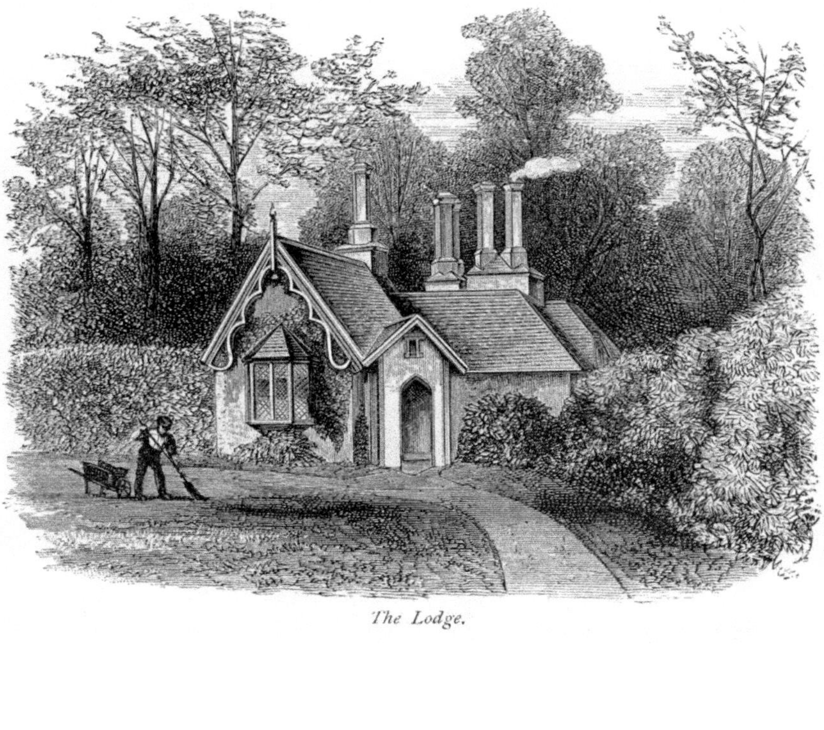

The Lodge.

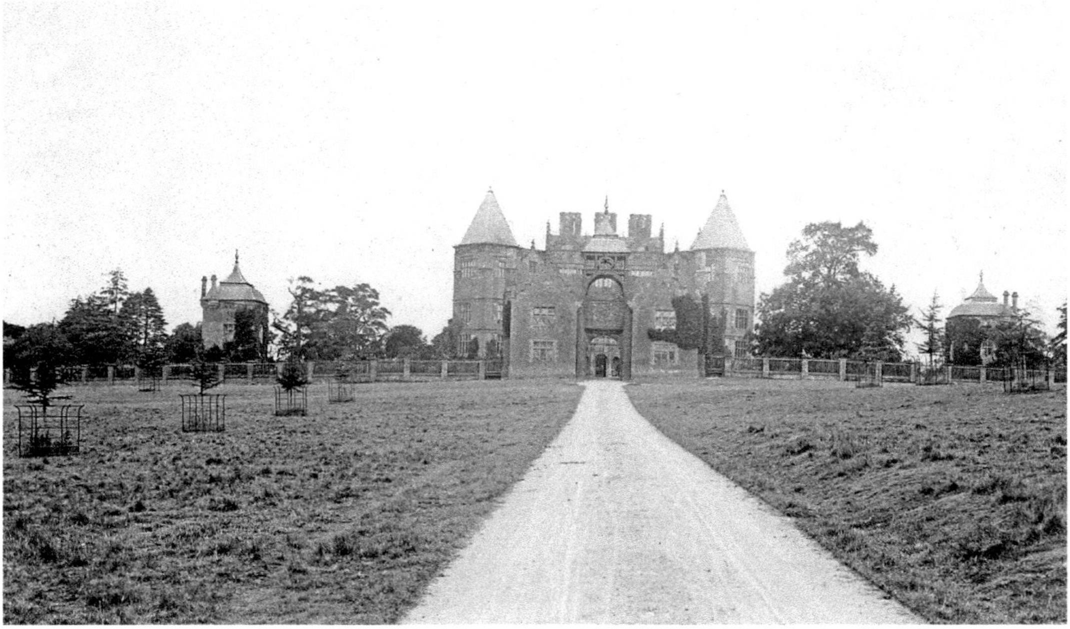

Westwood House

Two shots of Westwood House in the early 1900s are shown here, in which the gatehouse (below right) and pavilions (above left and right) can be seen. The tiny saplings that line the driveway in the image above are now a fine leafy avenue. The Pakington line died out at the end of the nineteenth century and the estate was then purchased by Edward Partington, who became Baron Doverdale of Westwood in 1917. This lasted until the death of third baron in 1949, and the estate was then split up into twenty-six lots and sold at an auction held at the Winter Gardens in Droitwich in October 1952.

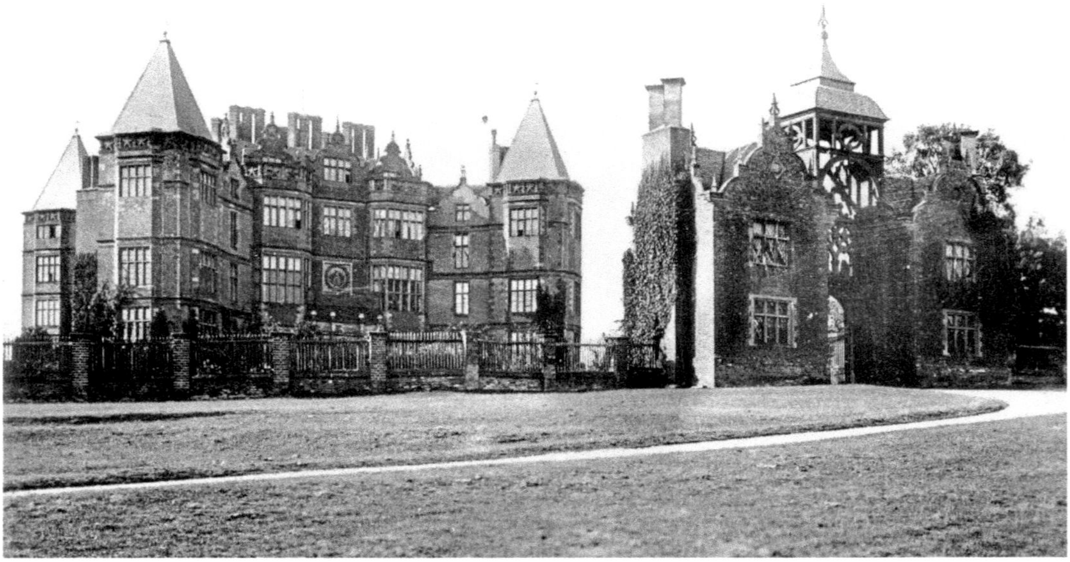

CHAPTER 9

VILLAGES AROUND DROITWICH

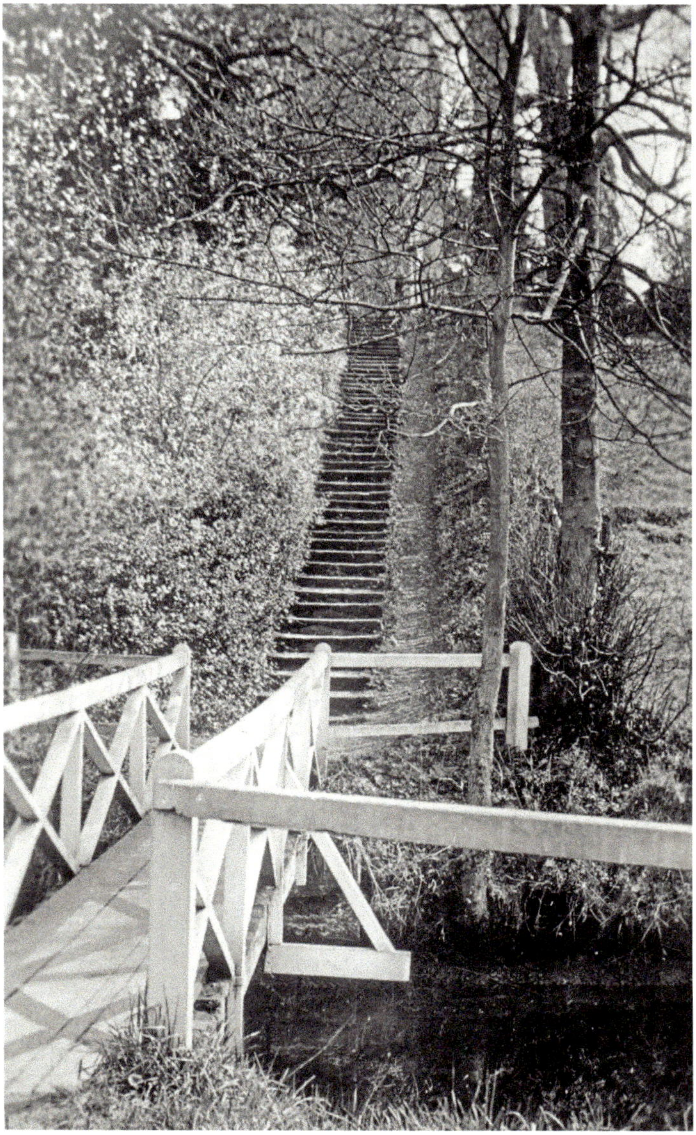

Salwarpe

For the tour of the villages around Droitwich, what nicer a spot to start than Salwarpe. The forty-nine steps, which are accessed from the north-west corner of the churchyard, are shown here. This particular card was posted in 1909, at a time when the charming bridge in the foreground still crossed the tailrace to the mill. The mill, tailrace and bridge have long gone, but the steps and nearby weir remain.

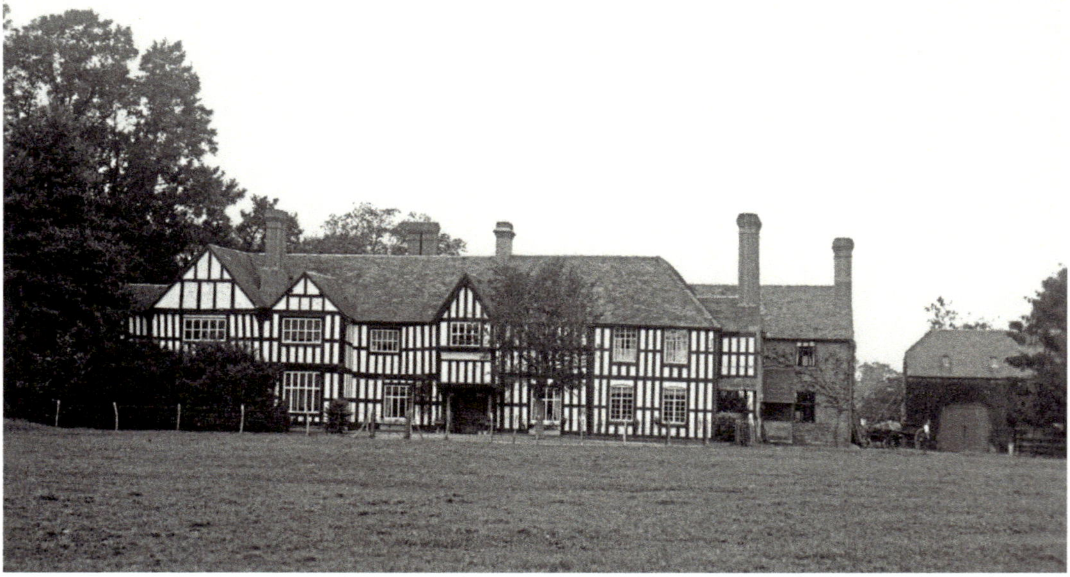

Salwarpe

Salwarpe Court in the early 1900s is shown above, which in more recent times has been restored to reveal the brick nogging. This type of timber framing is known as close studding as the timbers are very close together, meaning that a larger quantity of expensive timber was needed and so denoting a high-status construction. It is thought that the court was rebuilt for Sir John Talbot in around 1580. The colourised card below was posted in 1905 and shows part of the village of Salwarpe from the canal. The parapet of the church tower can be seen on the far left and a small boat floats to the right of the gate.

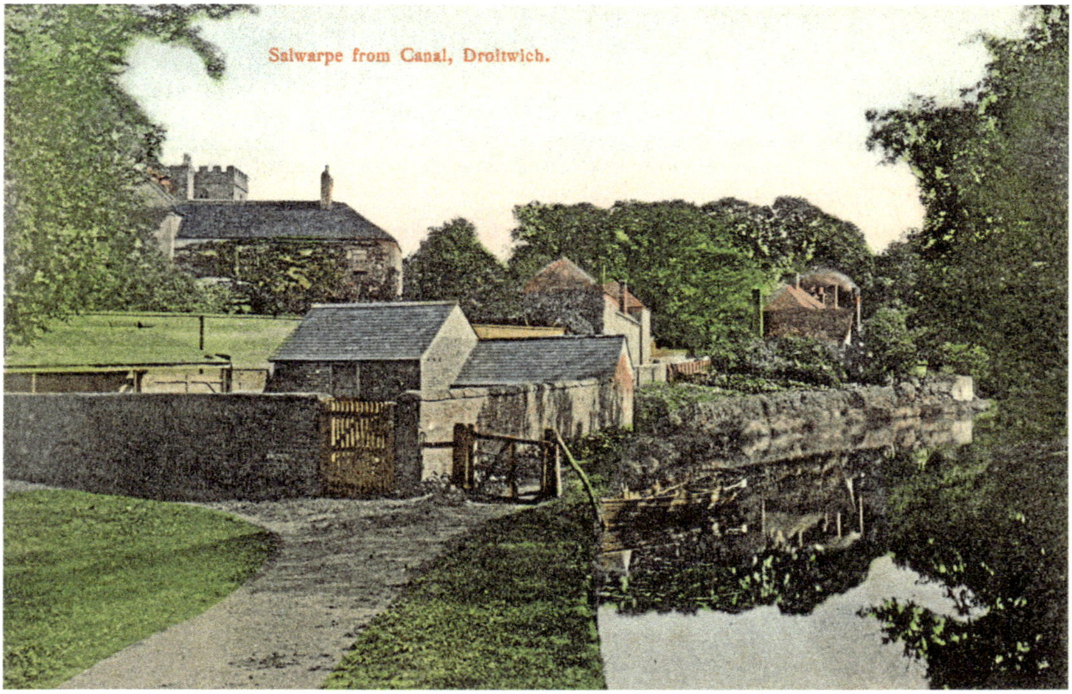

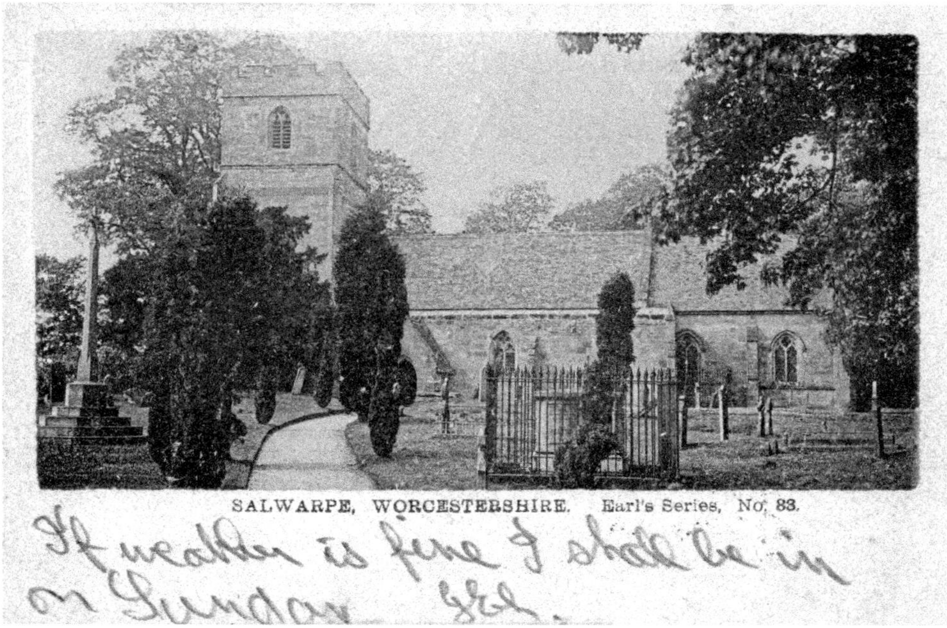

Salwarpe Church and Martin Hussingtree Church

The above card of Salwarpe Church was posted in 1904 and shows the Cypress trees long before they became the towering giants that they are today. The small tree right of centre blew down in a gale in February 2014 and seriously damaged the structure of the fourteenth-century south aisle, which thankfully has since been restored. The *c.* 1857 porch is dedicated to Lydia Ricketts and a stained-glass window dedicated to her husband Martin. Martin worked at his father's asylum in Droitwich, which adjoined what is now Ricketts Lane. The below card of nearby Martin Hussingtree Church also dates from the early 1900s.

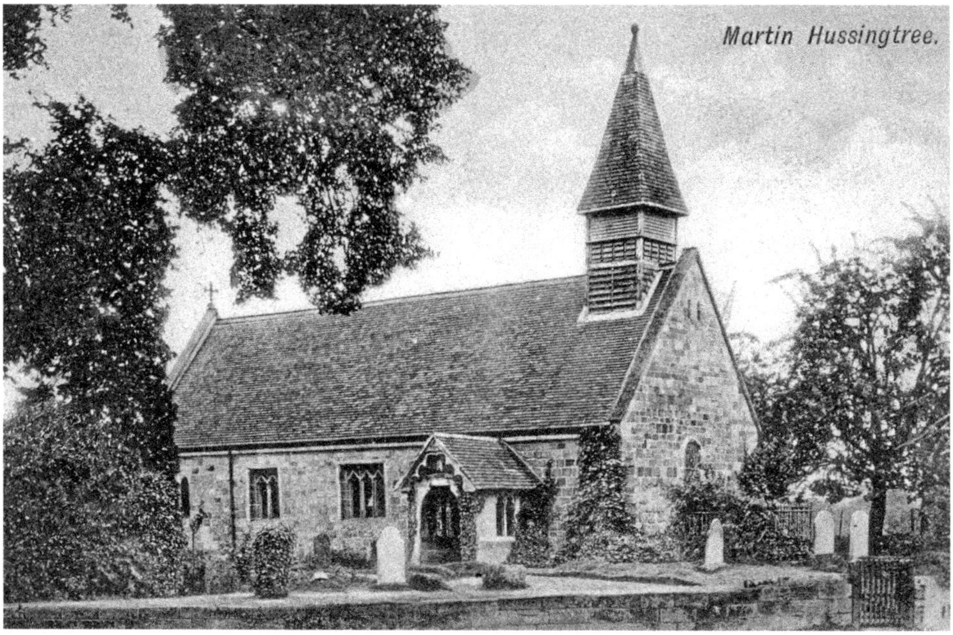

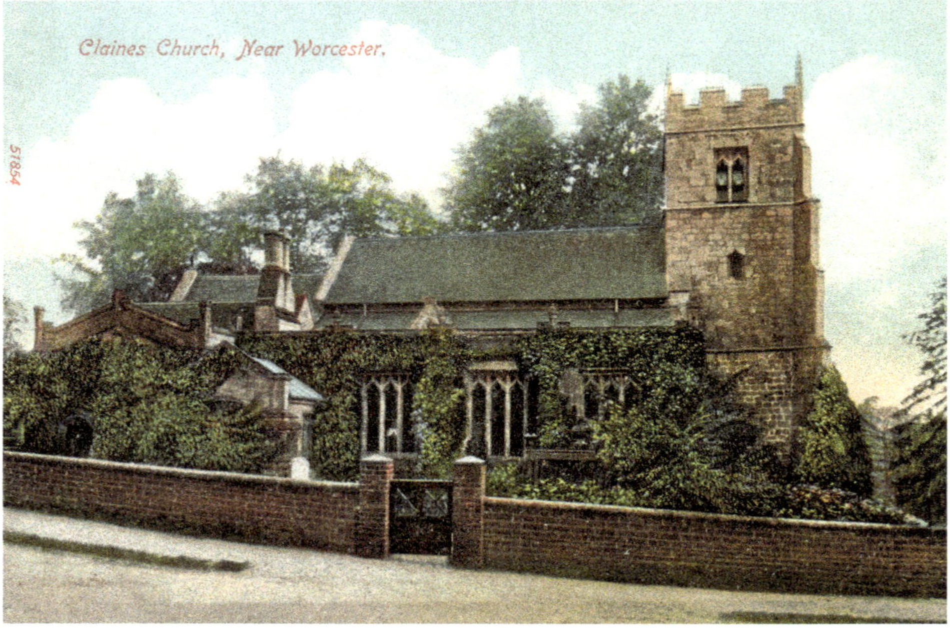

The Mug House and Hadley Bowling Green Inn

A rather overgrown Claines Church can be seen in the above image from the early 1900s. The Mug House Inn stands nearby, which was probably constructed in the sixteenth century as a church house, though some believe that it was the church alehouse. Apparently, there are only two pubs in England on consecrated ground, the Mug House at Claines being one of them. The Worcestershire historian Treadway Russell Nash lived nearby at Bevere. The Hadley Bowling Green Inn is shown below, which, like the Mug House, remains as popular as ever, and the mill at Hadley has survived with its original machinery and waterwheel intact.

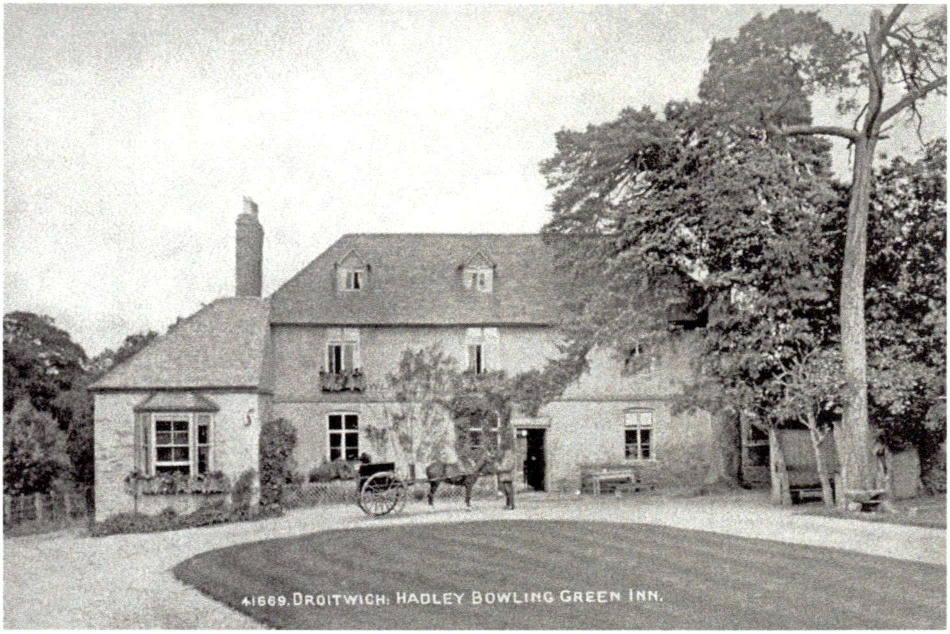

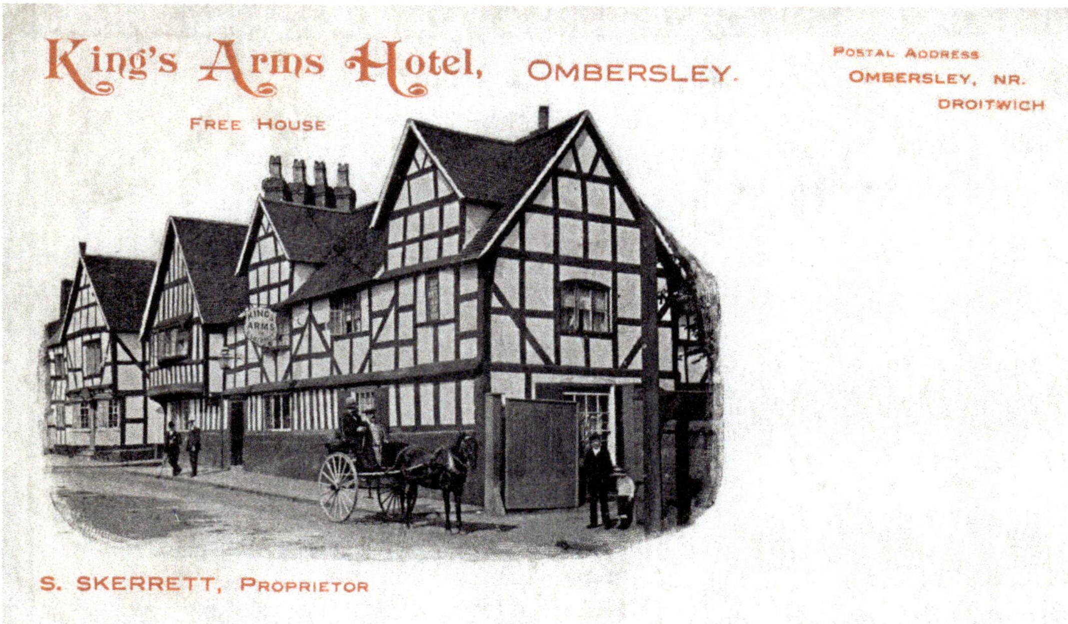

The Kings Arms

The above card of the King's Arms in Ombersley dates from the early 1900s, when Samuel Skerrett was proprietor. Samuel had been the proprietor of the Barley Mow in Droitwich in the late 1880s and moved to the King's Arms in the 1890s. Samuel's brother James (my great-great-grandfather) was the husband of Eliza Skerrett (*see* page 31), and Samuel's brother Philip resided at Albion House (*see* page 60). Their father William established his cab company in St George's Square Droitwich in around 1875. The Kings Arms in the 1890s is shown below, along with the Crown and Sandys Arms Hotel (centre).

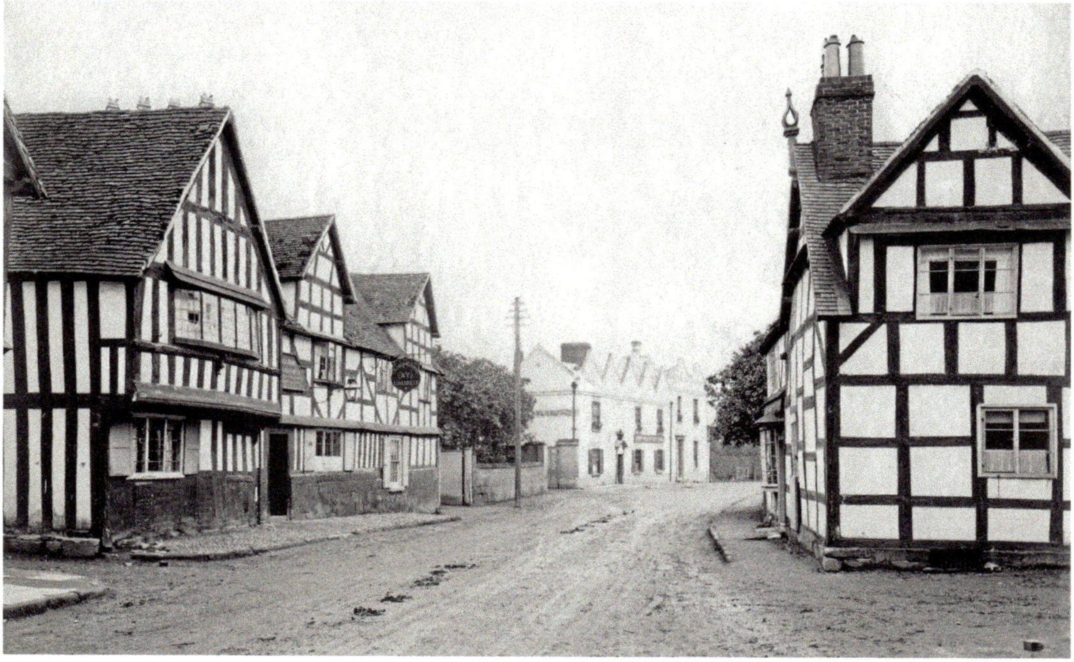

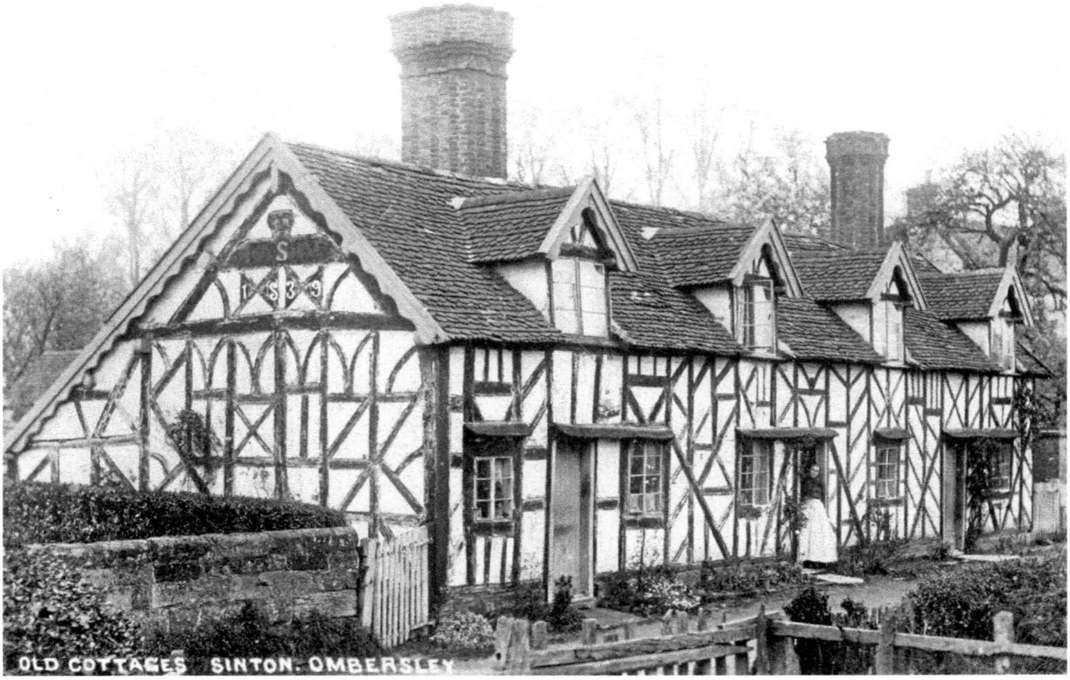

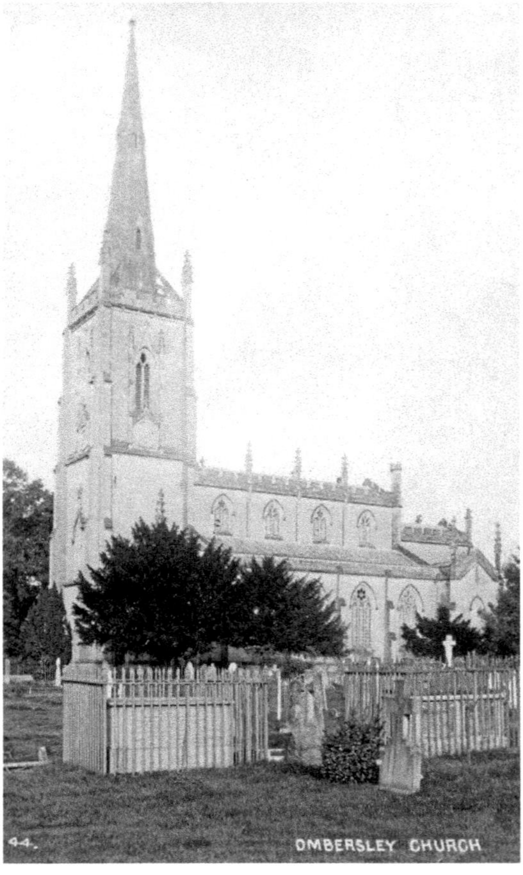

Ombersley

These lovely cottages in Sinton Lane Ombersley were demolished in 1972 to make way for the bypass. The date of '1539' is given on the gable end, and above this there is a wooden crown that – along with other parts of the structure – has been in storage at Avoncroft Museum of Historic Buildings since 1977. Also reproduced here is an early shot of St Andrew's Church in Ombersley. The Church of St Ambrose once stood just south of here, but was largely demolished and replaced with St Andrew's Church in the late 1820s. Part of the previous church's chancel survives, as it was converted into the Sandys Mausoleum.

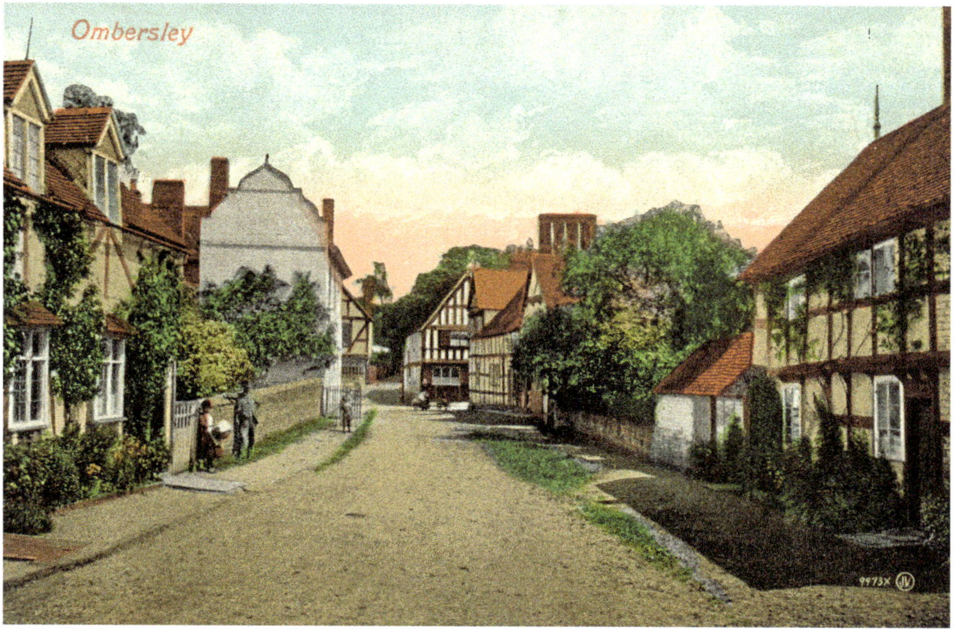

Ombersley

These two colourised postcards of Ombersley were produced in around 1905. The image above looks along Church Lane from the churchyard and towards the King's Arms. An old garage with petrol pumps has occupied the area behind the wall on the left for many years. The shot below looks towards Kidderminster from the Ombersley roundabout – the post office being the small cottage on the right, behind the cyclist in the foreground. This is another of Ombersley's lost buildings, as it was demolished around forty-five years ago. The timber-framed building on the left, however, is still standing.

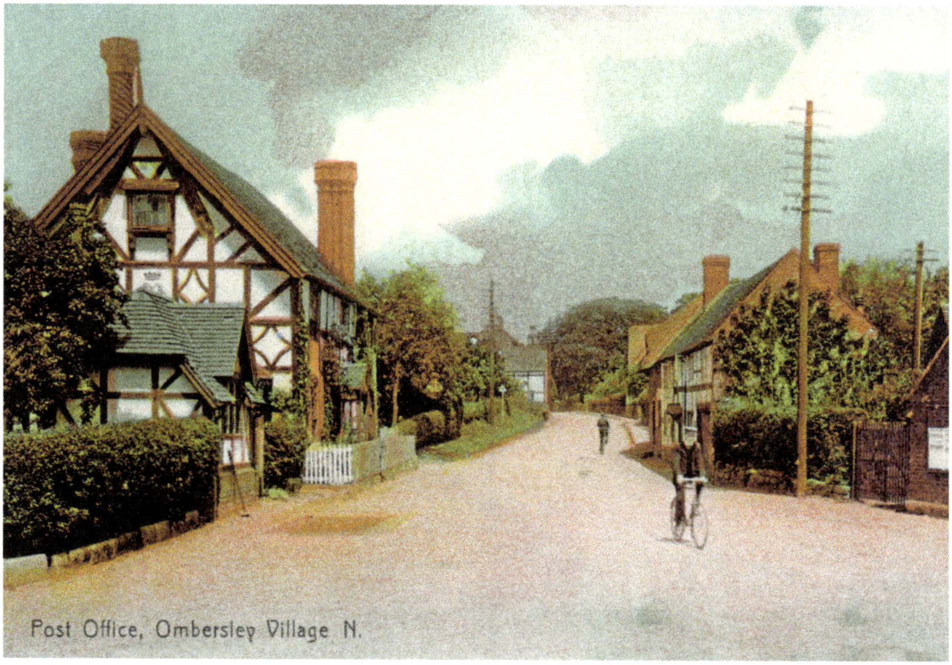

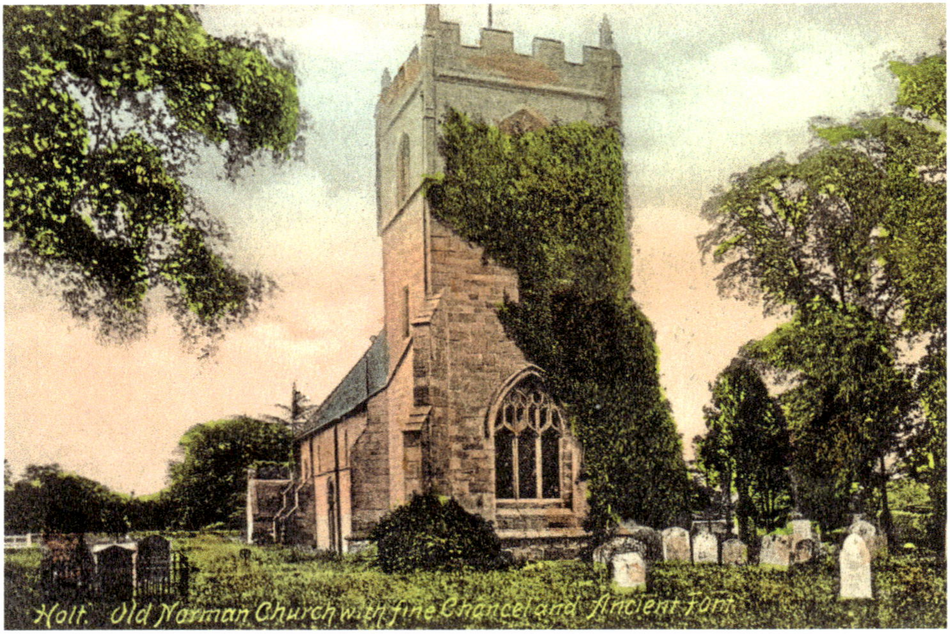

Holt

Holt Church in around 1900 is shown above, which is well worth a visit if you are interested in Norman architecture. The font is a wonderful example of the period, and the south doorway is also very fine. Opposite the church stands Holt Castle, which was held at the time of Domesday by Urso D'Abitot, who owned much property in the county – including salt works at Droitwich. The shot below also dates from around 1900 and was taken from Holt Fleet Bridge looking towards Droitwich. The building on the left contained a small roadside shop for many years, before closing in the 1990s.

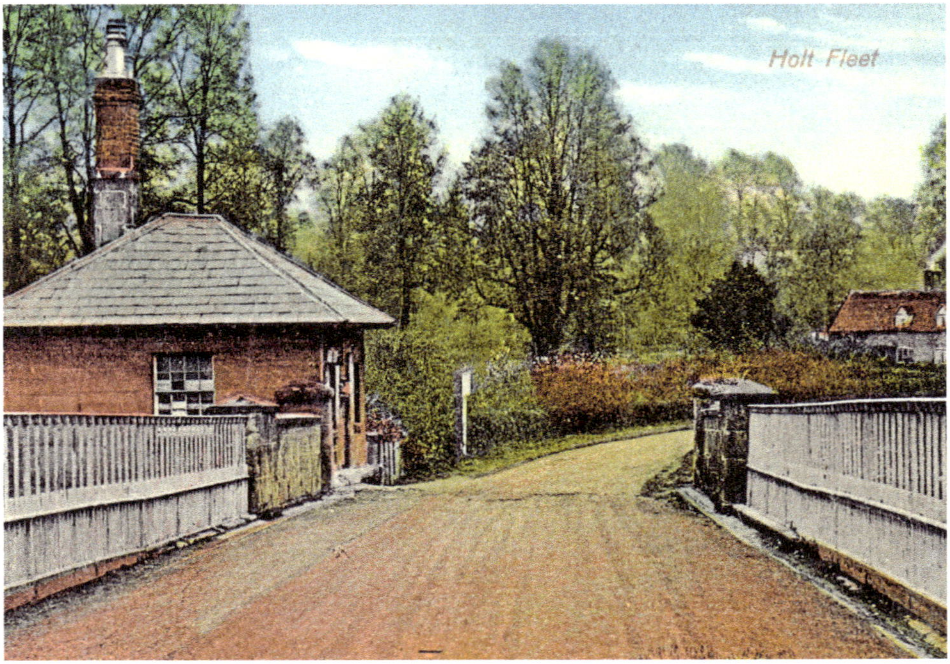

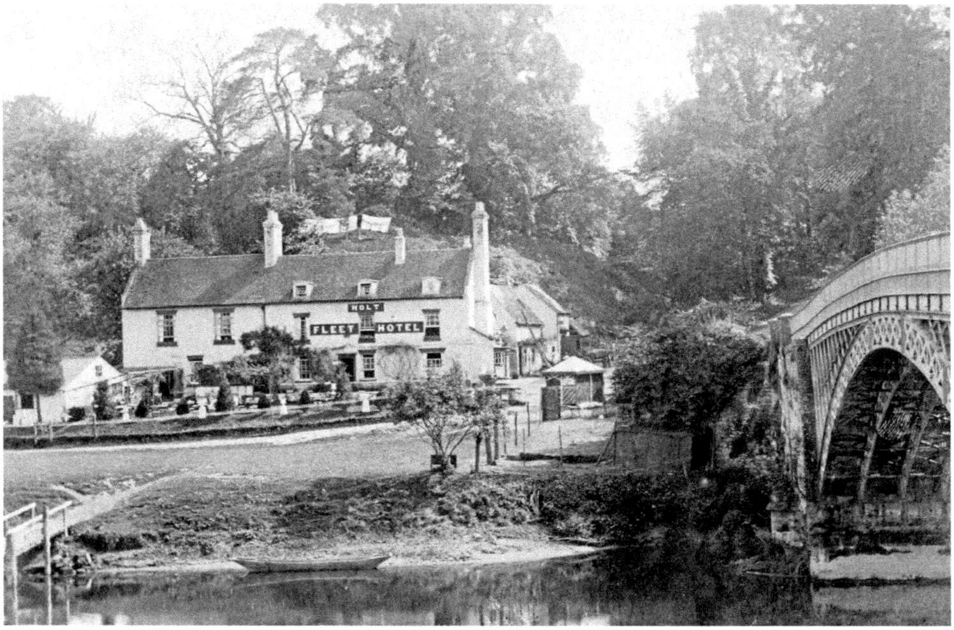

Holt Fleet Hotel and Bridge

The original Holt Fleet Hotel is shown above from a card posted at the end of the First World War. Many steamers would stop off here and the passengers would alight via the landing stage on the far left. This inn was demolished and replaced by the current brick and stone building in 1937. Holt Fleet Bridge below was designed by Thomas Telford and constructed in 1826–27. Cast in Shrewsbury, its single arch spans 150 feet, and it also has two smaller flood arches. It looks a little different today, as it was reinforced with concrete in 1928. A Second World War Hotchkiss gun emplacement stands nearby.

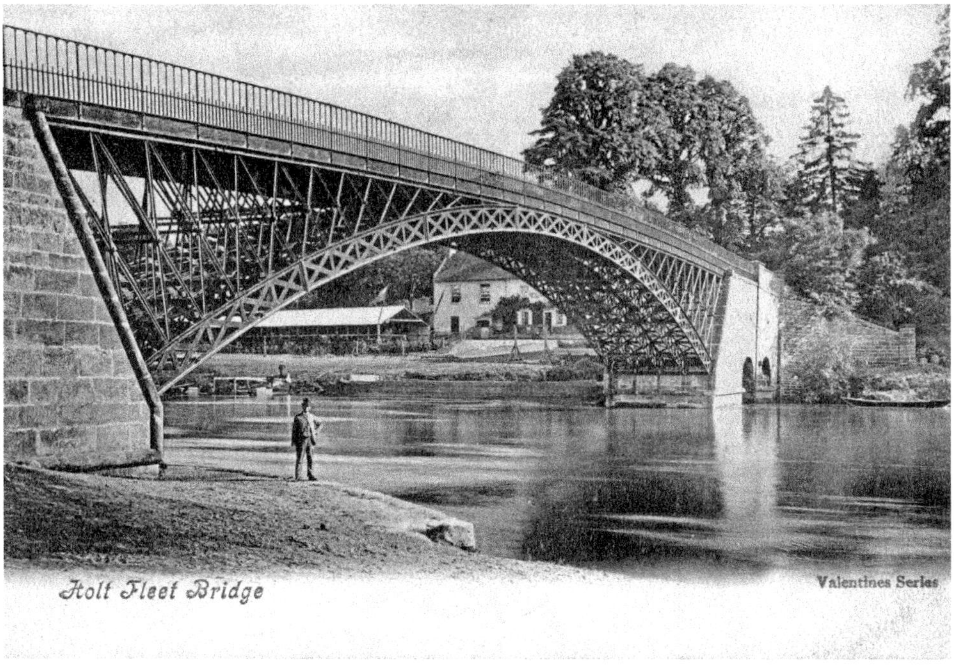

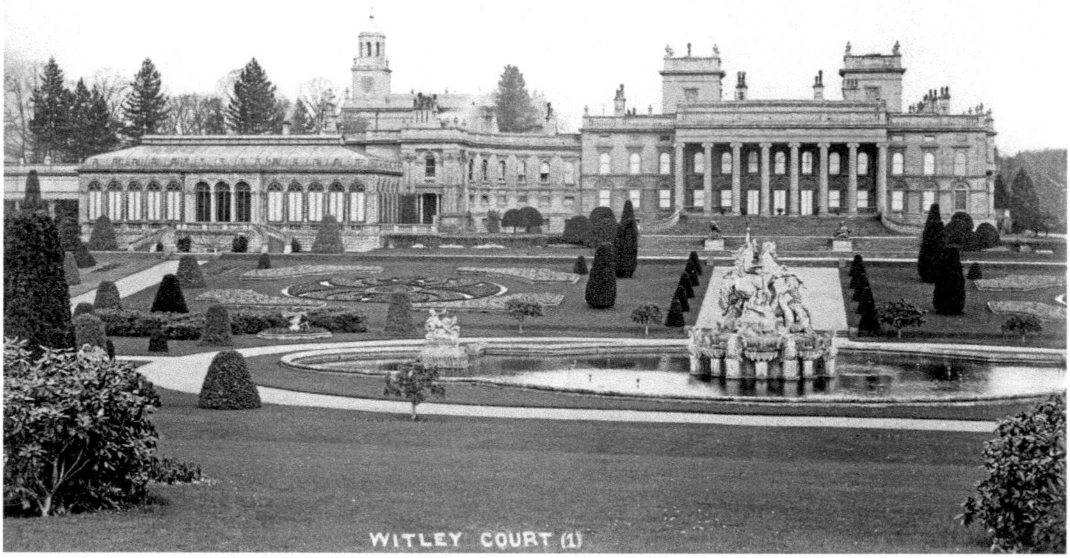

Witley

Witley Court in around 1910 is shown above, with the fountain that depicts Perseus saving Andromeda from Poseidon's monster right of centre. On the left stands the orangery, which, along with the house, is now nothing but a shell. Tragedy struck in 1937 when a fire raged through the house and much that remained was then sold at auction. It is, however, a wonderful place to visit thanks to English Heritage, who have restored the grounds and the fountain to their former glory. The old toll house at Great Witley in around 1910 is shown below. Once known as the Round House, it has long since been demolished.

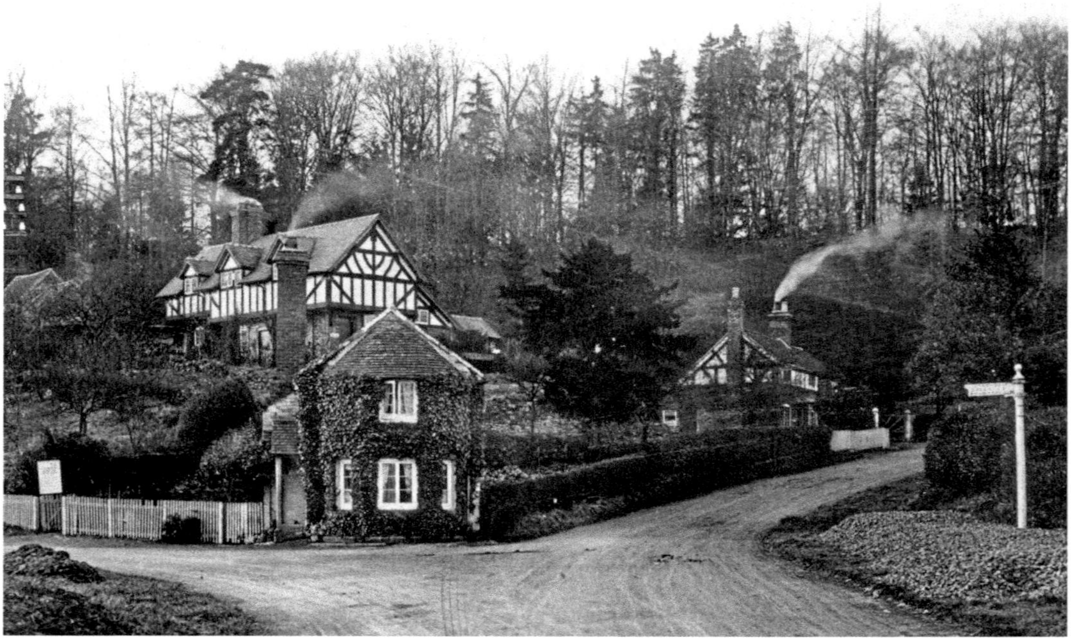

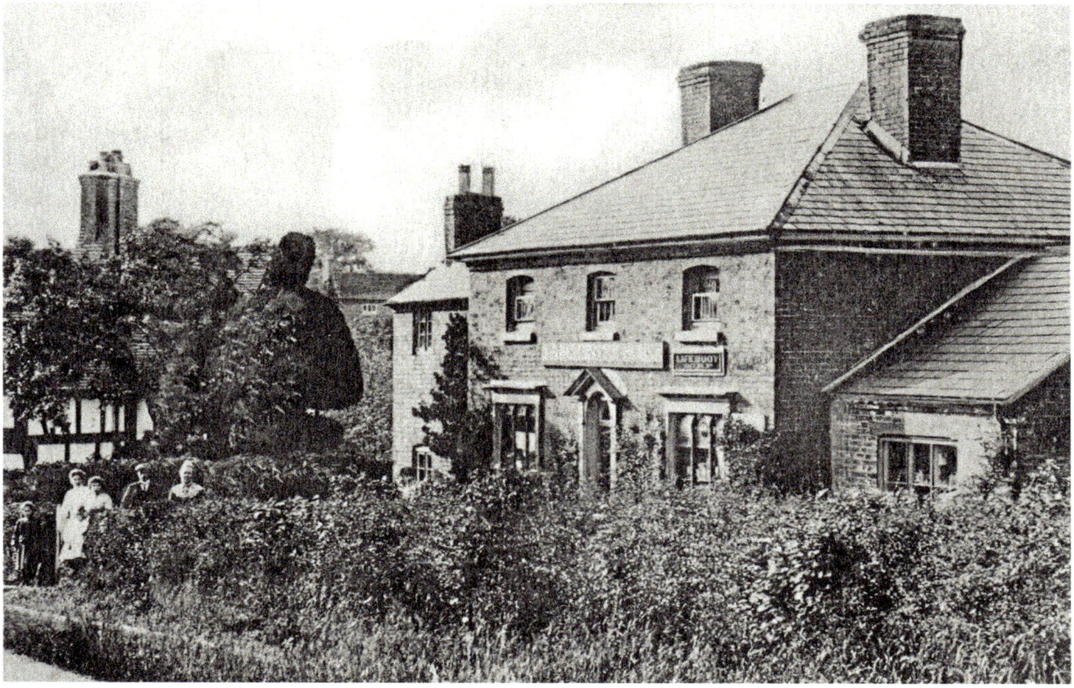

Abberley

The property at Abberley shown above was once known as Manchester House and was for decades the village drapery and grocery store run by George and Mary Quarterman with the assistance of their many offspring. By 1901, George was sixty-seven and Mary fifty-seven, and their time at the shop was drawing to a close. The family standing to the far left in this image could well be the Quartermans. By 1911, seventy-seven-year-old George and sixty-seven-year-old Mary were running a local farm. Also shown here is Abberley Clock Tower, which was constructed in 1883 and is still a familiar landmark today.

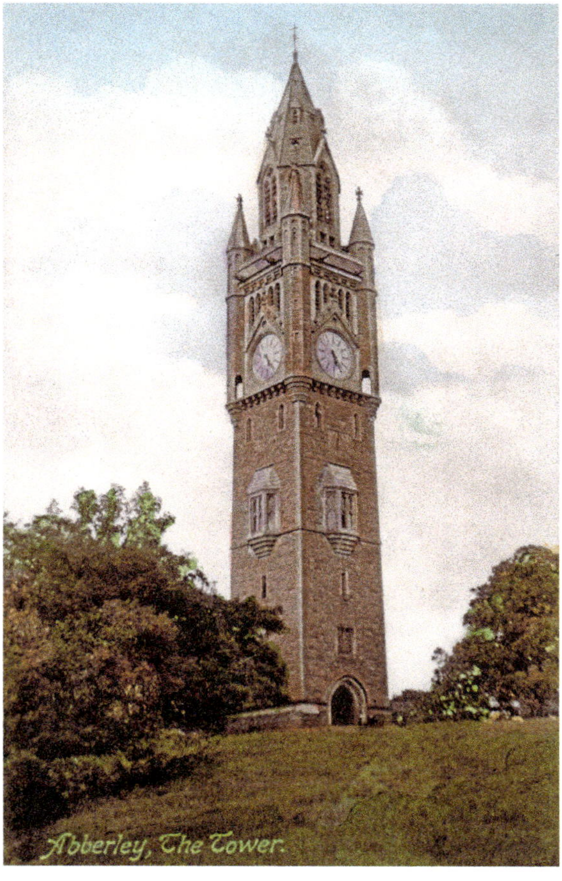

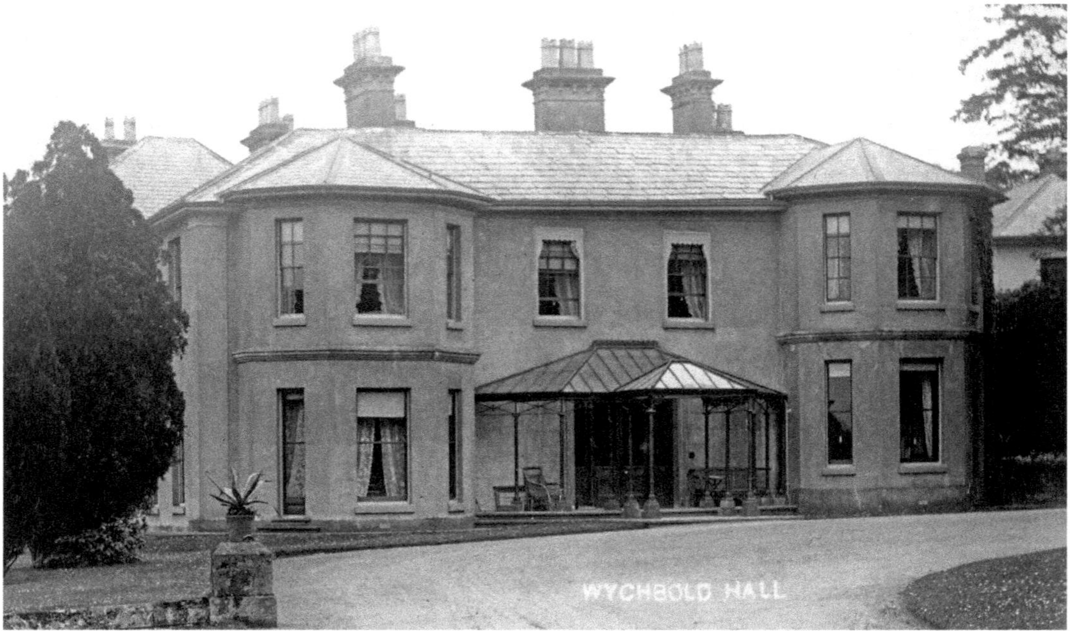

Wychbold

Two shots of Wychbold are reproduced here, both of which date from around 1910. Wychbold Hall (above) became a ruin in the late 1930s after the death of Sophia Amphlett. This was largely due to structural damage caused by a brine stream. In 1938, a second hall was built closer to the main road by Richard John Amphlett. This has also been demolished and the site is now a housing estate. The card below looks towards Bromsgrove, along the main road (the A38) that runs through the village. The lady left of centre is busy chatting to another person in the first-floor window of the property on the far left.

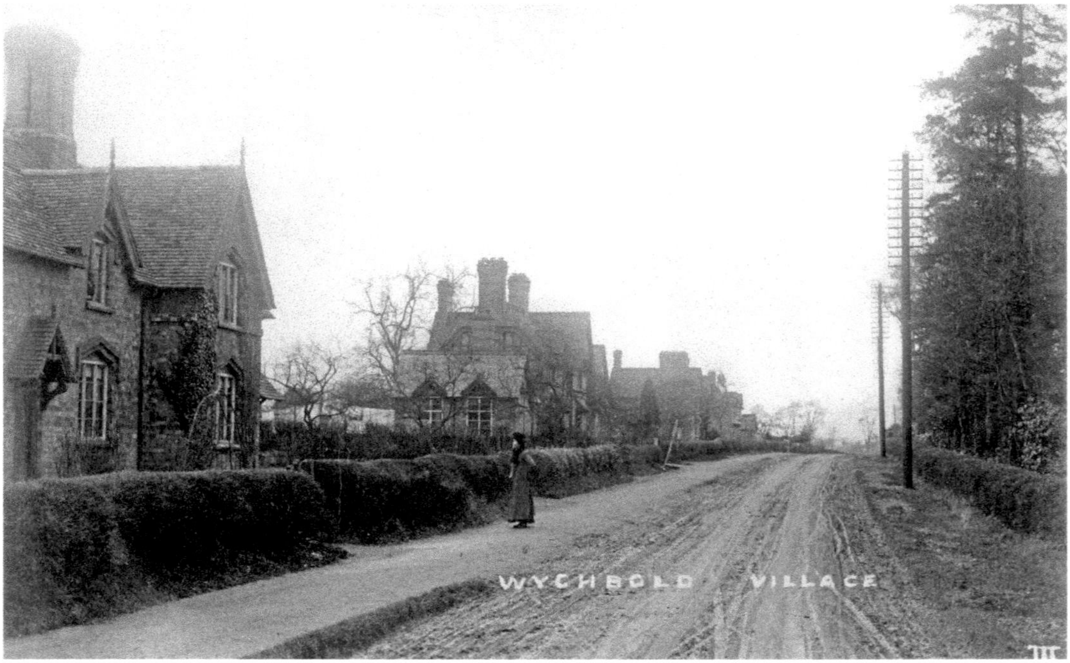

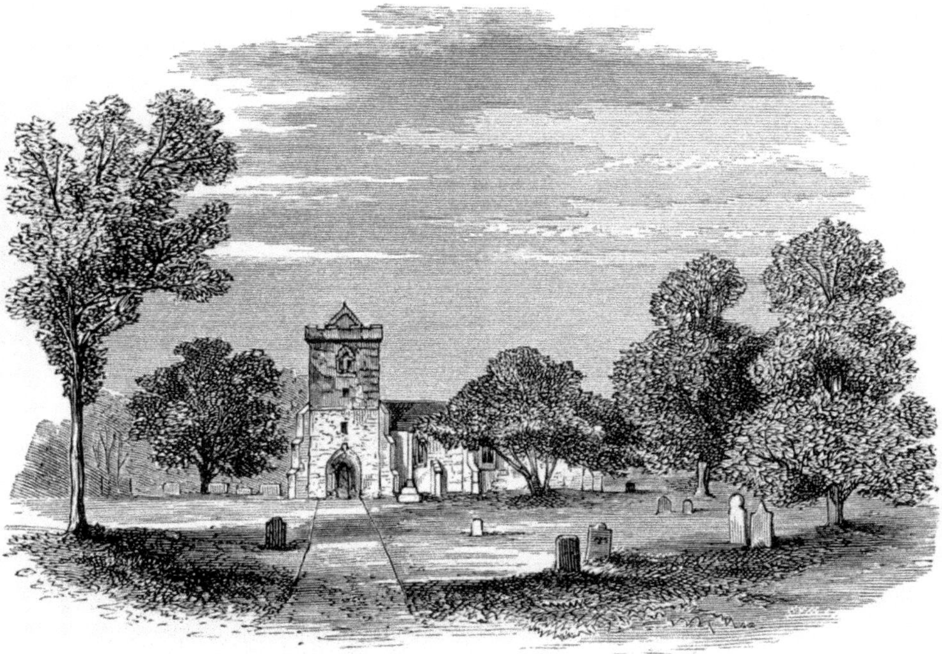

Hampton Lovett Church

Two images of Hampton Lovett Church are shown here – the first an engraving from 1875 and the second from a card posted in 1919. There is interesting Norman, Decorated, and Perpendicular work here, as well as a Victorian bier that was once used for conveying coffins at funerals. There is also very good fifteenth-century heraldic glass and fine Victorian glass by Hardman. Several monuments to members of the Pakington family can also be seen, and the Doverdale vault is in the churchyard. The lychgate seen in the foreground of the image below was constructed in the late 1850s.

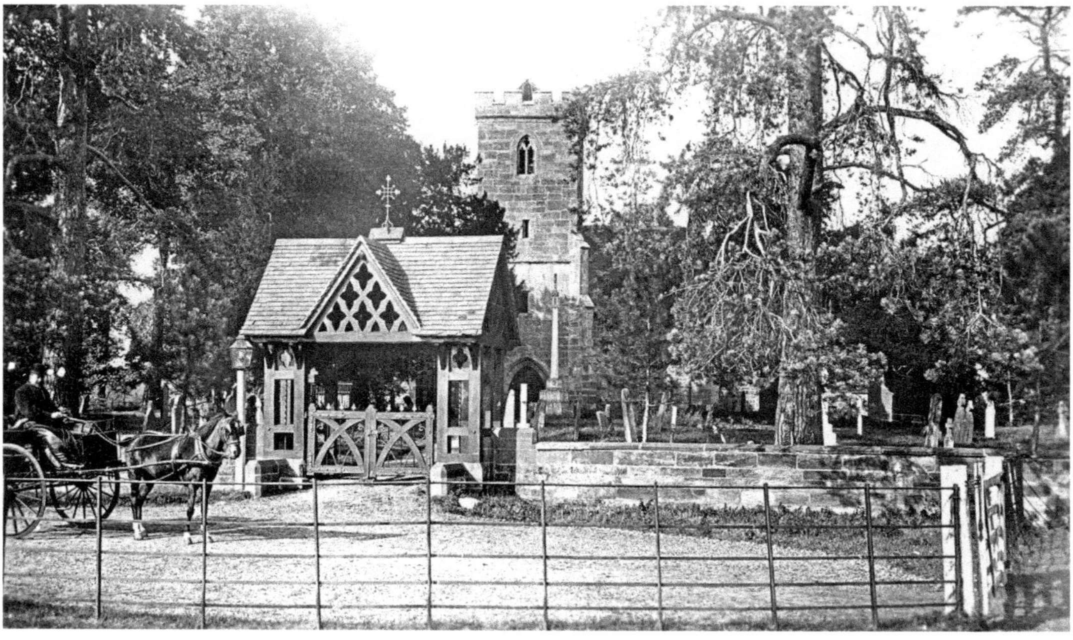

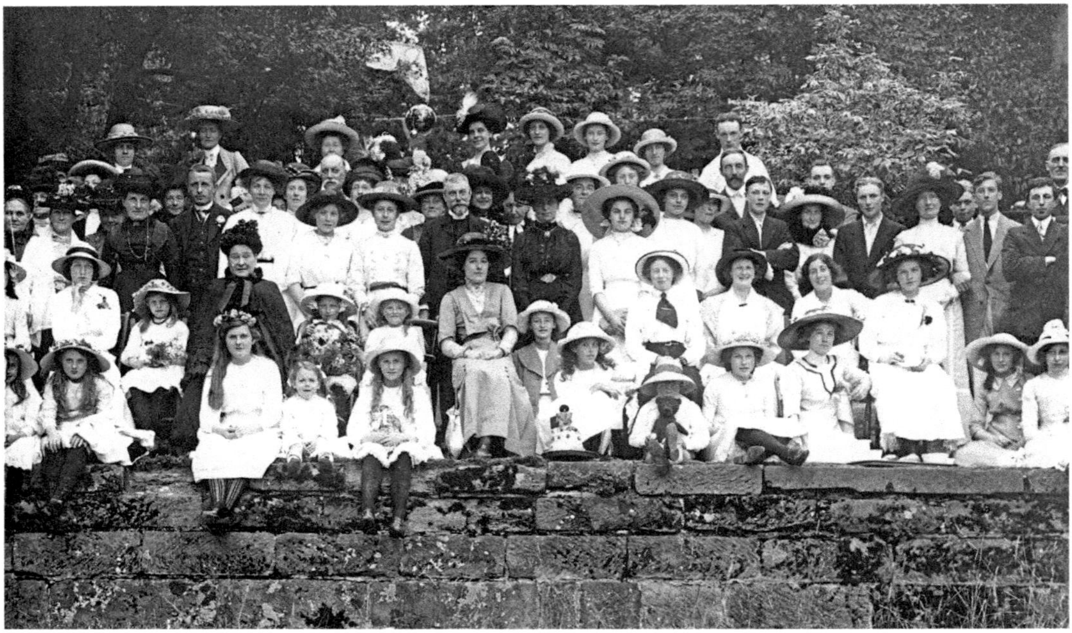

Hampton Lovett Church and Cutnall Green

The third Hampton Lovett image above dates from August 1913 and was taken by Droitwich photographer F. G. W. Sage during the rectory garden fête. The wall, on which some of the crowd are seated, is probably that of the churchyard as seen on page 81. Cutnall Green is shown below, from a card posted in 1912. According to an elderly relative who is no longer with us, the walk to Cutnall Green from Droitwich via the Kidderminster Road was once a very pleasant one, with orchards along the route. The orchards have now gone of course, and it is no longer advisable to walk along this very busy main road.

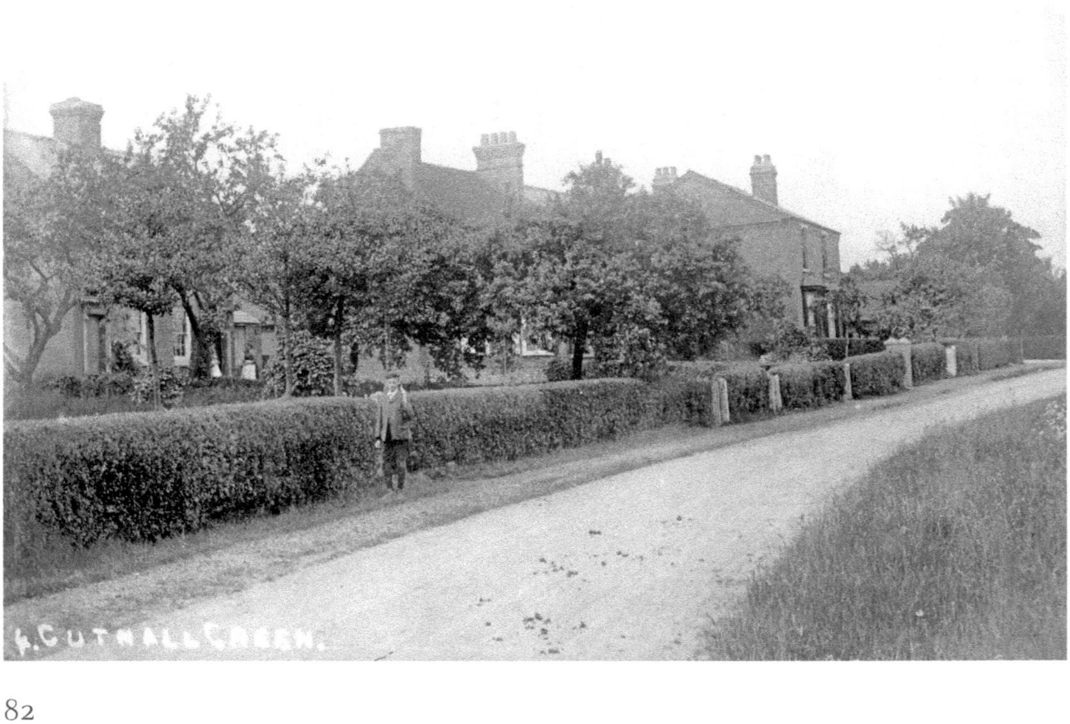

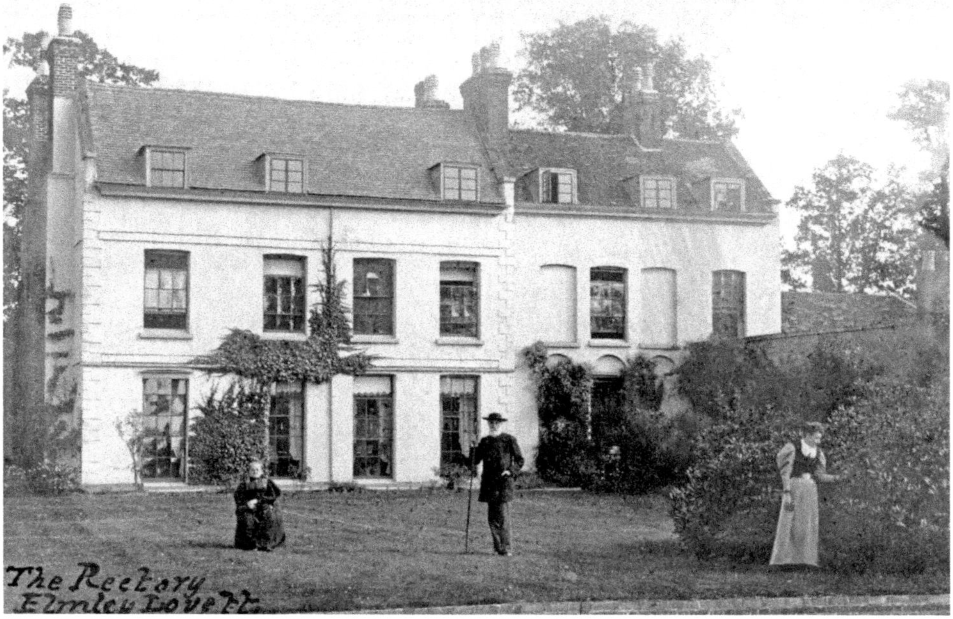

Elmley Lovett
Near to Cutnall Green lies Elmley Lovett, and its fine old rectory is shown above in around 1900. The man in the centre of the lawn is Revd W. T. Leeming, who is presumably accompanied by his family. The ground is rather rough to the south of Elmley Lovett Church, which is due to the fact that it is the site of a deserted medieval plague village. An avenue of trees stands to the south of the church, leading to where once stood a magnificent timber-framed property known as Elmley Lodge. This can be seen below in a very dilapidated state in an engraving from 1870. The remaining portions were demolished in around 1890.

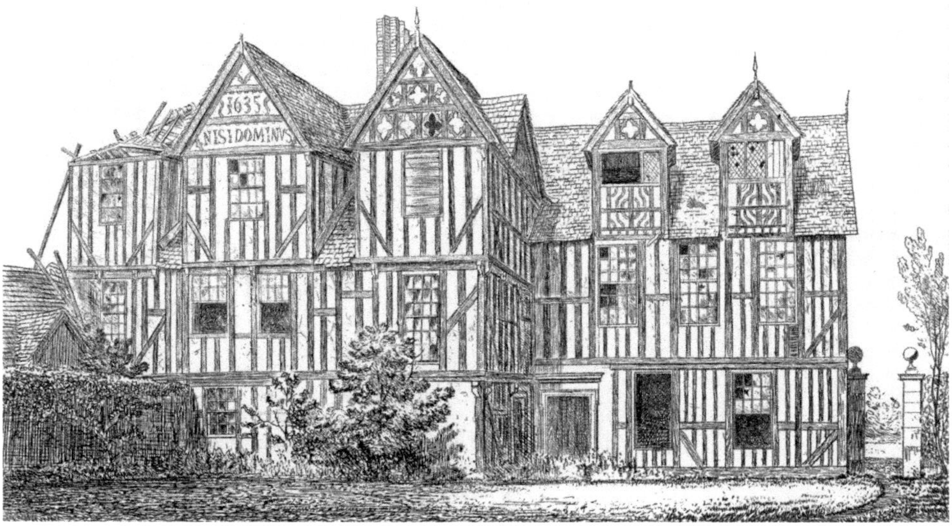

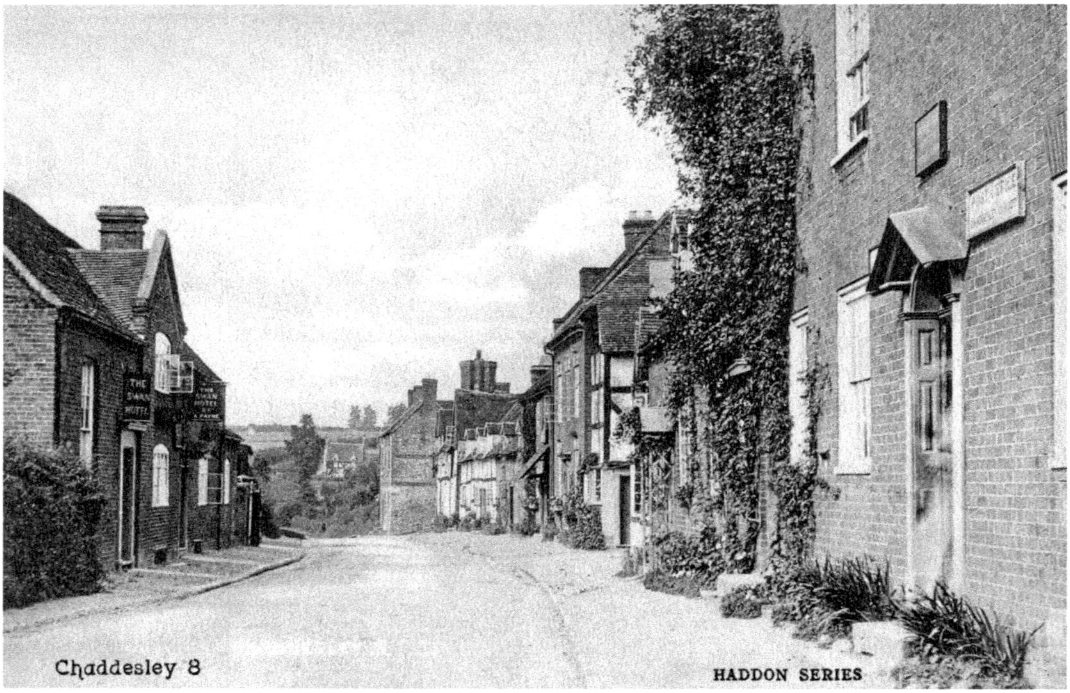

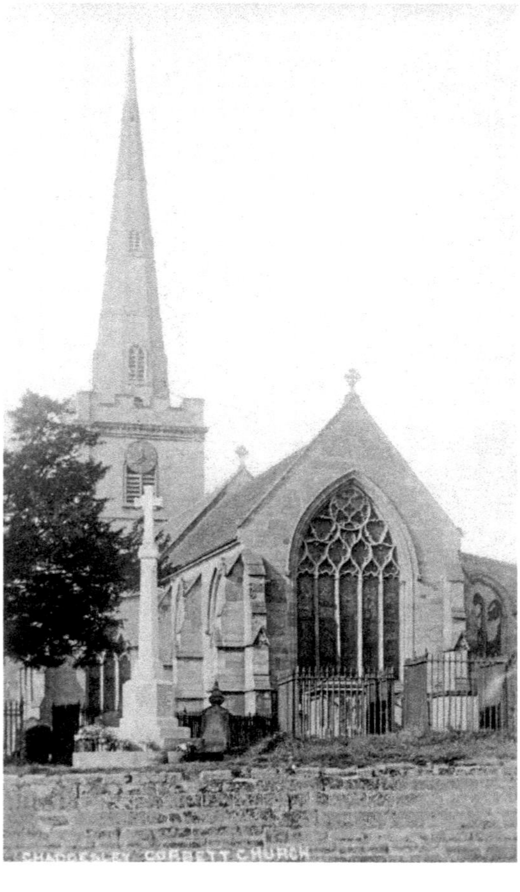

Chaddesley Corbett

The village of Chaddesley Corbett in around 1900 is shown above, in a shot that looks north towards Belbroughton. The Swan Hotel can be seen on the far left, and on the far right stands the village post office. Also reproduced here is a shot of Chaddesley Corbett Church, which is the only church in the country dedicated to St Cassian and is thought to be on the site of a Saxon minster. The Norman font, on which several dragons are beautifully carved, is of the Herefordshire School. One of the medieval effigies is of a knight in chainmail with shield and sword, and is probably a member of the Corbett family.

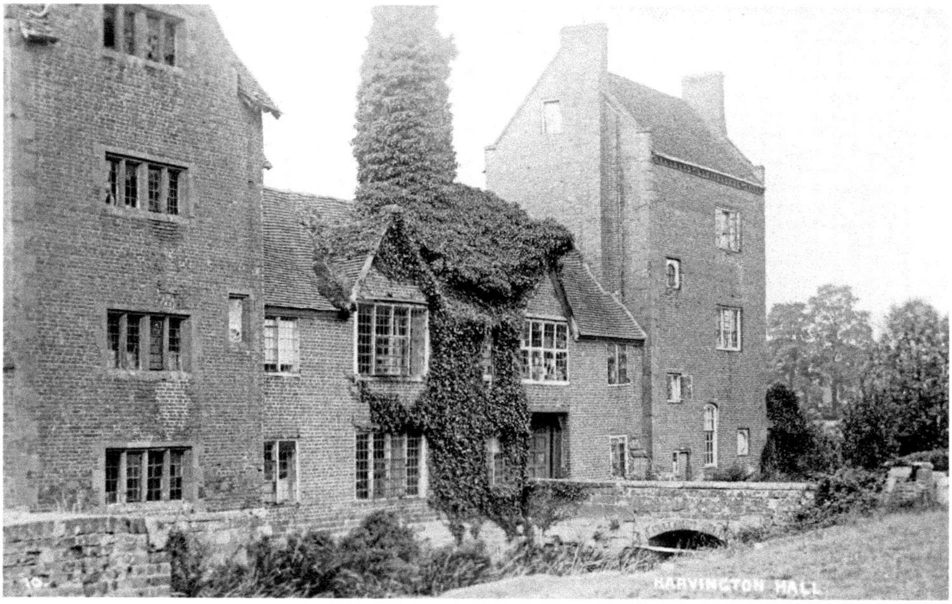

Harvington Hall

Only a few miles from Chaddesley Corbett stands Harvington Hall. The two photographs shown here date from the early 1900s at a point when this Elizabethan hall was in quite a perilous state. Above we see the main east entrance over the moat, and below, the rather overgrown south face of the building. Harvington Hall contains some fascinating priest's hides – probably constructed by Nicholas Owen in around 1600 – and was first restored in 1930–31. It is a wonderful place to visit; there is an excellent tearoom and it is also one of the most photography friendly halls in the county.

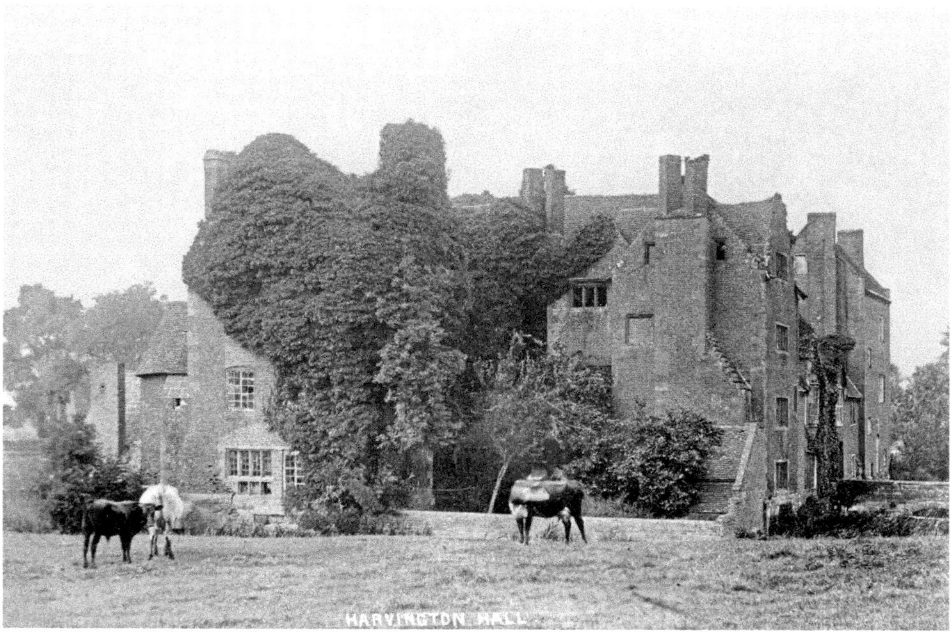

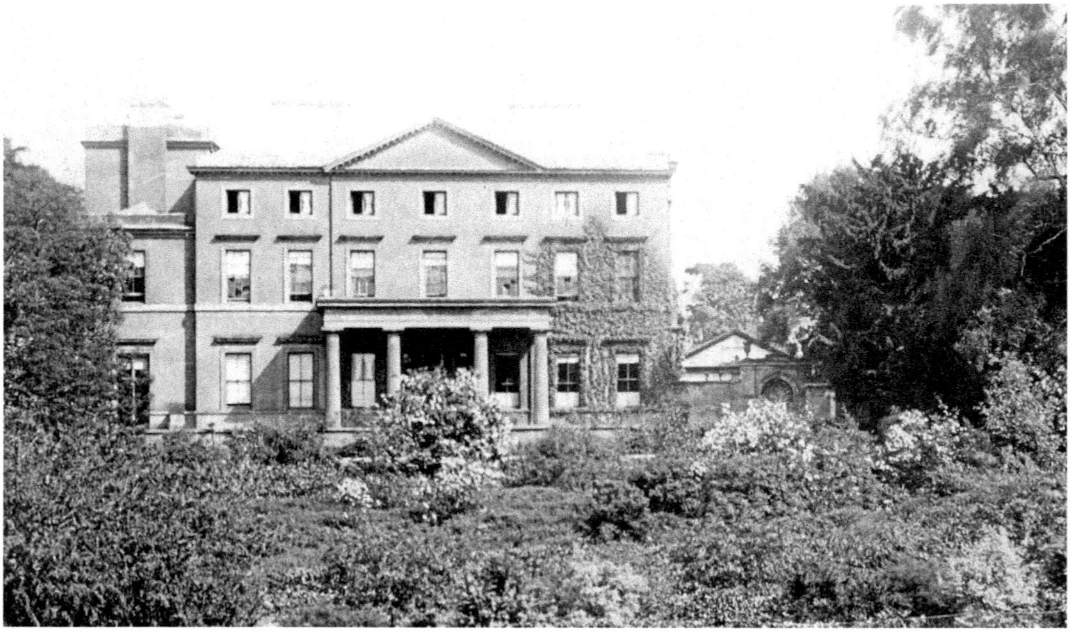

Hadzor Hall and Mere Hall

Two more local halls are shown here: Hadzor Hall (above), and Mere Hall (below). It is the west façade of Hadzor Hall (once Hadzor House) that we see here – probably at a time when the Dowager Lady Hindlip was in residence during the early 1900s. Prior to this, the hall was occupied by various members of the Galton Family, including Theodore Howard Galton in the nineteenth century who, among other things, was a local historian and author of two historical novels. The superbly timber-framed Mere Hall stands halfway between Droitwich and Hanbury, and was for centuries the home of the influential Bearcroft family.

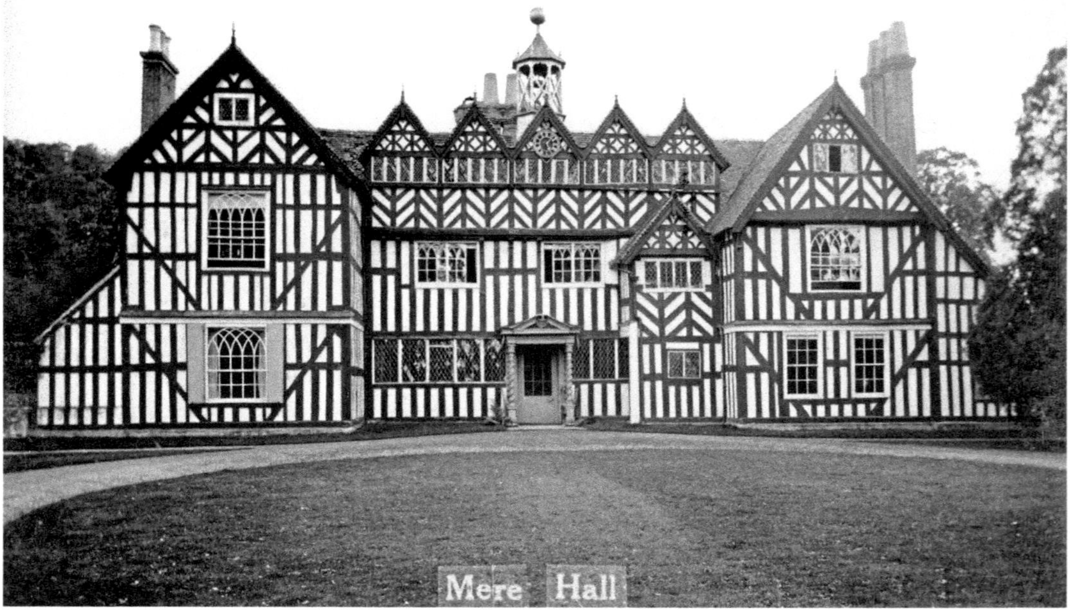

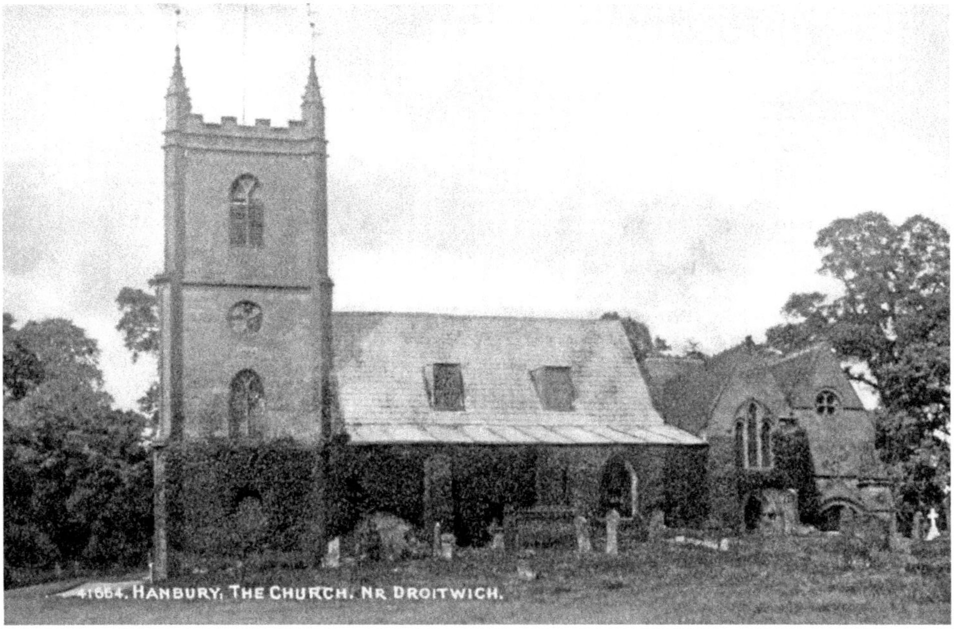

Hanbury Church and Rectory

The church and rectory of Hanbury are illustrated here – both shots dating from around 1905. Though the exterior of the church largely dates from the 1790s, fine medieval architecture has survived internally. The superb monuments include many to members of the Vernon family of Hanbury Hall. The rectory at Hanbury was demolished in the 1850s and replaced in 1861–62 with the new rectory shown below. It stands just to the east of the church and, when still functioning as a rectory, a straight path led from it to a set of churchyard steps. Though no longer in use, these steps are still in existence.

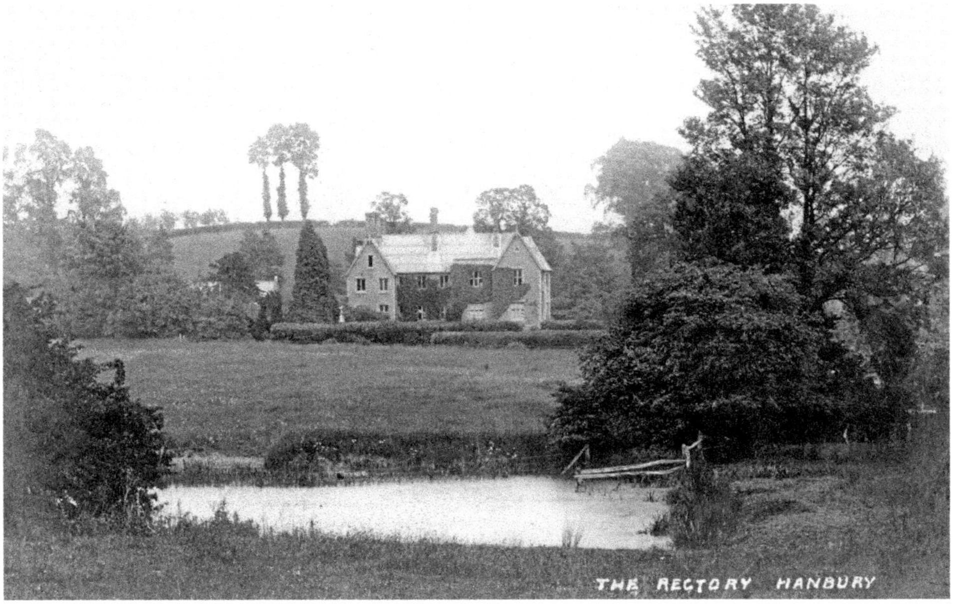

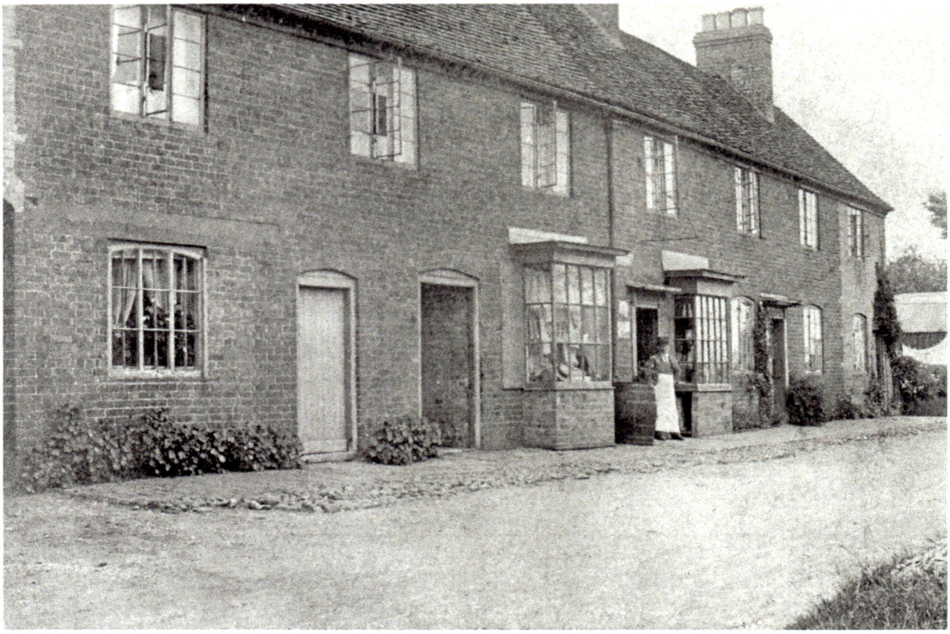

Hanbury and Feckenham High Street

The cottages that adjoin the Vernon Arms Pub on the main road at Hanbury are shown above in *c.* 1900. The shop, which is seen right of centre in this row, was once also the village post office. The image of Feckenham High Street below dates from around 1905 and shows the street's southern end looking north. At this time, needle, pin, and fish hook manufacturers were still in operation in the area. This scene has hardly altered, with the exception of the Alcester Co-operative Industrial Society Store on the far right (then managed by William Perks), which has since been replaced by modern housing.

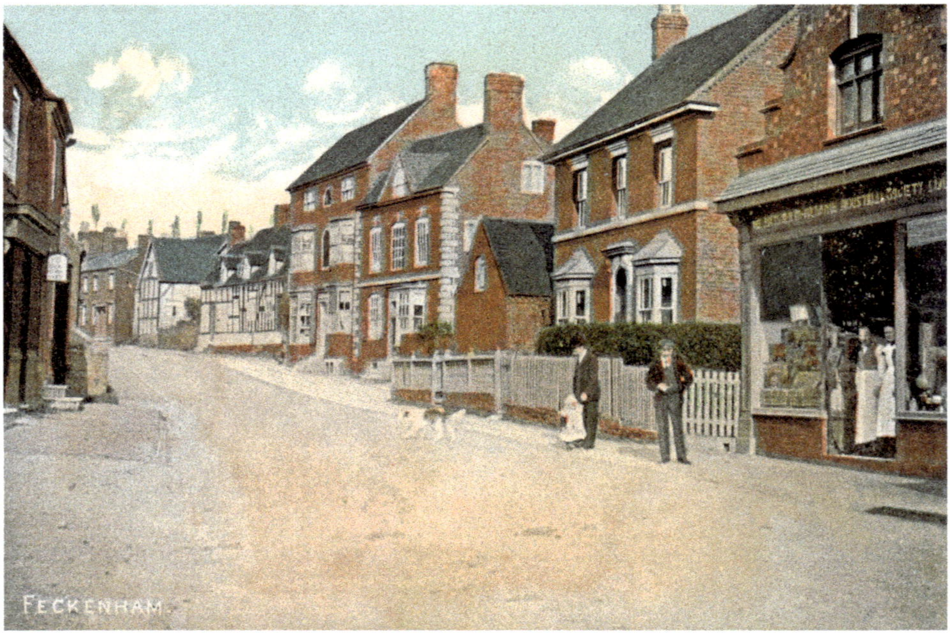

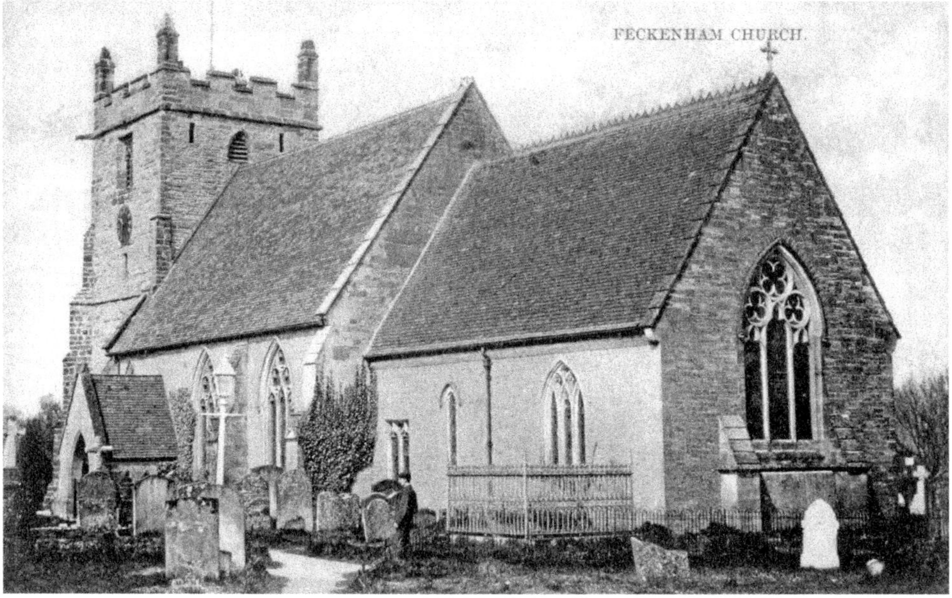

Feckenham and Stoke Prior Churches

Two churches in *c.* 1900 are shown here: Feckenham (above) and Stoke Prior (below). Feckenham Church has a fourteenth to fifteenth-century tower and the windows of various periods include two Norman windows in the chancel. The paintwork on the thirteenth-century north arcade largely dates from 1903–04. It was created from a small surviving portion of the original design and gives a good insight into just how lavishly our churches were once decorated. Stoke Prior Church is famous locally for being the final resting place of John Corbett of Impney, and it was he who funded the restoration of the church in the 1890s.

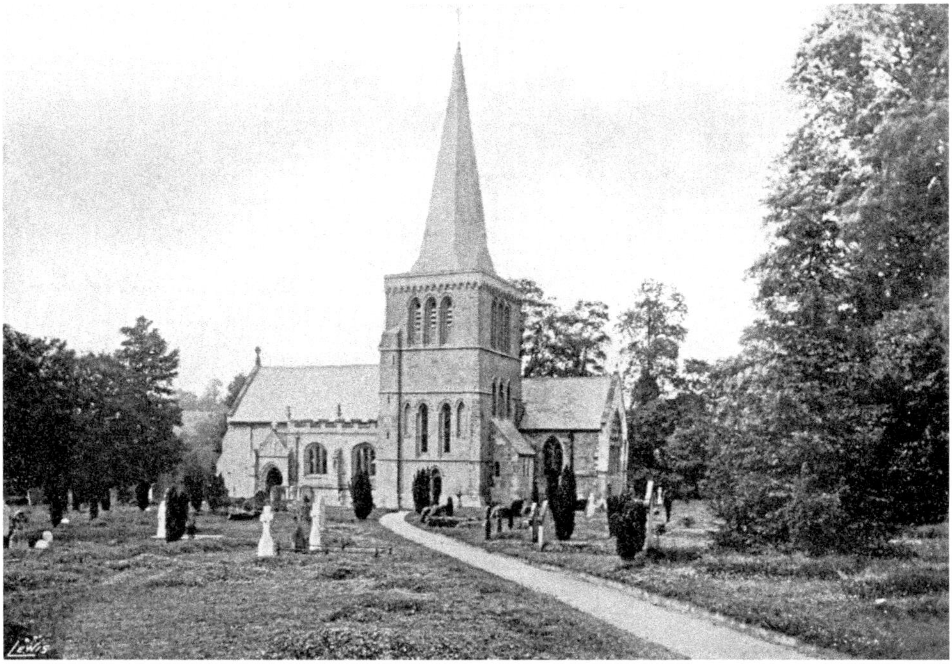

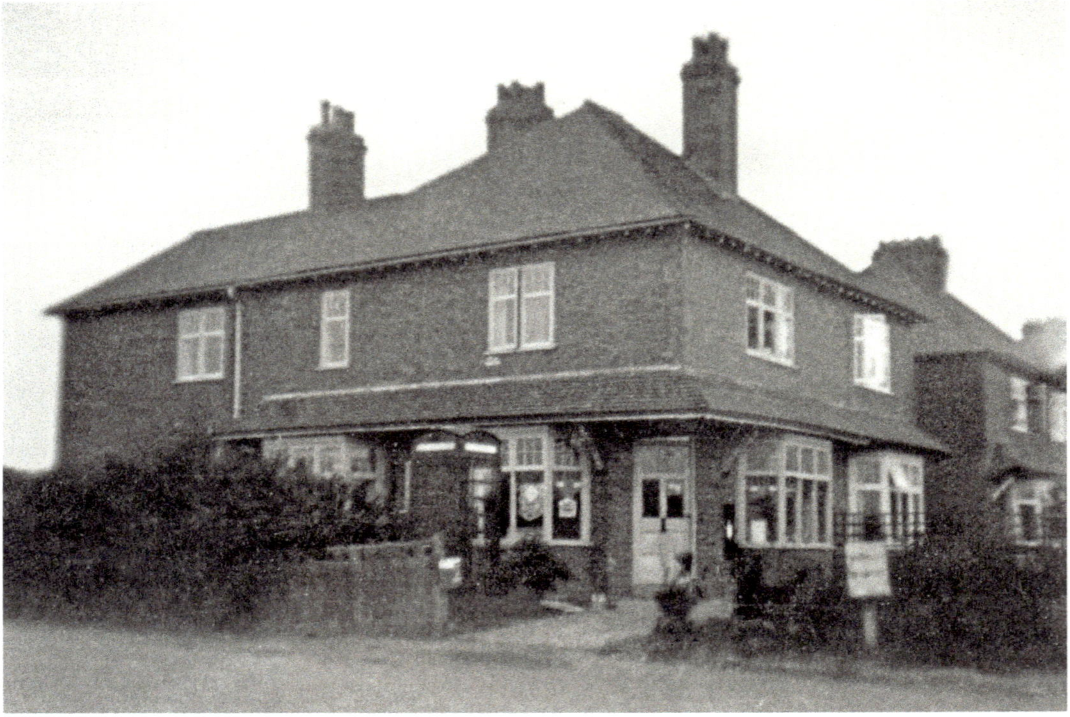

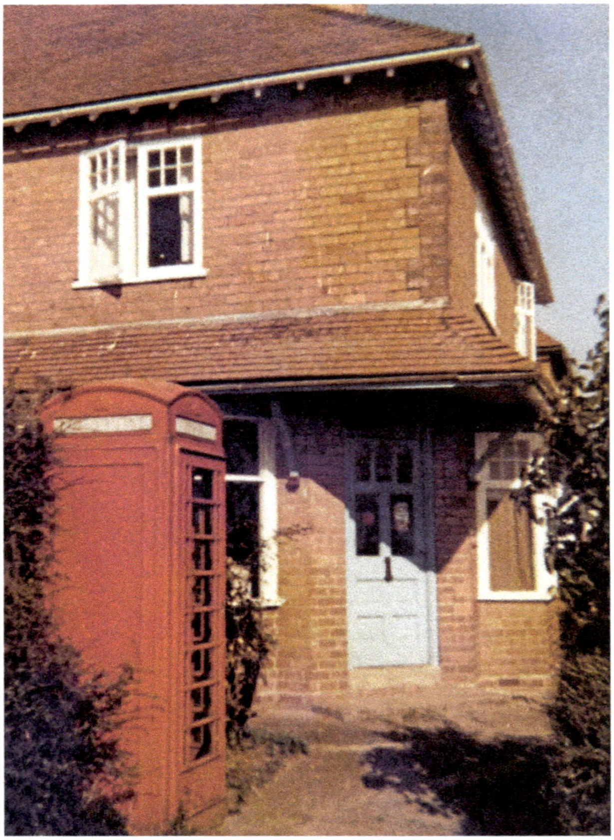

Oddingley Post Office

Two shots of Oddingley Post Office are shown here – the above dating from around 1960, and the colour image from the early 1980s. This row in Trench Lane was constructed by T. A. Everton Jr of Droitwich. In around 1933 his daughter Lilian Jackson and her family moved into this shop, with Lilian opening the post office in late 1930s. It was at Hanbury (*see* page 88) that my grandmother Margaret Jones learnt how to run a post office, and in 1951 she and her husband purchased the one in Oddingley and the land opposite from the Jacksons. My grandmother then ran the post office until it closed in around 1985.

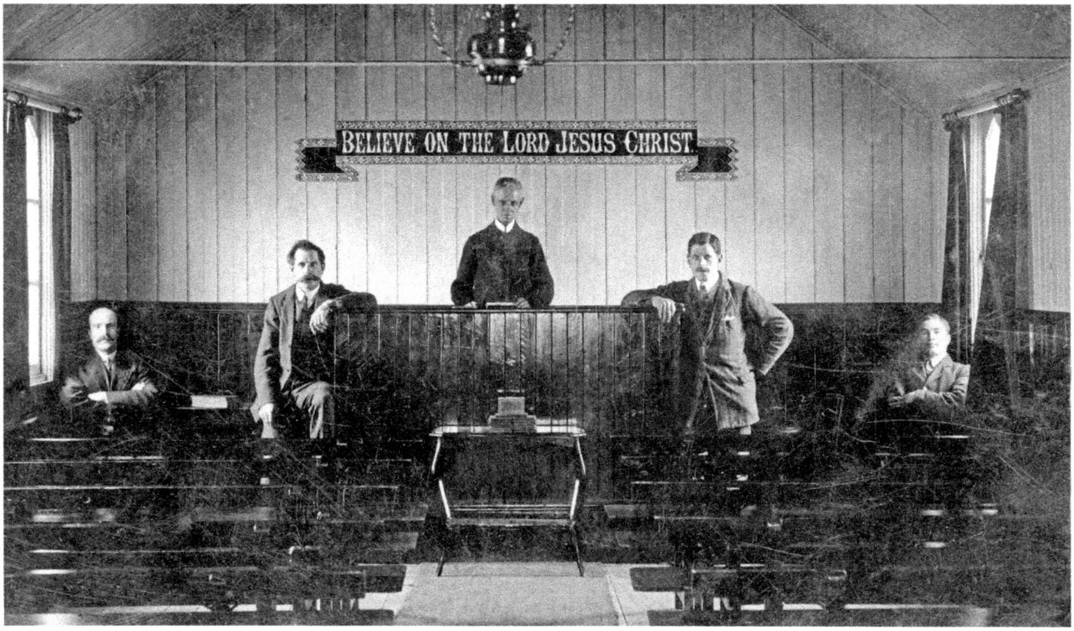

Crowle Mission Hall and Churchill Church

Crowle Mission Hall (later the Gospel Hall) on the Old Turnpike Road is shown above in around 1913, and the church of nearby Churchill in *c.* 1900 is shown below. Seated on the far right above is Albert Fincher (the brother of my great-grandfather) with four other members of the mission. Albert was killed during the First World War when the 2nd Battalion of the Worcestershire Regiment was among those ordered to attack the Hindenburg Line (known as the Action of Croisilles). In his last letter home he wrote: 'Let us dear sister, ask Him, who is God of Peace to speedily send us an abiding peace again among the nations of the earth.'

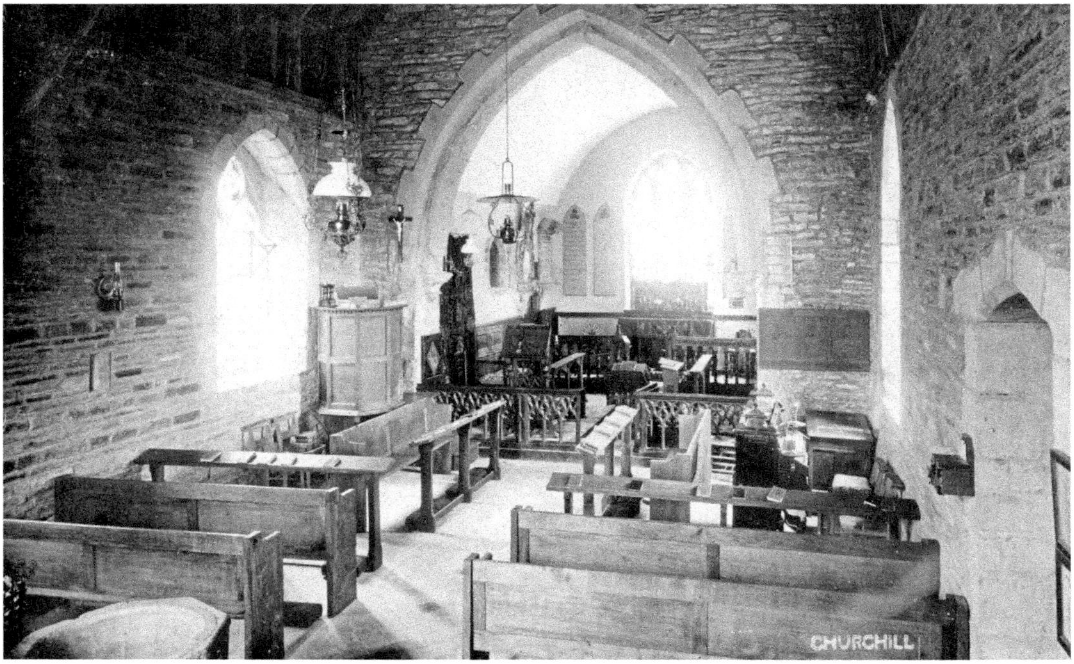

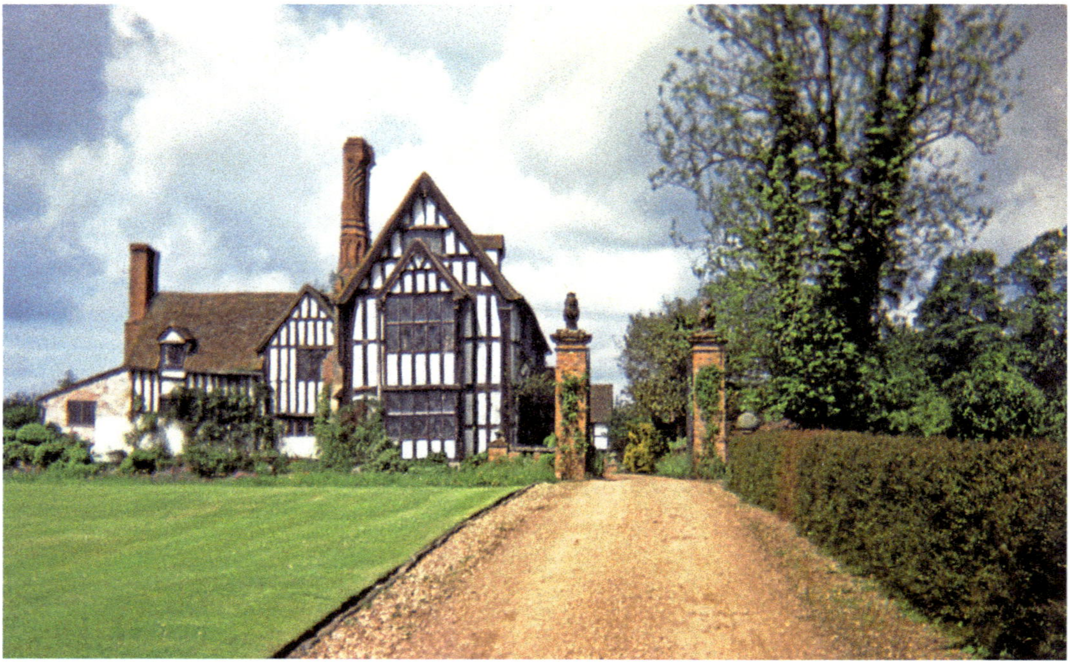

Huddington Court and Himbleton Church

The timber-framed Huddington Court is shown above from a shot taken by my mother in June 1967. Huddington Court is famous for its connection with the Gunpowder Plot, as the Catholic Wintour family – particularly Thomas, his brother Robert, and their cousin Robert Catesby – were heavily involved. Though this moated court is private, the delightful church stands just yards away to the south-east and is well worth a visit. Himbleton Church is shown below from the east in around 1900. This ancient church also has connections with the Wintours of Huddington and is another of the county's gems.

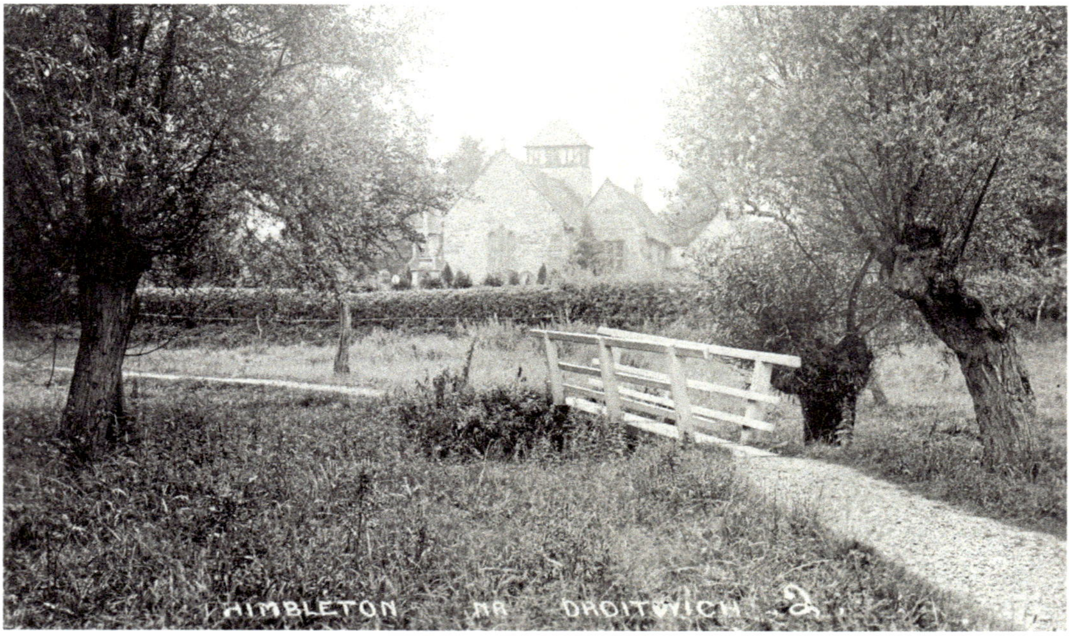

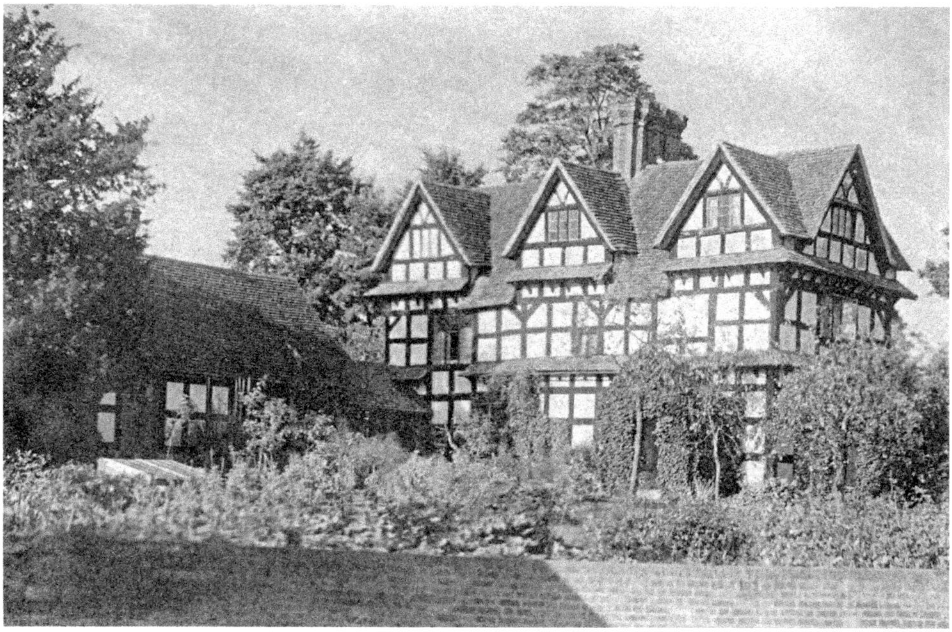

Dormston and Inkberrow

Moat Farm at Dormston is shown above and the church and vicarage of nearby Inkberrow below – both shots dating from around 1910. Around three-quarters of Moat Farm's moat is still in existence, and a timber-framed dovecote stands nearby to the south-west. Inkberrow Vicarage's west face (below) has altered considerably. This property ceased to be the vicarage several decades ago and was then split into two dwellings. The south portion (to the right of the gable ends) has since been demolished, but the castellated bay was reused on the building's south face. Another moat can be found here, just yards to the east.

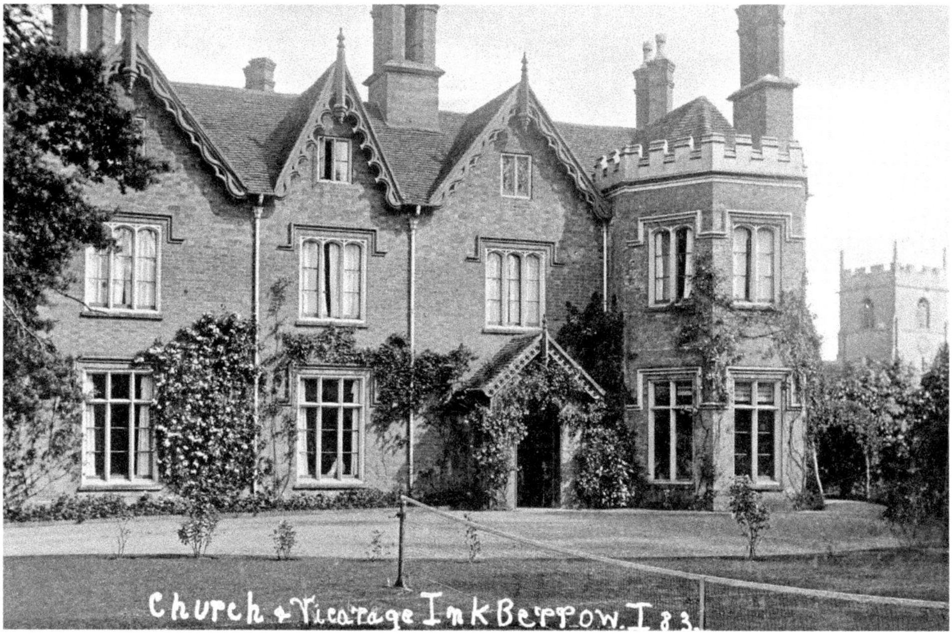

CHAPTER 10

MYSTERY IMAGES

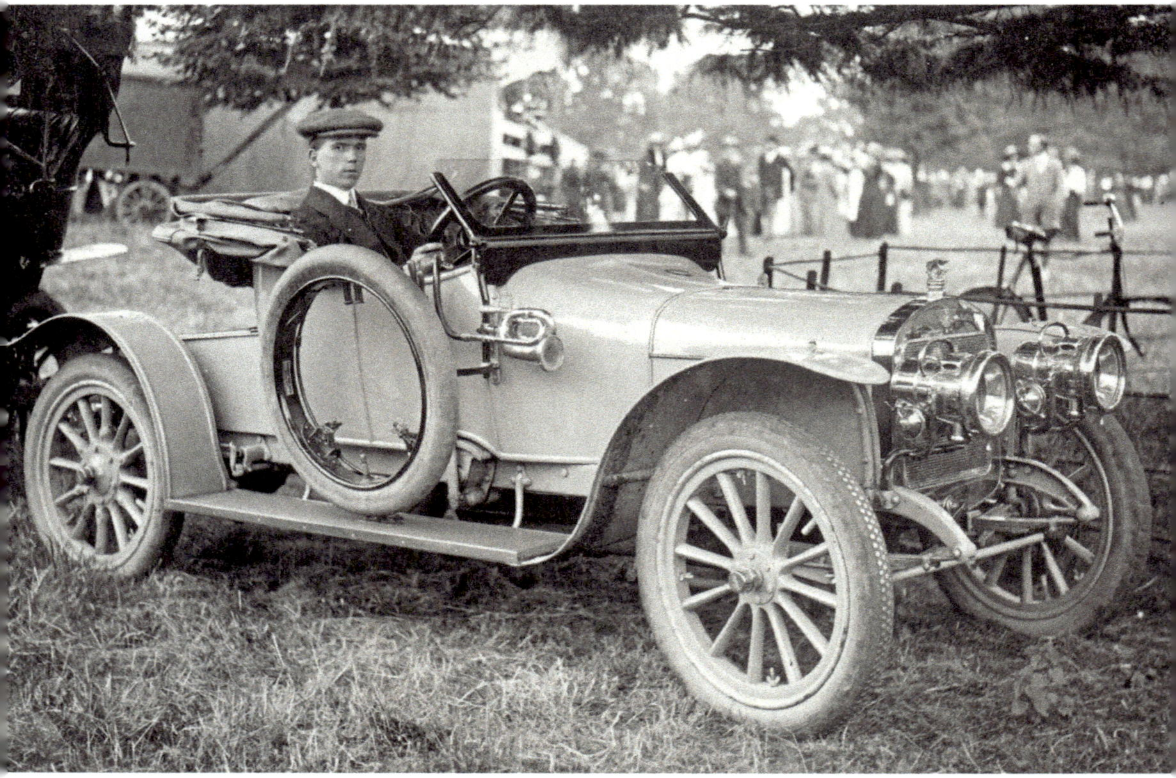

Local Events

This wonderful image was taken somewhere in the Droitwich area in around 1910. It seems to have been taken at a fête or flower show, and the person sitting in the car may or may not be its owner. The text printed on the back of the card reads: 'Photo by Wood and Guise, Droitwich'.

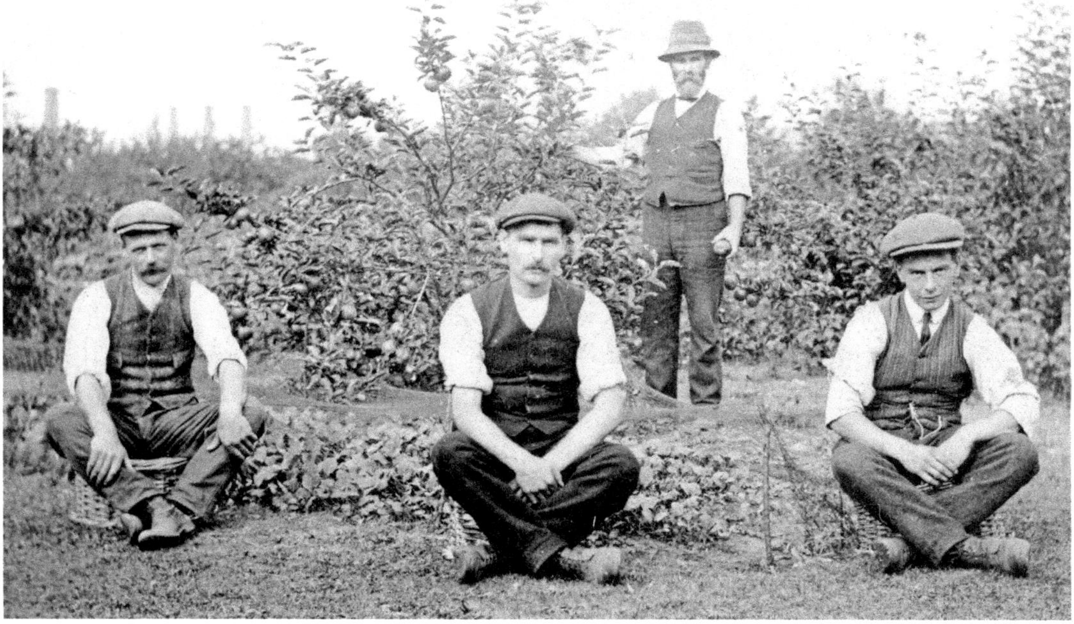

Local Workers

Both of these images were taken at unknown locations somewhere near to Droitwich. Chimneys are visible in the top-left corner of scene above, which may possibly be those of Covercroft Salt Works. The man at the back is standing next to an apple tree and holding one of the apples in his left hand. Local hop pickers are depicted below in a scene from a card posted at Droitwich in 1913. Up until the 1960s it was quite common to see hops growing on Worcestershire farms, and many families earned extra money by going hop picking. Several growers managed to survive beyond the 1960s, but most have now gone.

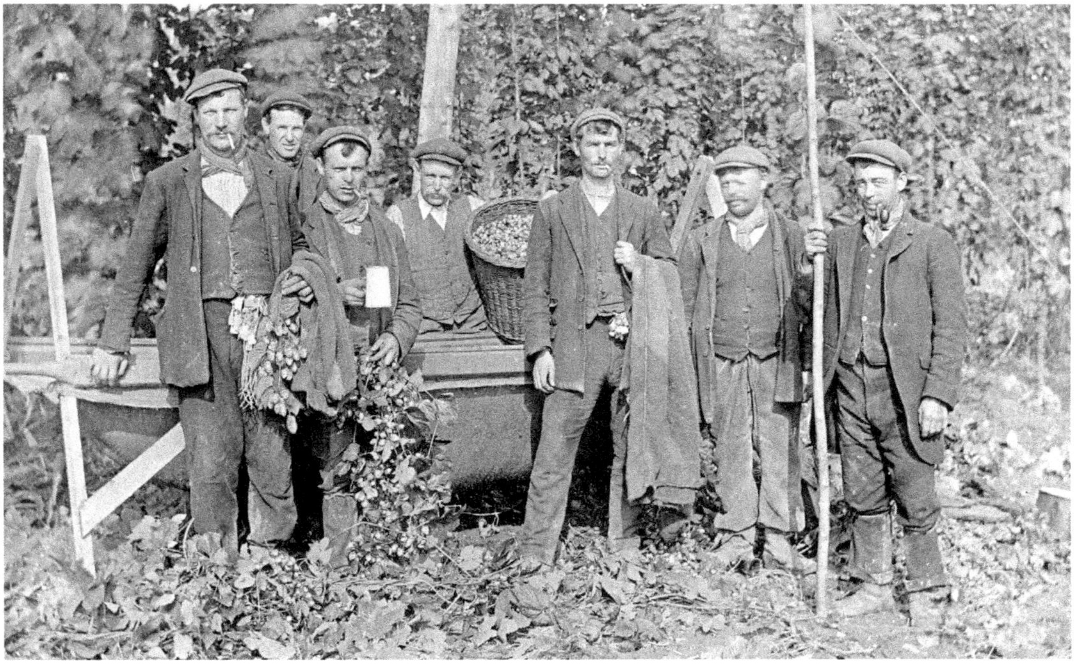

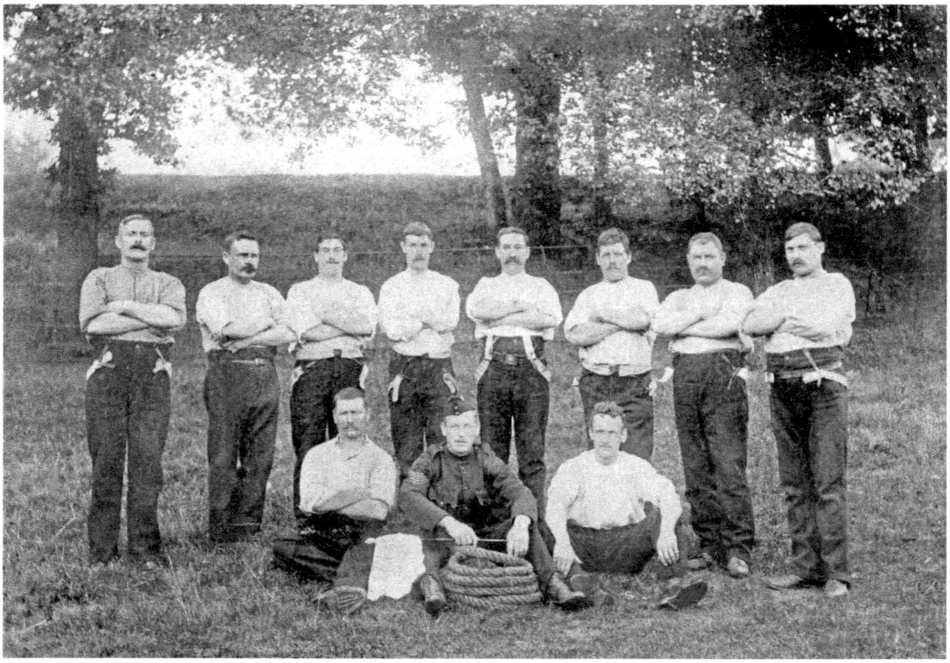

Local People and Places

The photograph above came from a collection of local images and I suspect that it could be that of a winning team of Volunteers (the Territorial Army was once known as the Rifle Volunteers or just the Volunteers), as described in the *Berrow's Worcester Journal* in 1889. In that year the Volunteers gathered at the Salters' Hall Droitwich and Captain Tombs pointed out that the Droitwich Volunteers had 'supplied six of the ten men who won the regimental tug-of-war prize in the brigade camp'. The man sitting behind the rope certainly seems to be wearing a Volunteer uniform (now the Territorial Army). The below image was taken by F. G. W. Sage of Queen Street Droitwich, but the location is unknown.

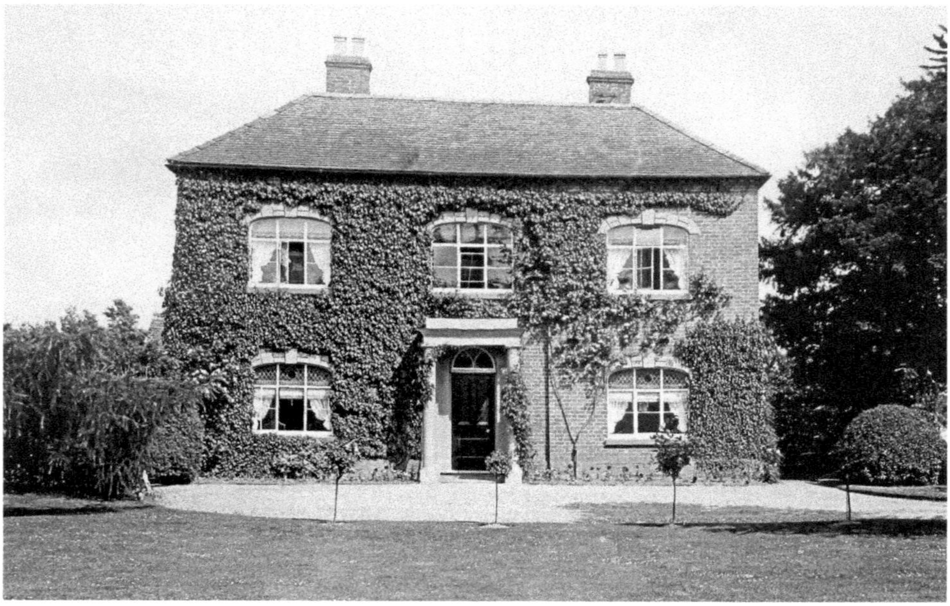